The Health Care Dilemma

Marie F. Santiago RN BSN)

The Health Care Dilemma

SECOND EDITION

Aubrey C. McTaggart
San Diego State University

Lorna M. McTaggart

HOLBROOK PRESS, INC. BOSTON

Library of Congress Cataloging in Publication Data

McTaggart, Aubrey C
    The health care dilemma.

    Includes bibliographical references and index.
    1. Medical care—United States. I. McTaggart, Lorna M., 1931–   joint author. II. Title.
    [DNLM: 1. Delivery of health care—U.S.
    2. Quality of health care—U.S. 3. Consumer
    satisfaction. WB50 AA1 M17h]
    RA395.A3M3 1976   362.1′0973   76–199
    ISBN 0–205–05446–3

Contents

Preface   ix

One   INTRODUCTION   3

Two   THE M. D.'s   11

*Becoming a Physician 11   The Trend Toward
Specialization 14   What Makes a Medical
Specialist? 16   Do You Need a Specialist? 20
Choosing a Physician 24   Maldistribution and
Primary Care Problems 31   Continuing Medical
Education for Physicians 33   Foreign Medical
Graduates 36   The American Medical
Association 37*

Three   DENTAL CARE   43

*Historical View 43   Becoming a Dentist 44
Distribution of Dentists 45   Specialization 46
Dental Auxiliaries 48   Choosing a Dentist 51
Dental Clinics 59   Overcharged or Dissatisfied?
59   The American Dental Association 61
Dental Trends 62*

Four   NURSING   67

*History of Nursing 67   Levels of Nursing Per-
sonnel 68   Characteristics of Nurses 71
The Hospital as Employer 73   Changing Roles
of Nurses 74*

Five   OTHER HEALTH PRACTITIONERS   83

*Osteopathy 83   Chiropractic 87   Podiatry
90   Christian Science 93   Homeopathy 96
Naturopathy 98*

Six   ALLIED HEALTH   105

*Trends 106   Careers 108   Physician Ac-
ceptance of Allied Health Personnel 128
Licensure 131   The American Society of Allied
Health Professions 131   Conclusion 132*

Seven   HEALTH MAINTENANCE ORGANIZATIONS
135

*The Three Cornerstones 135   Health Mainte-
nance Organizations 138   Advantages and Disadvantages of HMOs 147   HMO Results 151*

Eight   HOSPITALS   157

*Development of the Hospital 157   Federal Sup-
port of Hospitals 160   Classification of Hospitals
164   Organization of Hospitals 164   Hospital
Costs 168   Hospital Accreditation 171
Choosing a Hospital 175   The Right to Know
180   Being Hospitalized 182   Encouraging
Trends 183*

Nine   PRESCRIPTION DRUGS   195

*The Food and Drug Administration 195   A New
Drug On the Market 196   Patent Rights On a
New Drug 200   Quality of Drugs 201   Drug
Safety 203   Adverse Drug Reactions 203
Prescriptions for Controlled Substances 206
"The Name Game" 207   Drug Prices 210
Advertising 214   Your Doctor and Drugs 217
The Pharmacy 219   Is the Food and Drug
Administration Holding Up Progress? 220
Physician-Owned Pharmacies 223   What Can
You Do? 224*

Ten EMERGENCY MEDICAL SERVICES 231

Hospital Emergency Departments 232 The Emergency Medical Services Systems Act 233 An Effective Emergency Medical Services System 234 Rating Emergency Departments 239 Total Systems 240 What Can You Do? 245

Eleven MEDICARE AND MEDICAID 249

Medicare 249 Purchasing Private Insurance 261 Medicaid 264 Summary 267

Twelve NURSING HOMES 271

Alternatives to Nursing Home Care 272 Types of Nursing Homes 275 Licensure and Certification 276 Choosing a Nursing Home 277 Problems in the Nursing Care Field 284

Thirteen VOLUNTARY HEALTH AGENCIES AT WORK 291

The American Lung Association (Christmas Seal Organization) 292 The American Cancer Society 295 The American Heart Association 299 What Can Voluntary Health Agencies Do For You? 307 Funds 307

Fourteen THE PUBLIC HEALTH DEPARTMENT 311

The State Health Department 311 Local Public Health Departments 313 Family Planning 316 Child Health Conferences 317 Health Care Project 319 Public Health Nutrition 319 Records and Statistics 320 Environmental Sanitation 322 Public Health Laboratory 324 Public Health Nursing 325 Health Problems of Senior Citizens 327 Public Health Education 328 Other Programs 329

Fifteen CONSUMERISM IN HEALTH CARE 333

Health Education and Health Care 333 Public Health Facilities 334 Sources of Health and

*Medical Information 335   Free Clinics 339
Patient Noncompliance 341   Prospective Medi-
cine 342   The Hospital Experience 342
The Patient's Responsibility 343*

Appendix

A   ARRANGING THE FIRST VISIT   349

B   SOURCES OF INFORMATION ON HEALTH
CAREERS   355

C   PRIORITY ITEMS OF PUBLIC LAW 93–641
363

D   A PATIENT'S BILL OF RIGHTS   367

Index   370

Preface

"Caveat Emptor" is a good motto for you, whether you are buying a television set, a car, or health care. You will be better able to protect yourself when purchasing health care if you understand some of the pitfalls that await the unwary. An informed consumer usually makes some comparisons before buying—and the more expensive the item, the more careful the comparison. Yet, when it comes to something as important as health care, many people do not take the time to make comparisons, erroneously assuming that one healer is as good as another. It is true that excellent health care is available in the United States; it is also true that very poor health care is available. The purpose of this book is to provide useful information about the components of quality health care, and to suggest ways that will improve your chances of buying quality care.

We are indebted to many persons for assistance with this volume. Our thanks to the numerous authors and publishers who so readily granted permission to use copyrighted materials.

We are happy to acknowledge the assistance provided by Jack Damson, Executive Director of the San Diego Chapter of the National Lung Association; Pam Brennan, Education Director of the San Diego Chapter of the American

Cancer Society; Millie Crom, Executive Director of the San Diego Chapter of the American Heart Association; Dr. Donald Ramras, Acting Director, San Diego County Department of Public Health; and the patience and cooperation of librarians in the Documents Division of the library at San Diego State University.

Lorna and Aubrey McTaggart

The Health Care Dilemma

Chapter One

Introduction

Americans, accustomed to thinking they are number one and believing they should all be entitled to the best, are concerned and even angry when they realize that they do not always get the finest health care and are not necessarily the healthiest people in the world. In spite of enormous expenditures for medical care, it is becoming more and more evident to the consumer that the present situation is intolerable. The visibility of problems in our health care delivery has increased as the problems of implementing Medicare and Medicaid* become public knowledge. These programs have focused attention on the growing inflation in medical care costs, the inefficiency in the organization of medical care services, the lack of care for the poor and for those living in intercity or rural areas. Other problems include the scarcity of facilities for the elderly and the lack of quality control for physician and hospital services.[1]

The patient is the ultimate victim of the fact that medical care in the United States is a private business and not a public responsibility, as it is in all the other developed nations of the world. The U.S. method of health care delivery

* Medicare pays a part of the health care for those over 65; Medicaid pays for the health care of the poor. Both of these programs are dealt with in some detail in Chapter Eleven.

has been set up for the convenience of the providers—doctors, dentists, hospitals, and insurance carriers.[2]

Providing a basic human need such as health care for the people of this country should rest on something more substantial than the personal preferences of independent entrepreneurs, for this is indeed what the providers are: men in business for themselves. Many of our goods and services are distributed in this way, so why not medical care? Because it is a fact that the American marketplace has always done more for the provider than for the consumer. It works best for those with something to sell, but not so well for those buying. The consumer has always been shortchanged on price, availability, accessibility, convenience, and accountability. This may be tolerable for some commodities, but not for medical care.[3]

According to Jesse Steinfeld, former Surgeon General of the United States, "We have the world's best medical colleges, the best research, the best hospitals, best doctors, but we rank 15th in infant mortality. Women in eleven other countries live longer. The United States ranks 27th in life expectancy for men. The only category in which we rank first is in cost. We pay more per capita for health care than citizens of other industrialized nations, but we're getting less."[4]

Some skeptics contest the above statements and insist that we have special problems in the United States. For example, they contend that our infant mortality statistics make us look bad because they include minority groups. The answer to this is that even if we discounted the infant mortality rates for Blacks and Mexican–Americans, the United States would still not be in the top ten. Other skeptics say that there are discrepancies in methods of keeping statistics. David Rutstein, head of the Department of Preventive Medicine at Harvard and a specialist in internal medicine and cardiology, comments on this: "I should like to make the firm statement at this time that the differences in infant mortality rates between Sweden, other Western countries, and the United States are real ones. Sweden and the United States use the same World Health Organization criteria for the definition of a live birth. I have myself examined the use of this definition in Sweden, and I believe that the Swedes can count dead babies as accurately as we can."[5]

Dr. Martin Cherkasky, director of the Montefiore Hospital and Medical Center (New York) and chairman of the Department of Community Health at Albert Einstein College of Medicine, had this to say about health care in the United States: ". . . judging by the generally accepted indexes of infant mortality and longevity, . . . our record is not poor—it is disgraceful."[6]

We are leading the world in the production of well-trained surgeons *and* in tolerating needless surgical procedures. In many communities, elective surgery is done without independent consultation. Fortunately, most of the physicians in this country are dedicated, hardworking men of high integrity; but every profession has a few who are unethical. Our present inefficient system does not allow us to identify properly these unscrupulous, dishonest, or incompetent professionals.

According to the Committee for Economic Development, "the nation's health services have retained the organization—or lack of it—that may have been adequate for the health needs of an earlier era. As the major health problems shifted from acute to chronic diseases and toward conditions requiring more extended attention, the system failed to develop a continuous form of care to replace that based on episodic treatment. It also failed to shift from the concept of *sick* care to *well* care."[7]

Voluntary health insurance has helped millions of Americans to pay their medical bills. However, it has several serious shortcomings. To begin with, since the most prevalent kind of health insurance coverage is hospital care, expensive hospital facilities tend to be overutilized. Ambulatory care, which is much less expensive, is often poorly covered by insurance, and hence discouraged. Secondly, the present system of reimbursement of providers (doctors and dentists) has reduced or eliminated incentives for economy. Thirdly, many persons (up to forty million) are not covered by any health insurance. The majority of these are poor and near-poor, nonwhite, unemployed—in general, the disadvantaged.[8] According to Steinfeld, "Instead of encouraging preventive medicine and giving doctors a stake in keeping you well, we encourage the kind of private insurance system which requires that the doctor hospitalize patients for diagnostic tests, in order to make certain the insurance will cover the cost of the tests."[9]

It is generally accepted that what is needed is not more money poured into our present approach to health care delivery, but major changes to organize, administer, and deliver a system that will provide early care to each citizen regardless of his location or economic circumstances.[10]

We have yet to accept the humane fundamental principle that everyone prospers when a nation's people are concerned enough about each other and themselves to provide the opportunity for optimum health. It is, of course, a philosophical problem—a matter of priorities. The whole approach of medical care needs to be geared to keeping the citizen well. Until now, we have been crisis-oriented. We have treated diseases when they occurred, rather than concentrating on preventive care. We need to develop a system that can combine the talents of each health professional in such a way that both crisis and preventive medicine are available to all. This is a fantastic task, but other nations have done it—once they have accepted the idea that health care is a citizen's right.

How much longer are we going to be content to say that only those who can afford it are entitled to the best in medical care? Spiraling costs are reducing the number of people who feel secure about their ability to purchase care. People are getting anxious. When consumers become vocal enough about their concerns, working through their representatives, they will effect a change in the pattern of health care delivery. Consumer organizations are going to have to be very forceful to counteract the activities of the powerful lobbying groups representing the providers who, thus far, have had the most influence on government decisions.[11]

Consumers are concerned about the horrendous charges involved in health care. They are wondering why doctors are not available when needed, why the family doctor has disappeared and an impersonal stranger treats their disease but isn't interested in them as persons. The consumer is questioning the wisdom of licensing a doctor or any other health professional to practice for life without any evidence that he is remaining competent. The consumer also wonders about the advisability of doctors checking on one another's practices. He is asking why clinics are not more conveniently located; why some hospitals have a much better reputation than others; why old people don't have decent nursing homes they can afford; and why it takes so long to get an ambulance. If he lives in a rural or intercity area, he may also wonder why there are no doctors around.

As more people become aware of the inequities in our health care, one of the main motivators of reform will be the fear of the middle class that they cannot afford the cost of health care. These are the people who have access to the power structure. They can and will, when personally threatened, use their political power to instigate change. Some changes have already occurred. For example: medical schools are accepting more minority students and students from rural areas; students are being encouraged to view patients as whole entities; and entrance into specialties is being discouraged. Consumer suggestions are being solicited on such decisions as where to have clinics, what kinds of nursing homes are needed and in what areas, and how emergency medical care will be delivered in a particular city.

We are still struggling to obtain care under a poorly conceived system. No organization with the consumers' interests at heart has been responsible for systematic overriding continuity in the development of health care services. Experts from many disciplines will be needed to plan the most economical way of providing optimum service. Consumers will have to have more of a voice in letting the experts know what services they need, where they need them, and how they can be most effectively utilized. Health providers will have to be encouraged to work as a team, putting aside the old lockstep system which stifled individual growth, creativity, and advancement from one level to another. They will have to learn to work as associates with a common goal of providing optimum services. A cooperative sharing of knowledge and a concern for the total health picture will have to replace personal glory and acquisitiveness.

As you read the following chapters, you will become aware of your options as a consumer to obtain the most for your health care dollar. Once you become alert to what is happening on the health care scene, your contribution as an interested citizen and a consumer will be available to shape this country's first comprehensive health care system. The essential ingredient in the prescription for good health care in America is your concern.

ENDNOTES

1. David Mechanic, *Public Expectations and Health Care* (New York: John Wiley and Sons, Inc., 1972), p. 281.
2. David D. Rutstein, *Blueprint for Medical Care* (Cambridge, Massachusetts: The MIT Press, 1974), p. 23.
3. Abraham Ribicoff, *The American Medical Machine* (New York: Saturday Review Press, 1972), p. 137.
4. Jesse L. Steinfeld, Committee for National Health Insurance Newsletter, 1974.
5. David D. Rutstein, *The Coming Revolution in Medicine* (Cambridge, Massachusetts: The MIT Press, 1967), p. 25.
6. U.S. Congress, Hearings on Health Care in America, 90th Congress, 2nd session, 1969, p. 5.
7. Committee for Economic Development, *Building a National Health Care System* (New York: 1973), p. 12.
8. Ibid., p. 14.
9. Steinfeld, Committee for National Health Insurance Newsletter.
10. Mechanic, *Public Expectations and Health Care,* p. 281.
11. Ribicoff, *The American Medical Machine,* p. 137.

Chapter Two

The M.D.'s

Most of you have been faced with the need for medical care. When you were very young, your parents made the decision about which doctor to see and when to see him. How did they decide who would be the best one for you to see? Is there a reliable way to choose a physician? What kind of a physician should you choose? In this chapter, we will delve into the training of a physician, his specialization, hospital privileges, and level of competence, and provide you with some criteria for choosing your own doctor.

BECOMING A PHYSICIAN

The education of a physician usually involves nine years after completing high school. The premedical student must complete three years of undergraduate study to meet the minimum academic requirements to the nation's 114 medical schools. Actually, most of today's freshmen medical students have completed four or more years of college study.

The traditional approach to medical education has been to separate the first two years of preclinical science from the last two clinical years. In the past, a medical student in his first two years would spend his time in the classroom, library,

11

and the laboratory and would not be introduced to clinical (patient) care until his third and fourth years. The trend is now toward introducing the student to patient care during the first two years and even toward allowing him more elective time so that he can put some emphasis on the social sciences. Traditionally, the only patients that medical students would see were those in hospitals. Hospitalized patients, although not exactly a representative sample of a community's health problems, were used because they were in a convenient place and they would be in the hospital for several days, allowing the student to observe closely the results of various treatments. Now, students are introduced to patients in the community much earlier and they are able to observe the interplay of family, cultural, and economic factors on health and disease.

At one time, a separate year of internship in a hospital was required after medical school, and after completing his internship, the new physician was ready to take the state licensing examination.* Since 1975, the internship year has been incorporated into the residency program. Most physicians complete a residency program of from two to five years. During this time, they concentrate on patients with problems associated with their specialty area, be it obstetrics, orthopedics, or any of the other thirty-three specialties and subspecialties recognized by the American Medical Association.

The traditional medical school has come under much criticism for almost every phase in the preparation of a doctor. Changes have been called for to: enroll more women and members of minority groups, reduce the length of training, allow more flexibility in the curriculum so that it is not so scientifically narrow, change the pattern of training for the medical specialties, and put more emphasis on ambulatory care and comprehensive care. In an attempt to

---

* Licensure does not give a physician the privilege of practicing in a given hospital. Each hospital has a "Board," of which physicians are members, that decides on who shall practice in that hospital. Many such Boards require higher levels of competency than that required by state licensing regulations.

alleviate one of these problems, some medical schools have shortened their curriculum by one year. The medical school of McMaster University in Hamilton, Ontario, reduces it by another year. It accepts students after three years of college and graduates them with their M.D.'s after three years of medical school. To do this, summer vacations are reduced to one month and the curriculum is more condensed. Students receive their medical education in 112 weeks over a three-year period, rather than in the usual 120 weeks spread over four years.[1]

For several years, the University of Miami School of Medicine has been accepting students with Ph.D. degrees and turning them out with M.D.'s in two years or less. The students of the first classes had their doctorates in the biological sciences, but now they are being accepted with varied backgrounds, and their medical school performance is good. These students regularly finish in the upper 20 percent on national board examinations. The program would seem to be designed for those interested in medical research and teaching, but a surprising number of graduates of this program opt to practice medicine.[2]

The Association of American Medical Colleges would like to see medical education, from matriculation through specialty training, under university supervision. Currently, it is fragmented and varying in quality under the supervision of hospitals, service chiefs, and other interested parties. A step in the direction of a unified continuum under university supervision was the abandonment of the internship as an isolated freestanding entity in 1975.[3]

Federal aid to medical education is being reduced because the government has forecast a surplus of physicians by 1980. Since medical students can expect high remuneration after graduation, it is felt that they should be expected to pay more of the cost of their training. Even in 1980, there will be gaps in physician coverage; for example, general practitioners are expected to be in short supply, and physicians will not be evenly distributed throughout the population, with rural and inner city areas suffering the most. It is going to take time and considerable effort to develop a nationwide admissions system to medical schools that is responsive to both the needs of society and the medical profession. Medical schools across the nation are accepting a high proportion of applications from segments of the population that are underserviced, such as Mexican–Americans, Blacks, and Indians. These schools are placing more emphasis on a prospective medical student's socioeconomic background and attitudes.[4]

Other trends in medical education will involve a much greater output of physicians so that by 1980, if there is better organization of health care, we can expect an oversupply of doctors which will reduce the immigration of foreign medical graduates (dealt with in a later section). Also, more women and minorities will be accepted into medical schools; this may provide for a better distribution of health care providers.[5]

THE TREND TOWARD SPECIALIZATION

Medical education over the past half century has developed very close ties with the university hospital. Most university hospitals have certain common characteristics: they have specialists who serve as clinical faculty members; they have become referral centers for patients with complex diseases; they emphasize clinical research; and they are concerned almost exclusively with the hospitalized patient. Such characteristics make the university hospitals ideal environments for the training of specialists; in fact, "this evolution had a profound effect on the practice of medicine because the direct ties between academic medicine and the medical specialties hastened the deterioration of the status of the general practitioner. There were no general practitioner models in the teaching hospital. . . ."[6] Nor did the hospital in the past show any interest in what is now referred to as family practice. It was not until 1969 that family practice achieved specialty status and it has not been particularly successful in attracting large numbers of students. This paradox occurs in spite of the fact that almost all researchers acknowledge the pressing need for family practitioners.

Most professionals today, no matter what their field, have a very real sense of frustration. They realize that it is virtually impossible for them to keep up-to-date in a broad sense, so they have tried to stay abreast of new developments in a specialty area. Even to achieve relative competence and familiarity in a rather narrow area, one must be very diligent in keeping up with the ever-increasing mass of published material available today. This is especially true in the field of medicine, where there has been an explosion of knowledge. The trend toward specialization has been dramatic in the last fifteen years, with approximately 85 percent of physicians now classified as specialists.

As the trend toward specialization in medicine continues, we are losing our personal physicians who have traditionally had an interest in the whole person. With specialization, physicians tend to focus on a particular disease or a particular area without showing enough concern for the rest of the person.

Another problem is the availability of these specialists. We are frequently told, and it can be proven statistically, that we have more physicians per 100,000 population in the United States than ever before. This sounds great, but it is deceptive! With specialization, one physician does not care for one person—he cares for one *part* of one person—skin, gastrointestinal tract, genito-urinary tract, and so on. Obviously, many physician specialists are needed to care for a person with multiple problems. So, as pointed out by James L. Dennis, Dean of the University of Oklahoma Medical School, "the kinds of physicians we turn out are more important than the numbers we produce. If we doubled the physician population tomorrow and they were all limited specialists, we would not have solved any major problems."[7]

The intense focus on a disease or a specific part of the body tends to detract from the personalized, human interest with which physicians have traditionally been credited. Who is going to assume responsibility for the *whole* patient? The specialist may be so limited in his knowledge of other aspects of health and disease that he fails to note or suspect the presence of maladies outside his field.

Physicians now tend to go directly into a specialty after graduation. This means that they have never had a family practice in which they were able to relate to the problems of the "whole patient." Their medical education and their residency have certainly not encouraged an overall view of medical care. It is not surprising that the product of this system seems more interested in the disease than in the person. These specialists often think of themselves as dermatologists or psychiatrists first and as doctors second.

WHAT MAKES A MEDICAL SPECIALIST?

A physician has three main options open to him in his quest for a specialty rating. First of all, he may become interested in a specialty area such as pediatrics and decide to limit his practice to children. He is then a "self-styled" specialist. He has not had any prescribed extra academic preparation and is frequently considered "not a specialist" by his professional community. Secondly, he may actually serve one or two years of residency training in a given specialty and then call himself a specialist. A physician may decide not to limit his practice exclusively to a specialty and, under his name in the Yellow Pages, may list "general practice and surgery." He is then referred to as a part-time specialist. The third method of becoming a specialist is the most rigorous and the one that most people think of when they hear the term "specialist." This involves the completion of full residency training, which may be from three to five years, satisfactory completion of two years of full-time specialty practice, plus the passing of both written and oral examinations in the specialty field. A physician must also satisfy certain qualifications to become a candidate under this third option. He must have: a) satisfactory moral, ethical, and professional standing in the profession—but he does not have to be a member of the AMA or of his local County Medical Society; b) graduated from an approved medical school, and c) completed an approved internship program.[8] These latter qualifications are actually the same as the licensure requirements for physicians in general.

Once he has crossed all these hurdles, the physician receives a diploma in his specialty and is called a "Diplomate." He is now considered to be "Board-Certified" or "Boarded" in a given specialty. A Diplomate and a Board-Certified specialist are the same thing. A physician who has completed all the requirements *except* the oral examination is considered "Board-Eligible." This classification can be held for only three years, after which time the candidate must retake the written examination.

Some specialties set additional requirements for certification as a diplomate. The obstetrics-gynecology specialty, for example, requires that each eligible candidate, before taking his oral examination, must present "a verified duplicate typewritten list of *all patients dismissed from the candidate's care in each hospital* where he has practiced during the twelve months immediately preceding the month of application. The patients listed must be only those for whom the candidate assumed the major responsibility. Each list must show verification by the Record Librarian, or the Director of the hospital."[9]

Kinds of Specialists

There are thirty-five medical specialties and subspecialties which are recognized by the AMA. Emergency medicine, established in 1974, is the most recent specialty. We have listed only the twenty-one major fields of medical specialization; recognized subspecialties exist within some of these fields. The major medical fields include the following:[10]

Administrative medicine.   Administration of medicine: in business, health programs, and hospitals, for instance.

Anesthesiology.   Administration of various forms of anesthetic drugs necessary during surgical operations or diagnosis.

Colon and rectal surgery.   Diagnosis and treatment of disorders or diseases of the lower digestive tract.

Dermatology.   Diagnosis and treatment of diseases of the skin.

Family practice.   Evaluation of a patient's or family's total health care needs and provision of personal medical care in one or more fields of medicine, and coordination of other health services needed by patients.

Internal medicine.   Diagnosis and surgical treatment of diseases of the internal organs such as the heart, liver, and lungs.

Neurological surgery.   Diagnosis and surgical treatment of the brain, spinal cord, and nerve disorders.

Obstetrics and gynecology.   Diagnosis and treatment of diseases of the female reproductive organs and also the care of women during, and immediately following, pregnancy.

Ophthalmology.   Diagnosis and treatment, including surgery, of diseases or defects of the eyes.

Orthopedic surgery.   Diagnosis and medical or surgical treatment of diseases, fractures, and deformities of the bones and joints.

Otolaryngology.   Diagnosis and treatment of diseases of the ear, nose, and throat.

Pathology.   Study and interpretation of changes in organs, tissues, and cells, as well as alterations in body chemistry.

Pediatrics.   Prevention, diagnosis, and treatment of children's diseases.

Physical medicine and rehabilitation.   Diagnosis of disease or injury in the various systems and areas of the body and treatment by means of physical procedures, as well as treatment and restoration of the convalescent and physically handicapped patient.

Plastic surgery.   Corrective or reparative surgery to restore deformed or mutilated parts of the body or to improve facial or body features.

Preventive medicine.   Prevention of disease and promotion of health through epidemiological studies and public health measures.

Psychiatry and neurology.   Diagnosis and treatment of emotional disturbances, mental disorders, and organic diseases affecting the nervous system.

Radiology.   Diagnosis and treatment of disease through the use of radiant energy, including x-rays, radium, and cobalt 60.

Surgery.   Diagnosis and treatment of diseases, injury, or deformity by manual or operative procedures.

Thoracic surgery.   Diagnosis and operative treatment of diseases of the chest: those involving the heart, lungs, or large blood vessels within the chest.

Urology.   Diagnosis and treatment of diseases and disorders of the kidneys, bladder, ureters and urethra, and the male reproductive organs.

As a prospective patient, how can you tell which specialist took which option to achieve his specialty standing? When you phone a physician's office for an appointment, you can ask the receptionist if the doctor is Board-Certified. If he is not, ask where he took his residency training. Even if he did not take a residency, he may still be a very competent physician, and you may have had several people recommend him, and so you may decide to entrust him with your health care. The chances are, however, that a Boarded physician will be the best qualified specialist. Another option open to you is to check *The Directory of Medical Specialists,* which should be available in your public library. This compendium of approximately 2400 pages lists all the Board-Certified specialists in the United States and Canada and also provides a brief biographical sketch, including where each served his residency.

DO YOU NEED A SPECIALIST?

To answer this question, we might look at the doctors whom physicians choose for their own care. Doctors, remembering the old adage that "he who hath himself for a physician, hath a fool for a patient," usually seek the advice and care of another physician when they are ill. Doctors "tend . . . to go to specialists, especially to Board-Certified specialists; to choose medical school faculty members or directors of hospital departments; to choose internists as opposed to other specialties; and to avoid graduates of foreign medical schools."[11] A New Jersey study indicated that when physicians needed surgery for themselves or for a member of their family, they chose specialists.[12]

The degree of seriousness is the main consideration when deciding whether or not you need a specialist. For surgery, however, we would recommend a specialist in every case. Let us look more closely at surgery, a medical specialty which was mentioned in the Hippocratic Oath over 2500 years ago. Do you agree or disagree with the following statements?

1. Cutting skill is the most important ability of your surgeon.
2. The results of surgery depend on the dexterity of one person, and you should be sure that your surgeon does all the operating himself.
3. An older surgeon (one who has been in practice for twenty years or more) will be a better operator than a young one who has just finished his residency in surgery.

As strange as it may seem, all of the above notions are wrong! William H. Potter, in his book *You and Your Doctor,* posed these statements and then elaborated on each of them:[13]

1. He pointed out that diagnosis is the most important skill for a surgeon; a wrong diagnosis means wrong treatment. Judgment comes second: whether to operate, and if so, what operation to perform. Thirdly, preoperative and postoperative care, getting the patient ready mentally and physically for the operation and assisting in the convalescent period. Lastly, and least important, is surgical skill. This is the easiest to learn and can be taught within a few weeks. The development of the ability to decide why and when to operate, however, takes years. The actual surgery has been overdramatized to the public.
2. Surgery today requires tremendous teamwork, and your surgeon's job is to see that the skills of each member of the team are properly utilized. He may not make all incisions and sew every stitch, and it may be better that he "delegates these to others under his supervision who may be more eager and perhaps even more adroit mechanically, conserving his energies for the more significant activities of continual diagnosis, evaluation of

the changing situation, and making decisions as to the best next move."[14]

3. Surgical skill is necessary in a successful operation, and this skill generally improves as one does more and more operating. The senior surgical resident may well be the busiest surgeon, and although he may not possess the diagnostic ability or judgment of the seasoned veteran, he probably has excellent manual skills. Yet, when he completes his residency in surgery and opens his practice, a problem arises. How does he get his surgical patients? By referral from other physicians who have decided that their patients need the expertise of a qualified surgeon. To receive referrals, he must become known to other physicians, and while he waits for referrals, he spends his time doing things other than operating: physical exams for insurance companies and schools, and perhaps some teaching and research, and service on committees and organizations. Building up a referral system often takes years, and the young surgeon may grow rusty and may never again reach the surgical dexterity which he possessed as a senior resident. Some young surgeons find that the only way to get referrals is to split their fees with the referring doctor, a practice which is unethical. We must keep in mind, however, that the most important attributes of a surgeon are his diagnostic ability and judgment, and these are likely to be best in the experienced surgeon.

We have chosen the example of surgery because it provides an excellent basis for evaluation. Accredited hospitals (Chapter Eight) are required to analyze all tissue removed by surgery to determine whether or not it was diseased. Naturally, we may expect some errors in diagnosis, which means that some healthy tissue will be removed. A physician is generally allowed ten percent error. If, however, he consistently goes beyond that figure, he will be asked to justify his surgery to his colleagues. (He won't lose his license, however, and may not even lose his hospital privileges.)

That much healthy tissue is being removed from Americans at an alarming rate has been well documented.[15,16,17]

According to Dr. Martin Cherkasky, Head of the Montefiore Hospital in New York, "General practitioners take out bowels, gall bladders, and uteruses every day in our hospitals." To point out the importance of this practice, Dr. Cherkasky stated, "Let me give you one life-and-death statistic. In the hands of a qualified gynecologist, a woman with cancer of the cervix has an 80 percent chance of a cure. In the hands of an unqualified gynecologist, her chances are only 50 percent. I know of no more eloquent testimonial to being in the hands of a qualified doctor than that."[18] It is estimated that from 25 to 50 percent of all surgery in the United States is done by general practitioners, or unqualified surgeons (in some hospitals, it runs as high as 85 percent).[19]

Europeans do not tolerate such gross mismanagement. They allow only qualified specialists, on salary, to perform surgery in their hospitals. When surgery is done by these salaried surgeons, the rate of surgery drops dramatically. A study done in New Jersey revealed that the rate of tonsillectomies under Blue Cross-Blue Shield was twenty-seven children per one thousand hospitalized. The rate for the same operation by salaried doctors was nine—a two-thirds reduction![20]

We allow unqualified doctors to operate and do not provide adequate controls on their performance. Tissue is not examined in many of our smaller hospitals. One study showed that over 80 percent of surgery was done by non-specialists in hospitals of less than fifty beds. Another study by the United Mine Workers found that surgery was the major reason for the precipitous increase in hospital admission rates under their health care program. They limited surgery to salaried Board-Certified physicians as much as possible, and found that within ninety days their surgical rates fell 50 percent—and have remained at that figure ever since![21]

In spite of these rather dismal statistics in surgery, there are many general practitioners who make excellent personal physicians. They are able to handle most of the conditions which you may have. If they are willing to refer you to the appropriate specialist when the need arises, you will probably receive good medical care. Unfortunately, there is a reticence among some fee-for-service physicians to seek the consultation of another doctor. They may be concerned that this request will be viewed by the patient as a sign of weakness or of not being up-to-date. As a patient, you should be delighted when your physician seeks the opinion of another physician. It is generally agreed that many serious complications, and sometimes even death, could have been averted if the physician had sought help earlier in a case.

One solution to the dilemma of selecting a specialist is to choose an internist for your personal physician. Although he may be more expensive than the general practitioner, he is ideally qualified, through his specialty training, to handle all but the most unusual problems.

CHOOSING A PHYSICIAN

As mentioned in the Preface, when you were going to make a purchase of anything amounting to $25.00 or more, you would usually do some investigating. For instance, if you were going to buy a new portable stereo (substitute anything else you have bought recently), you would generally talk to your friends and find out what they liked and didn't like about their set. You would probably visit several stores where they were being sold and talk to salesmen about performance, durability, quality, and cost. You might even look at ratings made by private testing companies. Some of the more avid researchers might go to the public library or the newsstands for books or magazines which devote considerable space to sound equipment. You would try to become as familiar as possible with the merchandise that you were going to buy. As you learn more about stereos, you would find that you could discuss them more intelligently, and when you deal with salesmen, you would know what questions to ask. You would be better prepared to compare one view with another. You finally narrowed the choice down and made that last decision to buy a particular set. This example may not have adequately described your particular experience, but it demonstrates one approach. Considerable time and effort was invested to find what you considered the *right* stereo.

How carefully do you shop around for your medical care? If you are one of those people who has a prepaid group plan, to which your employer contributes, consider yourself lucky (this type of plan will be dealt with in detail in Chapter Seven). Most people have to do some looking around in the medical marketplace before they buy health care. Physicians are selling a commodity (time and service), and you are buying. It is like a business contract, and not all "wares" are the same. Some physicians are selling only sickness care, so be careful. The stereos used in the example above had varying levels of quality and costs. So do the physicians who dispense medical care. You can be certain you will be needing a physician one of these days, so why not do some investigating before an emergency arises? You didn't buy the first stereo you saw; why choose the first physician you hear about?

Usual Methods

You may have looked in the Yellow Pages under "Physicians and Surgeons" and found an overwhelming array listed. Even this is probably not a complete listing of the M.D.'s in your community. If there is a medical school in your city, the faculty members will probably not list their names in the Yellow Pages, although some of them may have a small practice. You may not find physicians listed who are members of a prepaid group practice. Obviously, the fact that their names are not in the Yellow Pages is no reflection on their competency—it simply means that they do not wish to have them listed. Also, telephone companies do not check the qualifications of those who are listed in the Yellow Pages. Since it is incomplete and certainly no indication of competency, the telephone book approach is not recommended except in an emergency. Situations vary, but most county medical societies have a special number that you can call in an emergency. In other areas, simply dial "0" and the telephone operator will assist you in locating a doctor.

Some suggest calling the county medical society for a recommendation, but like the Yellow Pages, it doesn't have a complete listing of the M.D.'s in your community. From this source you will hear only the names of those physicians who are members of the AMA and local medical society and who have indicated that they are willing to be recommended by the society. Such membership is no guarantee of competency, since many excellent doctors may not put themselves on such a list.

Recommendations of friends or relatives are often followed when choosing a personal physician. Assuming that they understand your preferences and that you respect their judgment, their suggestions can be a good starting point. But keep in mind that consumers are not particularly good judges of the quality of health care they receive; they are too easily swayed by a physician's personality.

If you are moving, ask your present physician if he knows of an internist or general practitioner whom he feels would make a good family physician.

Recommended Methods

The following suggestions are more likely to result in satisfaction in the quest for a physician.[22]

1. Medical school faculty

A call to the medical school will provide you with names of internists, pediatricians, and others on the clinical faculty. These are physicians who are in private practice, but who also teach the medical students. Clinical faculty members are carefully chosen by other doctors at the medical school. However, since there are only 114 medical schools in the

United States, this opportunity is not open to all. Everyone, however, does have a public library which will probably have a *Directory of Medical Specialists,* which was referred to earlier in this chapter. If you are looking for a Board-Certified specialist, the Directory will give you the information.

2. Hospital information

There are two ways to use information from accredited hospitals in choosing a doctor: to get names of good doctors from the hospital, and to check on names which you may already have. This may be difficult to do because hospitals are often reluctant to reveal information about their staff doctors. If you are really serious in your quest for information, this is a very valuable source, and should be worth some persistent digging. When there is more than one hospital in your area, you must decide which one to contact. Sheer distance may rule out some hospitals. Apparently, hospitals with the best reputation also tend to have the highest proportion of "Boarded" specialists on their staffs. In this case, you might listen to your friends and neighbors, as well as to professionals, to find out which hospitals are held in high esteem. When you have decided on an accredited hospital, call or write to ask for a list of doctors on its staff, with an indication of their rank or level.

Staff privileges.   Better hospitals are very careful in their selection of staff doctors, who have the privilege of admitting and treating patients at that hospital. A doctor may have staff privileges at several hospitals, but there are usually four different levels of staff privileges:[23]

> When a doctor is on the *consulting staff,* it means that he holds a position of esteem as an expert whose advice other doctors use. A good hospital has on its consulting staff men of considerable skill and experience. Consultants usually are Board-Certified specialists and/or have been given special recognition by the

award of fellowship in the American College of Physicians or the American College of Surgeons. One good way to select a physician or to get the names of potentially desirable ones is to use the names listed on the consulting staff of a well-reputed hospital.

The next rank is the *active staff* of the hospital. Active staff members are the doctors who spend most of their time at the hospital and who are responsible for the medical care there. In a city or a region where there are several hospitals and where one hospital has a good reputation among the townsfolk, the doctors who are on the active staff of that hospital are also good choices for you. Membership on the active staff of the hospital with a very bad reputation can be reason not to choose a doctor from that staff.

Associate staff is the next rank. It is a junior or apprentice staff, consisting of younger doctors without as much experience as active staff members. Members of the associate staff in good hospitals can be very well-informed and competent doctors. There is no reason to hold their youth against them; many will provide excellent service. They may even have more time for you because they are not so busy. In choosing a doctor, avoid selecting one who is on the associate staff of any hospital which has a bad reputation. *Courtesy staff* membership means that a doctor can admit patients to the hospital but that the doctor is not doing very much work in the hospital, either by participating in its medical staff organization or in admitting many patients. Little can be said about the qualifications of a doctor on the courtesy staff. In choosing a doctor you must find out at what hospitals the doctor does *most* of his work and at what hospitals he holds the highest rank, *i.e.*, consulting, active, or associate staff. The reputation of the hospital in which the doctor does most of his work is the important thing to consider.

Surgical privileges. In addition to the above four levels, doctors are also ranked on the kind of surgery which they are permitted to do. In better hospitals, doctors are "checked-out" very carefully by experienced doctors who actually observe the operative techniques of new men. A new doctor, if he is interested in surgery, will usually be granted *minor privileges.* This means that he can perform operations and other treatments that involve little danger to the patient and virtually no chance of disability. After he has been observed at this level during a number of operations and other physicians are convinced that he has the necessary skill, he may be granted *intermediate privileges.* This means that he can now perform operations that may involve some disability to the patient if the physician should make a mistake, but would not normally endanger life (with surgery, there is *always* that possibility!). Again, when he shows that he is competent at this level, he may be granted *major or "full" privileges,* which indicates that he can perform operations that could result in serious disability and even death if not properly done. Even when he has full privileges, he is limited to the kind of surgery that he can perform. A physician who has been approved to do major abdominal surgery, for example, cannot perform heart or brain surgery.[24] Normally, it takes a physician many months and sometimes years to move up to major surgical privileges. In some small hospitals, the above safeguards are not followed and a physician who has only minor privileges at a large well-run voluntary hospital may be doing major operations at a small or unaccredited proprietary (private) hospital.

It should be clear that both the staff level and surgical privileges of your physician in an accredited hospital can literally mean the difference between life and death. Since you are not qualified to judge a physician's performance and skill, you need to have other physicians rate the competence of a given doctor. Both the staff level and surgical privileges of a physician are evaluated in this way in our better hospitals.

If the information that you receive from the hospital lists some doctors as "Chiefs" or "Chiefs of Service," this means they are in charge of a department or major medical specialty. For example, a large general hospital will have departments of obstetrics, gynecology, medicine, surgery, and perhaps others. The chief of a department is usually a doctor who also is in private practice. In better hospitals, these key men are chosen with great care and represent a high level of trust. Such a man, if he is not too busy, would make an excellent personal physician. If he does not have the time to be your physician, he is in a good position to recommend well-qualified doctors whom he has observed practicing in his department. If the information from the hospital did not indicate which were chiefs, call or write and ask for it.

Meeting Your Doctor

When you have decided on a given doctor, make an appointment with him either for treatment of some minor problem, or for a routine physical examination. During the course of your visit, you can ask the doctor about house calls, fees, his hospital affiliation (if you don't already know), and these questions will probably lead to others. This will give you an opportunity to meet this doctor and decide whether or not you will be able to follow his suggested treatment. A doctor may be very competent and yet, if you dislike him, you would probably have better results if you found another physician with whom you felt at ease. The better the doctor-patient relationship, the more satisfied you will be. You may visit several doctors before you decide on one whom you really want for your personal physician. It may cost a few dollars to look around; try not to think of it as an expense, but as an investment in good health care. For some ideas about the first visit to your doctor, follow the suggestions in Appendix A and you will have a better understanding of the kind of care your physician will provide.

MALDISTRIBUTION AND
PRIMARY CARE
PROBLEMS

As mentioned in an earlier section, there is an uneven distribution of physicians across the nation. In order to provide proper medical service to people where and when it is needed, we must have additional physicians who are adequately distributed geographically and who reflect an appropriate mix of specialists, subspecialists, generalists, and family practitioners.[25] A recent conference in Canada dealt with the problem of an oversupply of physicians as well as a maldistribution of these physicians geographically and by specialty. A proposed solution was a National Manpower Advisory Council establishing "upper limits on the number of physicians by geographic region and by type of general or specialty practice."[26] It is probably inevitable that similar controls will be imposed on physicians in this country unless the medical profession takes steps to remedy the situation.

Although no one is certain of the outcome, attempts are being made to correct the distribution problem through innovations in medical education. At the University of Washington in Seattle, clinical clerkships are set up that allow students to spend six weeks with rural practitioners. Clerkships have been established in towns with 3500 to 10,000 residents in Washington, Alaska, Montana, and Idaho. The goal of the program is to encourage more doctors to practice family medicine and to choose rural locations for their practice.[27] Another example is a New York program which decentralizes medical education and locates physicians where the patients are and where the doctors ought to be. City University of New York is experimenting with a six-year program to train primary care physicians for practice in inner city areas. The goal is to provide students with an understanding of the community situation and help them realize the relationship between health, medicine, and society. Hopefully, the program will produce physicians who are broadly humanistic.[28] In another approach to the problem, the Navajo Indian Nation hopes to build a medical school for American Indians that would keep Indian students in an Indian community throughout their medical training. Hopefully, Indian doctors would become involved in the health problems in their own areas and remain in those communities.[29]

The federal government which heavily subsidizes medical education will be attempting to emphasize primary care and improve physician distribution by: (1) gradually lowering student grants, (2) providing bonuses to schools that emphasize primary physician training, and (3) providing scholarships to medical students who agree to serve in physician-scarce areas after graduation.

The number of counties in the United States without a practicing physician is increasing yearly and efforts are being made to remedy this trend. The National Health Service Corps (NHSC) is a federal program that places physicians and other health professionals in an area of critical need for a period of two years. Paid volunteers serve in urban as well as rural areas. Some eventually settle permanently in the communities that they served while with the NHSC.[30] There are many characteristics that hamper the ability of certain areas to attract physicians. To begin with, trends in medicine show that a smaller number of physicians are entering general private practice. Most M.D.'s are tending to specialize in hospital-based practice. Secondly, increased medical technology makes physicians feel dependent on specialized equipment, colleagues, and allied health personnel. In addition, there is a trend toward favoring group practice over solo practice, which requires locating the practice in a medium-to-high-density population area.[31]

The professional environment is not the only concern doctors have when they consider practicing in rural areas. They are interested in cultural activities for their spouses and good educational opportunities for their children. Small towns, unless they are adjacent to a large urban area, are usually unable to satisfy these needs.

Small towns have been studying physicians' reasons for

lack of interest in working in rural areas and have been advised to cooperate with adjacent towns in seeking medical assistance. Such a regional approach might establish a population base that could support not only one but several physicians. This would eliminate the intercity competition for physicians and provide for a better professional environment where physicians would not feel isolated from their colleagues. Some small towns that are so isolated that regional organization is out of the question have set up scholarship practice agreements in which medically needy communities sponsor financially needy students in return for an agreed amount of primary care service.[32]

The problem of maldistribution of physicians is also present elsewhere in the world. Some socialistic countries, such as Hungary, Poland, and the U.S.S.R. which have centralized health planning have dealt with the problem in the following ways. In the U.S.S.R., after graduation, medical doctors are assigned to a rural area for two or three years. In Poland and Hungary, financial incentives encourage doctors to practice in rural areas. Different approaches are used in Yugoslavia where health services are decentralized. Individual communes, aided by the government, offer high salaries, better housing, and longer vacations to physicians who are willing to work in rural areas.[33]

The problems of maldistribution in the United States and possible solutions are summarized in Table 2.1 on pp. 34–35.

CONTINUING MEDICAL EDUCATION FOR PHYSICIANS

In the past, a physician who received his license to practice never had to take another course unless he wished to—in spite of the fact that tremendous advances were being made each year in the fields of medicine and pharmacology. Li-

TABLE 2.1

Problem	Solution
1. Health science schools are located in urban areas and education is urban-focused.	1. Decentralize education geographically. Develop models and preceptorships of group practice with the team approach in rural areas.
2. Health science schools have not accepted responsibility for disproportionate distribution of manpower.	2. Recruit aggressively to meet rural manpower needs. Select students from rural areas. Develop monetary incentive programs. Provide models of attractive rural practice.
3. Health science schools have not accepted responsibility for the kinds of health care personnel needed.	3. Produce more family physicians. (Goal of 50 percent of graduates.) Produce more primary health care personnel at all levels. Adequately finance programs to produce primary personnel.
4. Health science schools focus on disease and in-patient management of health problems to the exclusion of primary care. Students are not taught team approach. There is little content in curricula in management, economics, and planning of health care systems.	4. Devise curricula to be comprehensive and patient-oriented. Emphasize primary and ambulatory care so that the patient is seen in the context of his own environment, rather than the environment of the teaching hospital. Involve other departments on campus to train students in administrative principles.
5. Health science schools provide isolated, fragmented education.	5. Develop programs for a broad spectrum of disciplines in the same setting. Provide models for team delivery developed by official consortium arrangements between administrations of different schools.

TABLE 2.1   (Continued)

Problem	Solution
6. Health science schools exclude rural practitioners from their faculties.	6. Appoint rural professionals to the faculties, gaining a two-way educational exchange between the schools and the rural areas.
7. Health science schools do not promote faculty interest in the study of health care delivery systems.	7. Reward faculty who do research in health care delivery systems with academic promotions.
8. Health science schools do not provide adequate continuing education programs.	8. Develop outreach education with joint planning by professionals and academics so that community needs are met. Institute problem-oriented records.
9. Technology is not applied in rural areas by health science schools.	9. Implement the technology available to make primary, secondary, and tertiary care available to rural people.

Source: Len H. Andrus and Mary Fenley, "Health Science Schools and Rural Health Manpower," *Medical Care* 12, March, 1974, 277–278.

censure for life has come under increasing criticism in recent years and changes are being made. Participation in continuing educational programs has been suggested as a requirement for periodic relicensure. Recently, medical practice acts have been amended in several states to give state licensing boards authority to require participation in educational programs as a qualification for relicensure.[34] Specialty boards are also taking a closer look at the need for recertification and a growing number of hospitals are requiring their medical staff members to participate in continuing education programs. Many hospitals now review staff members' voluntary efforts at continuing education before reappointing them.[35]

FOREIGN MEDICAL GRADUATES

In a recent year, almost half of the newly licensed physicians were foreign medical graduates (FMG). This was the seventh consecutive year that the number of FMGs has increased. These thousands of FMGs who were initially attracted by residency training opportunities in the United States have stayed on to become permanent additions to the U.S. manpower pool.[36] The migration of physicians from developing countries to the United States may be due to the westernization of medical education systems in such countries. The medical curriculum is a virtual carbon copy of the standard American curriculum often taught by American- or British-trained faculty. However, the medical problems facing the graduating physicians are far different from those reflected in their westernized training. For example, in developing countries "the urgent need is to achieve a better standard of family health care and to solve problems relating to nutrition and public health. Sophisticated refinement of diagnosis and therapeutic measures is but a vague goal in the unforeseeable future."[37] The medical training in developing countries is designed to propel the students toward migration to the west rather than to solve their own countries' health problems.

Foreign medical graduates are approaching 20 percent of all physicians in the United States and one-third of all current internship and residency training posts are filled by them. The Association of American Medical Colleges (AAMC) states that "this country should not depend for its supply of physicians to any significant extent on the immigration of FMGs or on the training of its own citizens in foreign medical schools." According to the AAMC, the foreign-trained physicians are less competent than those trained in the United States. The AAMC also objects to a special licensure provision for FMGs allowing them to practice in any state institutions. FMGs are working in areas that often are not acceptable to American doctors—city, state, and prison hospitals and institutions for the mentally retarded. The AAMC suggests that public institutions are depending on physicians who are not fully qualified but who are willing to accept poor working conditions and lower incomes. The AAMC would like to eliminate the services of the foreign medical graduates and replace them with auxiliary staff, educated and supervised by "U.S.-trained" physicians.

There are those who applaud the FMGs in our midst, feeling that they fill a gap in our medical ranks. Once qualified for practice in the United States, the FMGs tend to settle in metropolitan areas, seeking specialty training and Board certification in about the same proportion as American-trained doctors.[38]

In answer to the charge that foreign medical graduates are less competent, it has been proposed that the method of comparing the foreign-trained and American-trained graduate is unfair. Licensure failure ratios are often quoted without specifying that many of the FMGs who take the examination have been out of medical school for several years while American candidates are nearly always fresh from their studies of basic sciences. A more equitable comparison may emerge when all physicians are required to take examinations for relicensure.[39]

FMGs are discriminated against in many ways while pursuing their profession—from licensure laws, entrance into training programs, acceptance into specialties (especially surgery), and election to higher offices in organized medicine. The nonassimilation of the foreign physician, either due to his reticence to integrate or to prejudicial feelings within the medical profession is detrimental to all concerned.[40]

THE AMERICAN MEDICAL ASSOCIATION

The American Medical Association (AMA) was founded in 1847. It is the national organization of M.D.'s and approximately 175,000 (of the 375,000 doctors in the United States) are members. Its headquarters are located in a block-long, nine-story building in Chicago, where a staff of 900 persons (25 in Washington) directs various programs. Any physician who is a member in good standing of his local medical society may become a member of the AMA. Your doctor may belong to one of the over 1900 local medical societies. The 235-member House of Delegates, elected mainly from the state medical societies, is the policy-making body; it also elects the president, vice president, and other officers of the AMA to their annual terms. The AMA maintains numerous councils and committees to keep up to date in medical matters and to develop policies in the best interest of the organization.

The AMA publishes the weekly *Journal of the American Medical Association,* as well as ten monthly specialty journals dealing with psychiatry, otolaryngology, environmental health, pathology, ophthalmology, internal medicine, surgery, neurology, and children's diseases. It also publishes a monthly consumer magazine, *Today's Health,* and a weekly medical newspaper, *American Medical News.*

For biographical and educational information pertaining to a member of the AMA, look in the *American Medical Directory,* published biennially and found in most libraries. The information is coded to conserve space, so it will take some effort for you to learn what you want to know about a particular doctor. The information in the directory is obtained directly from each physician, and is sometimes supplemented from other sources. The directory also lists some M.D.'s who are not members of the AMA.[41]

ENDNOTES

1. V. R. Neufeld, Coordinator, Program for Educational Development, McMaster University Faculty of Medicine, personal communication, November 18, 1974.
2. "Ph.D.s to M.D.s," *American Medical News,* June 3, 1974, p. 9.

3. "Graduate Medical Education: Moving Toward a New Status Quo," *Hospitals* 48; August 16, 1974, 41–42.
4. "Schools Seek a Better Way to Select Medical Students," *American Medical News* 16; December 24, 1974, 10.
5. Robert H. Ebert, "The Medical School," *Scientific American* 229; September, 1973, 148.
6. Ibid., p. 141.
7. James L. Dennis, "The Establishment of Family Practice Department in Medical School," unpublished paper presented to the American Academy of General Practice, Kansas City, Mo., April 19, 1969.
8. The American Board of Medical Specialties, *Directory of Medical Specialists,* Vol. 16 (Chicago: Marquis—Who's Who, Inc., 1974–1975), pp. xvii–xix.
9. Ibid., pp. 522–523.
10. American Medical Association, *Horizons Unlimited* (Chicago: 1969), pp. 49–50.
11. Reprinted with permission of the Macmillan Company from Richard H. Blum, *The Commonsense Guide to Doctors, Hospitals, and Medical Care* (New York: Macmillan, 1964), pp. 47–48. © Richard H. Blum, 1964.
12. Martin L. Gross, *The Doctors* (New York: Random House, Inc., 1966), p. 205.
13. William H. Potter, *The Common Sense Guide to Medical Care* (New York: Duell, Sloan and Pearce, 1961), pp. 46–51.
14. Ibid., p. 49.
15. Alex Gerber, *The Gerber Report* (New York: David McKay Company, Inc., 1971), pp. 1–17.
16. David Mechanic, *Public Expectations and Health Care* (New York: Wiley-Interscience, 1972), p. 187.
17. Selig Greenberg, *The Quality of Mercy* (New York: Atheneum, 1971), pp. 187–189.
18. Roul Tunley, *The American Health Scandal* (New York: Harper & Row, 1966), p. 45.
19. Gross, *The Doctors,* p. 204.
20. Tunley, *The American Health Scandal,* pp. 116–117.
21. U.S. Department of Health, Education, and Welfare, *Public Health Service-Labor Seminar on Consumer Health Services* (Washington, D.C.: U.S. Government Printing Office, 1968), p. 108.

22. Blum, *The Commonsense Guide to Doctors, Hospitals, and Medical Care,* pp. 51–53.
23. Ibid., pp. 53–54.
24. Ibid., p. 54.
25. Robert E. Toomey, "Graduate Medical Education: Defining the Hospital's Role," *Hospitals* 48; August 16, 1974, 43–44.
26. John K. Inglehar, "Downs, Ups of Medical Education," *Modern Healthcare* 2; July, 1974, p. 79.
27. *San Diego Evening Tribune,* June 11, 1974.
28. "Training MD's to Help the Inner City," *American Medical News* 17; April 15, 1974, 18–19.
29. "Navajo Health Authority is Planning Pan Indian Medical School," *Public Health Reports* 89; September–October, 1974, 488–489.
30. "AMA to Recruit Physicians for NHSC," *American Medical News* 17; April 29, 1974, 12.
31. Ross Mullner and Thomas W. O'Rourke, "A Geographic Analysis of Counties Without an Active Non-Federal Physician, United States, 1963–71," *Health Service Reports* 89; May–June, 1974, 256–262.
32. "Small Towns Get New Rx," *American Medical News* 17; May 6, 1974, 1, 7.
33. Laurence Steinman, "Maldistribution of Physicians in Yugoslavia," *Journal of Medical Education* 49; February, 1974, 187.
34. "Relicensure and Recertification," *Journal of the American Medical Association* 229; July 22, 1974, 458–459.
35. "Focus in California Program: What are the Learner's Needs?," *Hospital Practice* 7; March, 1972, 51–56.
36. "Reliance on Foreign Graduates Hit," *American Medical News* 17; July 29, 1974, 1.
37. Mehdi Tavassoli, "Physician Migration," *Journal of the American Medical Association* 228; May 13, 1974, p. 825.
38. Arms C. McGuinness, "Performance of U.S. Citizen Candidates on the January, 1974, ECFMG Examination," *Journal of the American Medical Association* 229; July 22, 1974, 428–430.
39. *Los Angeles Times,* May 2, 1972, p. 7.
40. *Journal of the American Medical Association* 229; 434–435.
41. American Medical Association, *The American Medical Association* (Chicago: 1965), pp. 5–15.

Chapter Three

Dental Care

Dental disease is rampant in America; 98 percent of the population suffers or will suffer from it. More money is spent on this malady than on any other disease.[1] Decay is not the only problem that affects your teeth; you may also suffer from chipped and broken teeth, gum infections, impacted wisdom teeth, and the loss of one or more teeth. Such conditions or the desire to have a checkup generally motivate people to see their dentist.

HISTORICAL VIEW

Archeological reports suggest that from his earliest appearance man has been concerned about dental diseases. Skulls dating back to the New Stone Age indicate that prehistoric man may have taken care of painful teeth by knocking them out. Early attempts at diagnosis included the theory that tooth worms caused dental decay. A remedy of 50 percent arsenic was used to treat this condition. In early Egypt, the lawbreaker's front tooth was removed as a permanent and severe form of punishment for his transgression.

Modern dentistry was introduced by the Frenchman Pierre Fauchard with his two-volume work entitled *The*

Surgeon-Dentist. His facts and theories served as a guide for dentists for over a hundred years.

The world's first dental school, The Baltimore College of Dental Surgery, was founded in 1840. Prior to this, all dental practitioners received their training by apprenticeship. This system allowed a young man to associate himself with an established practitioner who taught the apprentice everything that he himself knew. After 1840, dental schools flourished, and set their own standards. Proprietary schools, which were more interested in showing a profit than in providing good quality training, spread rapidly. Professional dental leaders eventually became alarmed at these substandard schools turning out poorly trained graduates, whose useless degrees were accepted by many states. A concerned profession urged reform and, in 1926, a five-year study entitled *Dental Education in the United States and Canada* was published. It stressed the importance of dental school being affiliated with universities, the need for integrating the clinical and biological sciences, and the importance of research. This publication sparked reform in dental education and, one by one, the substandard schools were forced out of business. By 1930, only thirty-eight dental schools met or surpassed the new educational standards.[2]

BECOMING A DENTIST

Pre-professional Education

Before a student can enter a dental school, he must complete at least two, and preferably three, years of pre-dental education. Actually, over half of the dental students in the United States obtain their baccalaureate degrees prior to their entry into dental school.

Professional Education

After successfully completing their pre-professional education, students attend one of the fifty-eight schools in operation in the United States. Men predominate in the four-years program which graduates dentists with either the degree of D.D.S. (Doctor of Dental Surgery), or its equivalent, D.M.D. (Doctor of Medical Dentistry).

Dental education places emphasis on both clinical (or technical) skills and a sound understanding of the physical and biological sciences. The basic sciences and preclinical sciences are taught during the freshman and sophomore years. In some schools, medical and dental students are taught the basic science courses together. During the first two years, some basic skills of dental restoration and treatment are learned through practice on inanimate objects.

In the second two years, students actually treat patients under the supervision of clinical instructors. Students are also introduced to hospital dental procedures and the dental care of special patients, such as geriatric or chronically ill patients. Some dental schools are introducing students to the patient earlier in the curriculum so that they may better correlate knowledge of the basic sciences with the practical application of dentistry.

While in dental school, the students also learn how best to utilize the skills of the dental auxiliaries: the dental hygienist, the dental assistant, and the laboratory technician. During their professional training, dental students are exposed to approximately thirty different subject areas which include the basic sciences and the various dental specialties, as well as pharmacology, roentgenology, jurisprudence, and diagnosis and treatment.

DISTRIBUTION OF DENTISTS

Like doctors, dentists are not evenly distributed throughout the country. The District of Columbia has one dentist for every 1,137 people; Mississippi, on the other hand, has one dentist for every 3,446 people. The average for the nation is one dentist for every 1,682 persons. Within states, the dentist-to-population ratio also varies widely from area to area. Although these numbers reflect real differences in the availability of dentists in the nation, they do not tell the whole story. "Some dentists are more productive than others because they employ several auxiliary personnel. There is geographic variation in needs for dental care, economic conditions and appreciation of dental health. Also, residents of a given location may obtain dental care in another locality."[3]

SPECIALIZATION

Dentistry, like medicine, has recognized specialty areas. There are nearly 11,000 dental specialists in private practice in the United States, and approximately 800 in practice at the federal level—in the armed services, public health service, and the Veteran's Administration.[4] The eight dental specialties are listed below.[5]

1. *Dental Public Health* deals with the prevention and control of dental diseases and the promotion of dental health through organized community efforts. It serves the community as a patient, rather than the individual. It is concerned with dental health education of the public, with applied dental research, and with the administration of group dental care programs, as well as with the prevention and control of dental diseases on a community basis.

2. *Endodontics* is concerned with the cause, prevention, diagnosis, and treatment of the diseases and injuries that affect the interior tissues of the teeth. It includes pulp capping, the treatment of infected root canals, and the subsequent filling of these canals; the surgical removal of diseased tissue when indicated; the restoration of the natural appearance of the crown when discolored; and the replantation of teeth that have been knocked out.

3. *Oral Pathology* deals with the nature of oral disease through the study of its causes, its processes, and its

effects. The oral pathologist need not treat the disease directly, but through knowledge of the disease guides other members of the health services team to more effective therapy.

4. *Oral Surgery* deals with the diagnosis and surgical treatment of oral diseases, injuries, and defects of the human jaw and associated structures.

5. *Orthodontics* is the study of oral and dental development. It seeks to determine the factors which control growth processes so that the teeth are properly aligned. Persons under the care of an orthodontist usually wear metal or plastic appliances in the course of their treatment.

6. *Pedodontics* is the treatment of patients possessing a developing dentition (children). Such practice may include the use of pedodontic appliances to prevent malocclusions.

7. *Periodontics* deals with the health and diseases of the supporting structures of the teeth and oral mucous membrane.

8. *Prosthodontics* deals with the replacement of missing natural teeth and associated tissues via fixed or removable artificial substitutes (dentures).

How does a dentist become a specialist? Prior to December 31, 1967, it was possible for a dentist to notify the American Dental Association (ADA) that he was limiting his practice to one of the above fields. He was then considered a specialist in that area, even though he had completed no additional formal education or examinations. A second option is open to those who practice in a state which permits a dentist to take the American Board Examinations. On successful completion of written and oral examinations, the dentist is then considered a specialist in that field. The third way a dentist may specialize is by completing two or more academic years of advanced education in one of the above fields. If, after this, he sucessfully completes the American Board Examinations, he is classified as a Diplomate.

Unfortunately, when you go to a dental specialist, you probably do not know which of three methods he used to become a specialist. To improve your chances of receiving competent care, we would suggest the following. First of all, when you call to make an appointment, ask the receptionist if the dentist is a Diplomate. If he is not, ask where he received his specialty training. If he did not receive any specialty training, you can ask how long he has been practicing his specialty. Before phoning, you may also check the *Directory of Dental Specialists,* a listing of all dentists who are recognized as specialists by the ADA. It is available in most libraries.

DENTAL AUXILIARIES

There are three auxiliary members of the dental health team: the dental hygienist, the dental assistant, and the dental laboratory technician. In the last few years, the number of allied dental auxiliaries has increased more rapidly than the dentist supply. Dental auxiliaries now account for approximately three-fifths of the total dental work force.[6]

Dental Hygienist

Two types of programs are available for the education of dental hygienists. The first is the two-year curriculum which leads to a certificate in dental hygiene or to an associate degree in arts or applied sciences. At one time, dental hygiene programs were provided primarily by schools of dentistry, but now junior colleges and technical schools provide many of the programs. This two-year program qualifies hygienists for clinical practice in a dentist's office. The second approach is a four-year bachelor's degree program offered at approximately half of the dental hygiene schools. This curriculum is designed for those hygienists who wish to assume leadership positions in teaching and public health. Bachelor's level hygienists qualify for graduate programs leading to master's degrees in dental hygiene and related fields.

The dental hygienist works under the supervision of the dentist and assists both the dentist and the patient by scaling and polishing teeth and by providing dental health information. She may also expose and process dental x-rays, apply fluoride solution to children's teeth, and instruct patients in toothbrushing techniques and proper diet in relation to the teeth. Most dental hygienists (80 percent) work in private dental offices providing services to patients. Others are found in public and parochial schools, public and private clinics, hospitals, and other institutions. The dental hygienist is the only one of the three auxiliary members of the dental health team who must be licensed to practice. For every one hundred practicing dentists there are about sixteen active hygienists, although many of these are part-time.[7]

The American Dental Hygienists Association (ADHA) became a national organization in 1923. It works very closely with the American Dental Association (ADA). For example, members of the ADHA serve as consultants to the ADA council on Dental Education and as members of accreditation teams, as well as in other capacities. The official monthly publication of the ADHA is the *Journal of the American Dental Hygienists Association.*[8]

Dental Assistant

Over fifty years ago, the American Dental Assistants Association (ADAA) had its beginnings. The dental assistant of today has come a long way from the unskilled office girl of 1924 who received on-the-job-training. Today's dental assistant receives her training at one of the 250 accredited dental assisting programs around the country. To be accredited, a program must provide at least one academic year of training in dental assisting. Approximately 20 percent of these programs offer a two-year curriculum in which the required training in dental assisting is augmented by a year of general education. The two-year program leads to an associate degree. Students graduating from either one- or two-year accredited programs, or those who have completed equivalent training, are eligible to apply for examination and certification by the Certifying Board of the ADAA. To retain certified standing, the dental assistant must show annual proof of continuing education.[9,10]

At least two of every three dentists in private practice now employ one or more dental assistants. The main function of the dental assistant is to assist the dentist at the chairside; this includes preparing the patient for treatment, keeping the operating field clear, passing instruments, and mixing materials. Most dental assistants are being trained in the principle of "four-handed dentistry," that is, the efficient utilization of the chairside dental assistant. She may also serve as secretary-receptionist and handle office records and accounts.

The certified dental assistant is viewed by the profession as "a competent, perceptive, well-educated auxiliary, knowledgeable about scientific and technical principles, cognizant of a dentist's needs in operating procedures, and capable of performing many intraoral [within the mouth] functions herself."[11]

The ADAA's official monthly periodical is *The Dental Assistant*.

Dental Laboratory Technician

Since few formal education programs are available for dental laboratory technicians, most receive their training on the job in commercial laboratories. Approximately thirty-five accredited institutions offer the two-year academic program, consisting of one year of basic and dental sciences and a second year of supervised practical laboratory experience.

A voluntary certification program now exists for technicians who have completed the two-year accredited program and three years of employment (or equivalent experience in lieu of formal training). To obtain certification, a technician must pass an examination administered by the National Board for Certification in Dental Laboratory Technology.

Most dental laboratory technicians are employed in commercial dental laboratories that serve the majority of the nation's dentists. Technicians do not have direct contact with patients, but perform the work according to instructions received from the dentist. Technicians are highly skilled craftsmen who perform many tasks involved in the construction of complete and partial dentures, fixed bridgework, crowns and other such dental restorations and appliances.[12]

CHOOSING A DENTIST

Choosing a dentist should be done with great care unless you can afford, in terms of quality and price, to have dental work done by an inept dentist. There are four important reasons why self-defense is very important in the dental area.[13] First, at least 15 percent of dentists, by conservative estimates, are incompetent, dishonest, or both. Second, over 80 percent of dentists are in solo (individual) practice. This means that they work in their own offices and their work does not come under the scrutiny of their colleagues. Physicians receive some monitoring when they use a hospital because other doctors and hospital committees see what they are doing or observe their records. Thirdly, there is virtually no quality review of dentists by the dental profession. And lastly, in most states, there are no requirements for either formal standards of performance or continuing education for dentists.

The traditional approach to finding a dentist has been to call the local dental society. This will provide you with the names of dentists in your area who are members of the society, but does not indicate the levels of competence or incompetence. Dental societies usually take the view that all dentists are equally competent, but many studies have shown that this is not the case. Another traditional approach, which may prove effective, is to ask friends or relatives to recommend good dentists. However, for those who are serious about finding and keeping a competent dentist, the following suggestions should help.[14]

Where to Start

Begin with the professionals themselves. They are in the best position to know which of their colleagues are the most knowledgeable and proficient. The faculty of a university school of dentistry will be made up of dentists who are generally outstanding in their field. Dentists affiliated with the dental school usually have a private practice as well. If they are too busy to take on more patients, they will be able to recommend other highly qualified dentists. Unfortunately, there are only fifty-eight dental schools in the U.S., so this avenue may not be open to you.

Another approach is to call an orthodontist or an endodontist for their recommendation. These two specialists are interested in preventive dentistry and they tend to receive referrals from other preventive-minded dentists and are in a position to assess the quality of care that the patient has received.

If you can find out where dentists go themselves when they need dental work done, you will have some good prospects.

The Initial Contact

Most people make their first contact by phone, which may be fine if they have followed the preceding suggestions.

But if you make your choice from the Yellow Pages of the telephone book, it would be advisable to make a personal visit to your prospective dentist's office. This will enable you to "size up" his office. What kind of an atmosphere does it have? Does the dentist have up-to-date equipment? (If you want to get technical, two items a dentist should have are: (a) a high speed drill and (b) a special cleaning tool called a cavitron.) Does the office look clean and neat? If not, the things you cannot see may not be well cared for either.

Meeting the Dentist

Do you like the dentist? Do you feel confident that he knows what he is doing? Although you can be wrong about assessing the quality of dental work from the dentist's chair-side manner, you will certainly be less apprehensive about your treatment if you do have faith in him.

Does he take time to explain the various treatments and the possible benefits of any proposed dental treatment? For example, if a tooth has to be filled, does he explain the relative merits of silver (amalgam), gold, or plastic fillings?

Actually, the legal doctrine of informed consent requires a dentist to explain fully, in language you can understand, any treatment he proposes, including the risks, the alternative treatments, and any possible complications that may result. If he does not do this, legally you have not consented to the treatment and he may be liable for a malpractice suit.

Prior to treatment, a good dentist will ask questions about your past medical and dental experience. This will provide him with information about existing diseases or conditions, such as heart disease, diabetes, or drug allergies that might affect your dental treatment. If he neglects to take a history, he may neglect other important things as well.

Were you able to see the dentist reasonably close to the appointed time? A well-run practice usually enables the dentist to see you on schedule.

Getting an Estimate

It is always a good idea to know what dental treatment is going to cost. Ask the receptionist (or the dentist) *in advance* about fees. Reputable dentists prefer to have an honest discussion of charges so that later misunderstandings are avoided. If you find that a dentist or his receptionist hesitates to discuss fees, or becomes evasive, take your business elsewhere.

If you feel that an estimate is too high, get other estimates. Remember that it is not unusual for dental charges to vary somewhat in the same geographic area, even among good dentists, depending upon their experience, reputation, and specialty.

While we are discussing money, you should receive an itemized bill after the work is completed. On simple procedures, of course, an itemized bill is not necessary. But on any extensive work you should receive a description of the service and a breakdown of the costs. For example, x-rays and fillings should be listed separately on your bill. Since you are paying the bill, you have a right to know what each service costs you. Good dentists usually itemize.

Emergency Dental Care

Dental emergencies do not occur frequently, but when they do you will want immediate treatment. Your dentist should have a phone number that you can call in an emergency. If he is unavailable, he should have another dentist take his calls. A dentist who has been giving you routine treatment should be willing to take care of you in an emergency. In fact, Section 5 of the Principles of Ethics of the American Dental Association states, "The dentist has an obligation when consulted in an emergency by the patient of another dentist to attend to the conditions leading to the emergency . . . ."

In any case, the time to find out about the availability of emergency care is prior to an emergency. Don't hesitate to ask your dentist.

Preventive Care

Much is known today about preventing dental diseases. Most of the approximately sixty million teeth being extracted each year in the United States could have been saved by good preventive dental care. Since you will (hopefully) visit your dentist's office only one or two days a year, what you do the other 363 or 364 days will be vitally important to your dental health. Chose a dentist who is prevention-oriented. Does your dentist take the time to discuss prevention? Does he explain how to remove plaque (pronounced plack)? Plaque is that accumulation of food, salts, and saliva that provides a home for the bacteria. Bacteria turns sugar into the acid that is responsible for tooth decay. Most people need some encouragement to continue proper home dental care. Your dentist should provide this encouragement.

Living in a community that has fluoridated water will reduce the incidence of tooth decay in children by around 60 percent; it will also increase the resistance to osteoporosis (bones which break easily) in the elderly.

Extractions

Today most teeth can be saved by one of the various dental specialists. Your teeth should last a lifetime; removing a tooth should be done only as a last resort. If you have any doubts about having a tooth removed, seek a consultation from another dentist, one not associated in any way with your own dentist. Ask your dentist to forward your x-rays to the other dentist; this will avoid having to have other x-rays taken.

Often it seems cheaper to remove a tooth than to go to the expense of having a specialist work on it (for example, paying an endodontist to do root canal work). However, when all aspects are considered, that is, comfort, efficiency of chewing, and the stability of the other teeth in the mouth, most experts agree that saving a tooth is the best possible bargain in dental care.

X-Rays

Since radiation is potentially harmful, it is wise to avoid any excessive or unnecessary exposure to x-rays. Some x-rays are necessary, however, and detect many dental problems that would go unnoticed during a routine visual examination. For the average patient, having dental x-rays taken once a year seems to be a good rule of thumb. If problems are present, more frequent x-rays might be required. Every five years, it may be necessary to have full-mouth x-rays. If you have had recent x-rays for other purposes and you are concerned about overexposure, discuss it with your dentist. Alternatives may be available. The American Dental Association's Council on Dental Materials and Devices suggests that dentists "use leaded aprons on children and all patients in the reproductive age range as an additional precaution to prevent radiation of the gonads."[15] In addition, dentists are asked to have periodic radiation protection surveys of their office and to continue their education in the area of radiology.

Group Practice

Dentists who practice in a group are in a good position to evaluate the performance of their colleagues, and since those in the group usually share their expenses and profits, they are likely to get rid of incompetent dentists. Poor work by one dentist in the group reflects on all members in the group. Group practice may mean lower costs and better coverage during emergencies. Also group practice means that a greater variety of work can be handled under one roof.

Auxiliary Personnel

As pointed out earlier in this chapter, the dental auxiliary personnel are dental hygienists, dental assistants, and dental laboratory technicians. The dentist can improve efficiency and save a considerable amount of time by the proper use of the dental auxiliaries. He is most efficient when he does only the procedures that require his skill and delegates the other tasks to the appropriate auxiliary.

Board Certification

Although board certification is no guarantee of competence, it certainly improves your chances of receiving highly skilled care.

Wisdom Teeth

Wisdom teeth are the major cause of dental emergencies. Often, they only partially erupt in your mouth and they are difficult to see and to brush, so they are more likely to decay. Or, because of lack of room they may become wedged against another tooth (impacted). Wisdom teeth are often extracted even when they are not causing any problems. Why? It has been suggested that removal is "facilitated by the fact that surgery for removal of impacted teeth is generally covered by medical and surgical expense insurance, but other dental procedures are not covered. Blue Shield usually covers surgery for impacted wisdom teeth, so these teeth can be described as 'blue teeth.' The operation might be called the 'blue plate' special."[16] The answer? Get a consultation before having any wisdom teeth removed. We don't remove breasts on the chance that they might become cancerous, so why should we remove wisdom teeth on the chance that they may give us trouble?

Advertising

Section 12 of the Principles of Ethics of the American Dental Association states in part: "Advertising reflects adversely on the dentist who employs it and lowers the public esteem of the dental profession." Dentists who advertise are not members of their local dental societies or the ADA. Advertising guarantees neither competence nor training and tends to add a "hucksterish" air to the field of dentistry. Since dentists are in short supply in this country, you may reasonably ask: Why is it necessary for a dentist to advertise?

General

Some additional things to watch for:

- The people working in the dentist's office should be happy.
- The dentist should be relaxed, satisfied.
- He should have only two chairs, which means that he can take the time to treat you properly. More chairs may mean that he spends a lot of time moving from one to another. He needs long periods of uninterrupted work to do a good job.
- The dentist should be organized. His instruments should be readily available in a tray. If he is constantly looking through drawers for his dental instruments, watch out.

- He should be interested in giving you an annual or semi-annual checkup and will have his staff send out reminders or call you.
- He has another person working with him to assist him.

It is impossible in this chapter to cover adequately all the things to look for in a good dentist. By keeping the preceding points in mind, however, you will greatly improve your chances of receiving high-caliber dental care. But even the most careful search may result in dissatisfaction. If a dentist is not doing the job you expect he should, look for another dentist.

DENTAL CLINIC

For those who are close to a dental school and cannot afford regular dental care, the dental clinic of a dental school is a possibility. At such clinics, students are "practicing" the art of dentistry under the close supervision of a faculty member of the dental school. The work may be a little slower than elsewhere, but the price is right! Usually the level of care given at these clinics is good and often better than that found in the community.

OVERCHARGED OR
DISSATISFIED?

If you feel your dentist has overcharged you, or your are dissatisfied with his treatment, discuss the matter with him. If you are still not satisfied, send a detailed explanation of your experience to your county dental society, the Better Business Bureau, the State Board of Dental Examiners, and your state consumer agency. If you merely want sympathy, then complain only to friends and relatives; if you want action, complain to those who have enough influence (and perhaps power) to do something about your complaint.

County Dental Society

This is the local branch of the ADA and one of their objectives is to promote good dental care in their area. Their grievance committee will usually investigate legitimate complaints against a dentist. Most county dental societies are interested in bringing errant members into line. Of course, if your dentist is not a member of the county dental society, you may be referred to the State Board of Dental Examiners (see below).

The Better Business Bureau

The Better Business Bureau (BBB) will file any written complaint against a business (and doctors and dentists are in business). The BBB has no legal power; it is merely an information-dispensing organization. If a person calls in and asks if the Bureau has received derogatory information about a particular dentist, he will be told the number of complaints the Bureau has on file.

The State Board of Dental Examiners

The name of this organization may vary from state to state. It may be called the Bureau of Professional and Occupational Licensing. Call your local dental society for the correct name and address. In any case, this organization is in charge of licensing dentists and has the power to discipline those who have been proven to be overcharging or doing unsatisfactory work. Many complaints against a dentist will mean closer scrutiny when his license comes up for renewal.

State Consumer Agency

Many states now have an official consumer agency designed to help consumers by providing educational material and assistance in disputes over the quality and/or price of work done.

Don't expect miracles. Although most organizations are becoming more sensitive to consumer complaints, the results may be less than satisfactory and the discipline meted out may be nothing more than a reprimand. However, if complaints against one dentist keep coming in, legal avenues may be used to block his unethical and/or illegal practices. You owe it to yourself and other consumers to put your problem in writing. Only by concerted consumer complaints will changes be made.

THE AMERICAN DENTAL ASSOCIATION

The American Dental Association (ADA), with headquarters in Chicago, is the national organization for the over 125,000 dentists in the United States. Your dentist may belong to one of the 485 local or 54 state and territorial dental societies. The objectives of the ADA are "to encourage the improvement of the health of the public, to promote the art and science of dentistry, and to represent the interests of the members of the dental profession and the public which it serves." These objectives are carried out in three broad categories: 1) improvement of dental health through research, dental care programs, health education, and the promotion of water fluoridation; 2) reporting of scientific and technical information through professional meetings and various pamphlets, films, and publications; 3) service to the public and the profession by testing and evaluating drugs, inspecting and accrediting dental schools, doing surveys and special studies, as well as working with allied dental groups and representatives of other health professions.[17]

The official publication of the ADA is the monthly *Journal of the American Dental Association*.

DENTAL TRENDS

Several areas of dentistry are changing rapidly as our population grows and the need for dental care increases. One indication of change is the expansion of the duties performed by the dental auxiliaries, especially the dental hygienist and the dental assistant. These expanded duties include such procedures as removal of sutures and dressings, placement and removal of rubber dams (used for fillings), and taking impressions for study casts. One recent nationwide study showed that many states permitted these and other expanded functions for dental hygienists and dental assistants.[18] A study conducted on four private dental offices indicated that "the utilization of an expanded duty dental auxiliary is economically feasible for private offices; the dentist is permitted to deliver more services in less time."[19] A study of patients at the University of Iowa College of Dentistry compared dental treatment performed by dental school students with that done by expanded function dental hygiene students. "Dental hygiene students received higher ratings from patients than did dental students on preventive periodontal functions."[20]

Another area of change is in the rapid expansion of third-party programs. During 1974, some twenty-two million persons were covered by dental insurance.*[21] The "third party" is the insurance company which acts as the middleman ("fiscal intermediary") between the patient and his den-

* By 1980, it is estimated that there will be thirty-five to forty million people covered by dental insurance.

tist. For patients on Medicaid, the third party may be a government agency. Some dentists have not participated in dental service plans and others have refused to treat patients under Medicaid. These professionals will have to review their positions and may come to realize that these programs will bring better dental care to the public (and incidentally, will increase dentists' incomes). Dentists will have to become better acquainted with insurance terminology and benefits allowed by various policies so that they can explain the extent of coverage to their patients, before treatment starts.[22]

Peer review has been referred to as one of the top priorities in dentistry today. It may be that the dental profession is moving on this idea so that the government will not intrude. Peer review, that is, review of quality of dental work by other dentists, certainly needs to be established. It should help the consumer separate the incompetent dentist from the competent ones. As one dentist stated, "The best and only way to answer our critics and maintain any semblance of private practice is to bridge any existing credibility gap with an effective review system in every state."[23]

ENDNOTES

1. Thomas McGuire, *The Tooth Trip* (New York: Random House, Inc., 1972), pp. 223–226.
2. Shailer Peterson, *The Dentist and His Assistant* (St. Louis: The C. V. Mosby Company, 1972).
3. American Dental Association, *Distribution of Dentists in the United States by State, Region, District and County* (Chicago, 1974), p. 1.
4. *Distribution of Dental Specialists in 1973 by Region and State* (Chicago: The American Dental Association, 1974), mimeographed material.
5. *Definitions of Specialty Areas of Dental Practice as Submitted by the Council on Dental Education to the 1966 ADA House of Delegates,* unpublished material, American Dental Association.

6.   U.S. Department of Health, Education, and Welfare, *Health Resources Statistics* (Washington, D.C.: U.S. Government Printing Office, 1974), p. 68.
7.   Ibid., p. 69.
8.   Wilma E. Motley, *Ethics, Jurisprudence and History for the Dental Hygienist* (Philadelphia: Lea & Febiger, 1972), pp. 104–121.
9.   Bee Helgeson, "1924–1974: American Dental Assistants Commemorate 50th Anniversary," *Journal of the American Dental Association* 89; September, 1974, 539–544.
10. *Health Resources Statistics,* pp. 69–70.
11. *Journal of the American Dental Association* 89, p. 544.
12. *Health Resources Statistics,* pp. 93–94.
13. Herbert S. Denenberg, *A Shopper's Guide to Dentistry* (Harrisburg: The Pennsylvania Insurance Department, 1973), pp. 3–5.
14. Ibid., pp. 6–19.
15. Council on Dental Materials and Devices, "Recommendations in Radiographic Practices, May, 1972," *Journal of the American Dental Association* 84; May, 1972, 1108.
16. Denenberg, *A Shopper's Guide to Dentistry,* p. 18.
17. American Dental Association, *Membership in the American Dental Association* (Chicago, n.d.)
18. Council on Dental Education, "Report on the Education and Utilization of Dental Auxiliaries," *Journal of the American Dental Association* 88; May, 1974, 1039–1040.
19. Dale Redig et al., "Expanded Duty Dental Auxiliaries in Four Private Dental Offices: The First Year's Experience," *Journal of the American Dental Association* 88; May, 1974, 969–984.
20. Nancy L. Sisty and William G. Henderson, "A Comparative Study of Patient Evaluations of Dental Treatment Performed by Dental and Expanded-Function Dental Hygiene Students," *Journal of the American Dental Association* 88; May, 1974, 985–996.
21. Nancy A. Resnick, "Trends in Health Care Delivery: Private Practice Conference Explores Issues," *Journal of the American Dental Association* 89; September, 1974, 546.
22. Robert I. Kaplan, "Third Party Programs: Implications for the Future," *Journal of the American Dental Association* 88; May, 1974, 894.
23. *Journal of the American Dental Association* 89, p. 546.

Chapter Four

Nursing

The American Nursing Association has stated that "providing the best nursing care possible is and always has been the primary concern of professional nurses."[1] Indeed, some nurses have kept pace with the technological and scientific changes in the health care field; others have allowed themselves to be bypassed by these advances. In this chapter, we will discuss the development and education of nurses, their changing roles in health care, and some of the growing pains that the nursing profession is now experiencing.

HISTORY OF NURSING

Nursing has been considered a respectable profession for approximately one hundred years. Before the appearance of Florence Nightingale, the nursing needs of the country were met by religious groups or mothers in the home. "It was not until Florence Nightingale's time that the concept of nursing became one of vocation."[2] Early in the nineteenth century, the need for personnel in hospitals provided a focal point for nursing services. Gradually, hospitals began to train their own nurses and the vocation of nursing slowly began to take on the attributes of a profession. Just as government agencies began to evaluate and award accreditation to hospitals, so agencies evaluated and accredited the diploma schools of nursing.

Toward the end of the nineteenth century, nurses began to organize. One of these organizations was the National League for Nursing Education. One of its main purposes was to improve nursing education in schools across the United States.

Since the 1950s, there has been much controversy about the education of nurses. This controversy has paralleled three developments: the emancipation of women, the realization by communities that they were responsible for the care of the sick, and the recognition by nurses of the need for a greater body of knowledge.[3] During the past twenty years, many diploma schools of nursing have closed. (See Figure 4.1) Those remaining have changed their program from an orientation of service to the hospital to one of education, where the student spends more time learning and observing.

LEVELS OF NURSING
PERSONNEL

The consumer is often confused about the preparation of registered nurses (R.N.'s) and the duties of the personnel they see wearing a uniform, whom they assume to be R.N.'s. In any hospital, there are several levels of nursing personnel.

Nursing aides, orderlies, and attendants are auxiliary nursing workers in hospitals and nursing homes, and serve as assistants to nurses. These auxiliary personnel provide many services associated with the comfort and welfare of patients. There are no definite educational requirements for these positions, but most institutions provide on-the-job training which may include classroom instruction and practical application of principles learned in class. *Nursing aides,* usually women, assist both registered and practical

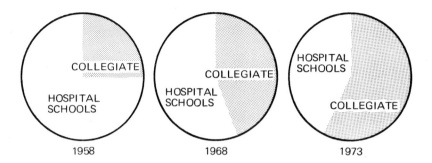

FIGURE 4.1 Changing patterns in nursing education: institutional shifts, 1958–1973. *Source: From Abstract Into Action* by Jerome P. Lysaught. Copyright © 1973 by McGraw-Hill, Inc. Used with permission of McGraw-Hill Book Company.

nurses by doing less skilled tasks related to patient care. *Orderlies and attendants,* usually men, perform various duties for male patients and provide assistance when heavy work is required for proper patient care. There is no national organization for persons employed as aides, orderlies, and attendants.[4] The National League for Nursing, however, would like to see some form of licensure for all persons involved in nursing care.

Psychiatric aides usually receive on-the-job training, but unlike nursing aides and orderlies, they are licensed in three states, Arkansas, California, and Michigan.

Licensed practical nurses (L.P.N.'s)* provide actual patient care and treatment under the supervision of an R.N. or a physician. They provide such services as catheterization, routine medication (in some cases), taking and recording of temperature, blood pressure, and respiration. In addition, they may assist with the supervision of nursing aides, orderlies, and attendants. At least two years of high

---

* In California and Texas they are called licensed vocational nurses (L.V.N.'s).

school (or completion of high school in a few states) are required prior to entering a practical nursing school. The training may be offered in trade, technical, or vocational schools or in private schools controlled by hospitals or colleges. After completing a program of twelve to eighteen months and passing a state board examination, the practical nurses become licensed. Licensure of practical nurses is required by law in all states and in the District of Columbia. The National Federation of Licensed Practical Nurses is the association for licensed practical nurses.[5]

Registered Nurses (R.N.'s)[6] are responsible for the nature and quality of all nursing care that patients receive. In addition, they are responsible for carrying out the physician's instructions and supervising practical nurses, aides, orderlies, and attendants. About 70 percent of active R.N.'s are employed in hospitals, nursing homes, and related institutions. Another 10 percent work as public health, school, and occupational health nurses.

There are three major types of nursing education programs that prepare persons for licensure as R.N.'s, and all require graduation from high school for admission: (a) Diploma programs are provided by hospital schools and usually require three years of training; (b) Associate degree programs usually offered by community colleges are two years in length; (c) Baccalaureate programs require four and occasionally five years of study in a college or university.

Since the majority of states offer a master's degree in nursing, and some institutions offer a doctoral degree, many nurses are electing to continue their education past the baccalaureate level.

All states and the District of Columbia require a license to practice nursing. Licensure as an R.N. is obtained by graduating from a school of nursing approved by the State Board of Nursing and passing a state board examination.

The professional organization for registered nurses is the American Nurses Association. With approximately 200,000 members, it is the largest professional women's organization in the world (although its membership does include male nurses).

CHARACTERISTICS
OF NURSES

The most obvious and important single personal charac-
teristic of nurses is the great proportion of women. The
American Nurses Association reports that less than 2 percent
of all licensed R.N.'s are men. Why aren't men attracted to
the field? The nursing profession, in spite of recent improvements, still does not match the financial and career opportunities of competing professions. Society views nursing as
a "nurturant" position and men in our society have not been
encouraged to play this part. Those men who do enter and
remain in nursing advance quickly. Approximately 8 percent of all male nurses are administrators or administrative
assistants compared with 4 percent of all nurses; approximately 16 percent of male nurses are supervisors or assistants compared with about 10 percent of all nurses. In addition, only 31 percent of male nurses serve as general duty
nurses compared to 56 percent of all nurses fitting into this
category.[7]

Counselors aware of these figures encourage medical
corpsmen to enter nursing. Also, the Department of Health,
Education, and Welfare has moved toward recruiting men
into nursing. In 1974, eighty-seven policemen and firemen
graduated from Hunter Belleview School of Nursing, New
York. They were the last class to graduate in an experimental program to prepare these men for a second career after
retirement. It was hoped that by having men from so-called
"manly" careers complete training as nurses, the public
stereotype of the nurse might be changed.

Other than these two examples, men are not being actively recruited into nursing, but then there is at this time
no vigorous recruitment of nurses in general since the American Nurses Association believes that there is no shortage
of nurses, merely a maldistribution of them.[8]

There is, however, a high withdrawal rate from the
profession of nursing. In fact, nationally, R.N.'s have a turnover rate of 70 percent. This means that during a twelve-

month period, the average facility must replace seven out of every ten nurses.[9] Figure 4.2 indicates that almost half of all R.N.'s who receive their license to practice are not practicing. Another 20 percent practice only part-time.

No doubt nursing has suffered in the United States by being almost exclusively a women's profession. Low salaries, poor working conditions, and lack of professional status have contributed to a lack of commitment to nursing as a lifelong career. In the past, the majority of women left the profession to marry and have families, rarely considering nursing as a career. A spokeswoman for "Nurses Now," a task force of the National Organization for Women, suggests that ". . . the disparity between nursing as it is taught and nursing as it is practiced is so great as to lead inevitably to job dissatisfaction and that leads to job turnover."[10]

Student nurses express a desire to "help people" as

FIGURE 4.2 Professional activity level among American nurses. *Source: From Abstract Into Action* by Jerome P. Lysaught. Copyright © 1973 by McGraw-Hill, Inc. Used with permission of McGraw-Hill Book Company.

their motivational force for entering nursing. The pyramidal structure of most health care institutions, however, moves a nurse up the organizational chart until she is removed from most personal contact with the patient. If the nurse rejects this role, few avenues of upward mobility are open to her. Provisions are now being made to allow better access to the educational process, so that nurses' aides can become practical nurses, practical nurses can become R.N.'s, and those R.N.'s with a baccalaureate degree can continue in postgraduate work.[11]

In recent years, pressure exerted on hospital administrators by the nurses' professional organizations has resulted in substantial salary increases for nurses. Also, the salary differentials paid to the various levels of nurses (associate degree, diploma, and baccalaureate graduates) are spilling over into salary differentials for work performed.

Improved manpower planning and a reexamination of the basic satisfactions of the profession could eliminate much of the so-called shortage of nurses. Such a reexamination should include: the personnel needed for optimum quality care, the high turnover rate, and the reason for large numbers of inactive nurses.[12]

THE HOSPITAL AS EMPLOYER

The nursing labor market has been dominated and may continue to be dominated by one employer, the hospital. Approximately 70 to 85 percent of employed professional nurses work in a hospital or related institution.[13,14] This concentration of the nursing labor market plus the lack of mobility of married female nurses has had a negative effect on wages. In addition, it is difficult to entice nurses above the age of forty back into the profession, not only because of the difficulty of keeping abreast of recent changes in health care, but also because of lack of sufficient economic incentives. As wages catch up to those in other professions, not only will more nurses remain in nursing, but more will be enticed to reenter the profession. Some believe that the problem is not the supply of nurses, but in the satisfaction achieved by nurses. If the reward systems can be improved, both extrinsically (pay) and intrinsically (satisfaction), then nurses will stay in the profession.[15]

A nurses' strike in the San Francisco area in 1974 established a precedent in hospital labor relations: Collective bargaining took place over issues such as nurse staffing, assignment of nurses to critical care areas, and the expanding role of nurses in management.[16] The striking nurses felt trapped on a plateau of professional progress with little chance for job mobility or upgrading. They wanted a major voice in the decision-making process of staffing and the delivery of nursing care. The hospitals maintained that these issues should be handled by the physicians, hospital administrators, and nursing service administrators.

In the 1960s, more professional administrators began running hospitals, lessening the input on hospital policy from physicians and nurses. Nurses commonly feel that since administrators are removed from patient care, their decisions may not reflect the actual needs of the patient. Some other issues that were raised during the San Francisco strike were staffing and the quality of patient management, independence, and portability of pension plans, as well as the role of clinical specialists in nursing. These issues will continue to be subjects during subsequent negotiations.

CHANGING ROLES
OF NURSES

Nursing needs to change and, hopefully, it will as health care delivery improves. These changes should follow social and cultural variations in our society, advances in health science and research, and improvements in the financing of health care. The American Nurses Association endorses a program of national health insurance benefits. The implementation of such a program may put health care emphasis on "wellness," increasing the demand for health services outside the hospital. These services could be provided in less expensive settings, such as neighborhood out-patient clinics and even home care. Nurses will probably be the ones to provide this service in the roles of family nurse practitioners, pediatric nurses, nurse associates, or midwives. This will necessitate a change in the doctor-nurse relationship. Historically, physicians have assumed they were the appropriate persons to say what and how much medical services should be provided. Members of other health groups which emerged were considered merely as doctors' assistants. "Today's nurse is no longer resigned to being merely a handmaiden to physicians."[17] Nursing is moving from a procedure-oriented profession to one of background knowledge, teaching and organization, and delivery of the social and psychological aspects of health maintenance and care.[18]

Nurses are increasingly challenging the physician's role as controller of and entry into the nonsystem of doling out medical and hospital care. In addition, there has been outspoken criticism by consumers of the current approach to medical services. Physicians and nurses need to work closely together as associates with a concept of teamwork in delivering health services. The needs of the patient, rather than the needs and images of professional disciplines, should be foremost in order to solve the problems of comprehensive care.[19]

Few nurses in the past were expected to participate in decision making beyond the actual nursing itself. It is going to take time to initiate nurses to the concept that the profession has an obligation to participate in and initiate planning for health services. When the nurse assumes a role that requires independent initiative and responsibility, the doctor and nurse must collaborate as equals. This is a new role for each of them and can be achieved only with the full cooperation of mature, psychologically secure participants. In this new role, the nurse has direct access to the patient, teaching, listening, advising, and providing support. The doctor serves in the role of consultant, establishing a colleague relationship with the nurse rather than the old restrictive master-servant association. In this setting, the nurse becomes an "associate" rather than an "assistant" to the physician.

There are over one million R.N.'s in the United States, making nurses by far the largest available group of trained health practitioners. The changing role of this large professional group will be an important factor in the improvement of health care throughout the country.[20]

Examples of
Expanded Nursing

A majority of states now have certificate programs that prepare R.N.'s for expanded roles in nursing. These programs usually vary in length from four months to one year and have specialty titles, such as pediatric nurse practitioner, medical nurse specialist, family health practitioner, nurse midwife, and adult health associate.* We will look at a few examples of these programs.

The University of Rochester offers a four-month *pediatric nurse practitioner* program. Recruitment has concentrated on married nurses with families on the premise that their own experience with children would provide valuable insight into their role as pediatric nurse practitioners.

The Kaiser-Permanente Medical Care Program is using nurse specialists to help implement one of the basic goals of the preventive medicine program. The nurse specialist

---

* For detailed information on the types of programs available in the various states, consult *Preparing Registered Nurses for Expanded Roles,* published by the U.S. Department of Health, Education, and Welfare, Bureau of Health Resources Development, Division of Manpower Intelligence, 9000 Rockville Pike, Bethesda, Maryland 20014. This booklet gives information on entrance requirements, length of program, when classes begin, and sources of financial aid.

and the physician work as a team. In this program, the largest group of nurse specialists will be in the medical care program. They are called *medical nurse specialists* and after six to nine months of full-time training, work in one of the following areas: (1) taking medical histories and performing routine physical examinations; (2) caring for patients who come to the clinic with certain acute conditions, such as cuts, abrasions, and minor communicable diseases; and (3) giving continuing care to patients with chronic illnesses, such as arthritis, asthma, and diabetes. Nurses at Kaiser are also being trained as pediatric nurse specialists and obstetrical and gynecological nurse specialists.[21]

In the early 1970s, programs developed for the preparation of qualified public health nurses as *family health practitioners.* Graduates are expected to be able to identify health problems, initiate treatment, and determine when patients should be referred to physicians. Family health practitioners are found in community health centers, hospital clinics, medical group practices, and in individual physicians' offices.

Studies have shown that patients were as satisfied or more satisfied with the care delivered by nurse practitioners when compared to that delivered by physicians. Openings for nurse practitioners are now appearing in many professional journals; for example, the following listing appeared in a recent newsletter.[22]

Family planning nurse practitioners. Ventura County Health Services Agency is interested in employing trained family planning nurse practitioners to work in family planning in abnormal cytology clinics and to become involved in a number of new community projects.

Other examples of the expanded nursing role are found in the team approach in family practice. *Family practice* ideally emphasizes primary care and tries to deal with the whole spectrum of the patient's life: his work, his family, and his community. The team approach uses the services of the physician, the nurse, the nutritionist, and the social worker to provide complementary care. In such a team setting, the health care providers hopefully will set aside competitive feelings and work toward a common goal: that of good patient care.[23] In many states, nurse practice acts legally limit the scope of care a nurse can provide. Often the act states that a nurse must work under supervision of a physician. "For nurse practitioners in adult health, no legally constituted body or published methods of examination and certification exist at present. Considerable differences in training and orientation of nurse practitioners have resulted from lack of agreement on the level at which they should perform and on how much basic knowledge is needed for the tasks delegated to them."[24] In time, the necessary legal guidelines will be drawn up to protect both patient and nurse practitioner. Most states are now examining ways to extend the authority of the nurse practitioner.

The Georgetown University School of Nursing in Washington, D.C., offers a *nurse midwife** certificate program.[25] A licensed R.N. with one year's experience in obstetrics, preferably in labor and delivery, is eligible for the program. Upon completion of the course, the nurse midwife usually functions as a member of the obstetrical team in medical centers, hospitals, and community health projects. She cares for the mother during pregnancy, stays with her in labor, evaluates progress, and manages the labor and delivery, watching for signs requiring medical attention. "She evaluates and provides immediate care for the newborn. She then helps the mother to care-for herself and her infant, to adjust the home situation to the new child, and to lay a healthful foundation for future pregnancies."[26]

Another area opening to nurses is in a potentially more restrictive role as physicians' assistants. When the AMA unilaterally proposed recruiting nurses as physician assistants, the 200,000-member American Nurses Association

* The *lay midwife* on the other hand, is usually a woman with little formal education who learns mainly through apprenticeship. She usually serves in rural areas where babies are often delivered in the home.

(ANA) reacted quickly. They objected to this independent action of the AMA and to the attempt to meet the shortage of physicians by depleting the supply of nurses.[27] The ANA demands recognition for nurses as members of an individual profession, distinct from and not dependent upon medical practice. Many nurses resent the fact that physician assistants (P.A.'s) with less education than R.N.'s receive the higher salary (P.A.'s are generally men). Though physicians seem to see the P.A. role as a step up the ladder for the nurse, the ANA views it as a subservient position. Of course, not all nurses agree with the ANA.[28] Physician assistants are a reality. Whether R.N.'s will fill this role or whether a new type of health professional will emerge will probably be determined in the next decade. The view of the nursing profession has been summed up as follows: "A large part of the work ahead is to convince nurses and physicians still locked in master-slave, king-handmaiden, or authority-subordinant relations that there is a better, more productive way to work. Co-equal is far more functional in the long run, but in the short run, it does raise anxieties by threatening the status quo."[29]

County health departments employ a wide array of health professionals and provide a variety of services. The public health nurse is, for many people, their most personal contact with the Health Department. The public health nurse assists families and individuals to resolve difficulties which prevent them from pursuing a healthy life. Some specific examples of her work are dealt with in Chapter Fourteen.

The Licensure Problem

Once a license to practice has been awarded, a registered nurse seldom needs to demonstrate her fitness to practice professional nursing. Yet health care knowledge and skills are current for only a limited time because of rapid advancements in the medical field. There is a great need to identify competency in nursing in terms of current concepts and techniques. A license issued under a nursing practice act designed thirty-five years ago may be a license to practice incompetently. The idea of a one-time licensure to practice in any of the healing arts is obsolete. Accountability helps insure excellence;[30] therefore, many states are moving toward the implementation of a periodic review of the nurse's qualifications for practice as a condition for license renewal.

ENDNOTES

1. U.S. Department of Health, Education, and Welfare, *Preparing Registered Nurses for Expanded Roles* (Washington, D.C.: U.S. Government Printing Office, 1974), p. 4.
2. Lillian DeYoung, *The Foundation of Nursing* (St. Louis: The C.V. Mosby Company, 1972), p. 65.
3. Ibid.
4. U.S. Department of Health, Education, and Welfare, *Health Resources Statistics* (Washington, D.C.: U.S. Government Printing Office, 1973), p. 215.
5. Ibid., pp. 214–215.
6. Ibid., pp. 213–214.
7. Jane S. Shaw, "A Man's Place: At the Bedside?" *Modern Health Care* 2; July, 1974, 66–77.
8. Ibid., p. 67.
9. Jerome P. Lysaught, *An Abstract for Action* (New York: McGraw-Hill Book Company, 1970), p. 132.
10. *Modern Health Care* 2, p. 66.
11. Stuart H. Altman, *Present & Future Supply of Registered Nurses* (Washington, D.C.: U.S. Government Printing Office, November, 1971).
12. Lysaught, *An Abstract for Action,* p. 129.
13. Altman, *Present & Future Supply of Registered Nurses,* p. 2.
14. DeYoung, *The Foundations of Nursing,* p. 99.
15. Jerome P. Lysaught, *From Abstract into Action* (New York: McGraw-Hill Book Company, 1973), p. 143.
16. Donald F. Phillips, "New demands of Nurses," *Hospitals, Journal of the American Hospital Association* 48; August 16, 1974, 31.

17. *American Medical News* 17, No. 25, June 25, 1974, 3.
18. Edith P. Lewis, *Changing Patterns of Nursing Practice* (New York: The American Journal of Nursing Company, 1971), p. 6.
19. Ibid., p. 115.
20. Kaiser Foundation Health Plan Inc., "Nurse Specialists Assist Permanente Physicians," *Planning For Health* (Los Angeles, Spring, 1973).
21. Ibid.
22. California Interagency Council on Family Planning, *Newsletter* 5, No. 4, Summer, 1974, 3.
23. *American Medical News,* June 24, 1974, p. 3.
24. Steven L. Taller and Robert Feldman, "The Training and Utilization of Nurse Practitioners in Adult Health Appraisal," *Medical Care* 12, No. 1, January, 1974, 40–48.
25. *Preparing Registered Nurses for Expanded Roles,* p. 5.
26. *Health Resources Statistics,* p. 209.
27. Lewis, *Changing Patterns of Nursing Practice,* p. 9.
28. "A Nurse by any Other Name . . . ," *Medical World News* 13, No. 2, January 14, 1972, 73–75.
29. Shirley A. Smoyak, "Seeking a Co-equal Status for Nurses and Physicians," *American Medical News* 17; February 11, 1974, 13.
30. Lauraine A. Thomas, "A Solution to the Licensure Problem," *Nursing* 48; July 16, 1974, 77–80.

Chapter Five

Other Health Practitioners

In choosing a practitioner of the healing arts, a prospective patient should understand the underlying philosophy of that method of healing and the professional preparation required for becoming such a practitioner. Some practitioners, although legally and professionally permitted to use the title "doctor," may not be qualified to use the full range of treatment (such as medicine and surgery) available to an M.D. Although we have spent some time discussing M.D.'s, there are other systems of healing which also should be explored when studying health care in this nation. We will examine approaches used by the following: osteopaths, chiropractors, podiatrists, Christian Science practitioners, homeopaths, and naturopaths.

OSTEOPATHY

Around 1850, a country doctor from Virginia named Andrew Taylor Still lost three of his children during an epidemic of spinal meningitis. As a result, he became very critical of medicine as it was practiced in his day and sought a different basis for the treatment of disease. He reasoned that a body cannot function properly unless it is structurally sound.

He concentrated on the proper alignment of bones, the proper functioning of the nervous system, and good circulation of the blood to all parts of the body. He claimed that removal of spinal "lesions" would restore the body's structural integrity and allow the nervous system to function efficiently. This in turn would enable the vital fluids (blood) to flow freely. For example, in treating a patient with a cold, Still would reason that he need not treat it directly, but by manipulation would raise the nerve (or blood) tone, which would hasten the cold's departure.[1] He carefully avoided the use of drugs and serums in his treatment. Osteopathy readily gained acceptance because many people had back problems which benefited from manipulation, and the actual "laying on of hands" was very therapeutic in itself for those whose illness was predominantly psychic in origin.

In 1892, when he was 66, Still founded the first school of osteopathy at Kirksville, Missouri, and by 1910, there were twelve such schools. In that year, the now-famous Flexner Report entitled "Medical Education in the U.S. and Canada" appeared. Flexner, a teacher who graduated from Johns Hopkins University, documented the proliferation of doctor "diploma mills." His report shook the medical profession and it soon adopted his suggestions, which ranged from emphasis on basic science, the need for research, and a full-time medical faculty, to making the university hospital a center for training the developing physician.[2] Flexner's report also had a salutary effect on osteopathy, and after 1910, the number of osteopathic schools decreased (as did the number of medical schools). Today, there are nine colleges of osteopathy in the United States, which have granted the degree of D.O. (Doctor of Osteopathy) to the nearly 16,000 practicing osteopaths in the nation.[3]

Osteopaths are licensed to practice medicine and surgery in all states and in the District of Columbia. They have the same professional rights and responsibilities as M.D.'s. Doctors of osteopathy practicing in Canada have received their education at one of the colleges of osteopathy in the United States; their practice rights, as in the U.S., are determined by the particular province in which they reside.

The osteopathic view of disease and treatment has changed considerably since Still founded the first osteopathic college and now, in most cases, is closely aligned with that of orthodox medicine. Entrance requirements to osteopathic colleges are comparable to those for schools of medicine. In half the states, the osteopath takes the same licensing examination as an M.D. Since there are approximately twenty-seven M.D.'s practicing in the United States for every D.O., osteopaths probably care for about 4 percent of American patients.[4] In spite of this small patient load, the D.O. seems to be a thorn in the side of organized medicine and the AMA has approached the osteopaths and proposed a merger which would conveniently do away with the osteopathic profession. The American Osteopathic Association (AOA) has steadfastly refused such a union, contending that the AMA merely wants to abolish the competition so that it will have an even tighter grip on the American public's health care. The AOA has no quarrel with individual M.D.'s and respects them as professional colleagues, but it does differ with the AMA in terms of philosophy and policy in the deliverance of health care. For example, the AOA feels that osteopathic medicine "goes beyond general medicine in its distinctive recognition of the function of the musculoskeletal system in health and disease."[5] The AOA points out that some specialties in medicine—orthopedic surgery, rehabilitation therapy, and physical therapy—are incorporating the techniques of manipulation in their therapy.[6] Another basic difference is in the approach to medical education. The AOA emphasizes the role of general practice rather than specialty training, with more than 75 percent of osteopaths serving as general practitioners (approximately 85 percent of M.D.'s are classified as specialists).

In spite of the above differences, there are certain trends which indicate the public's lack of differentiation between D.O.'s and M.D.'s. Something that galls the AMA is the realization that the general public has an abysmal ignorance of the difference between D.O.'s and M.D.'s. Some even confuse orthopedics with osteopathy and consider it a medical specialty! There is also evidence that legislators are more frequently including the osteopathic profession on the same basis as orthodox medicine when they are making appropriations. Insurance programs are also removing preferential treatment of M.D.'s over D.O.'s.

These facts, combined with the growing acceptance of D.O.'s within orthodox medicine, have resulted in recent changes of the AMA posture toward osteopaths. In 1960, the Joint Commission on Accreditation of Hospitals (see Chapter Eight) decided to accredit hospitals with osteopaths on their staffs. In 1961, the AMA said that state medical societies could determine whether associations between an M.D. and a D.O. would be considered unethical. The criterion would be: Does the D.O. use the same scientific principles in his practice as the M.D.? At the same time, it was pointed out that graduates of foreign medical schools were being accepted for internship and residency programs even though there was a suspicion that some of these students were receiving an education inferior to that received by the osteopaths trained in the United States. In addition, D.O.'s have the advantage of the United States's cultural background and the knowledge of medical English as used in the United States. In 1968, many of the American Medical Specialty Boards expressed a willingness "to consider certification of doctors of osteopathy when they had had appropriate specialty training." In 1969, the AMA approved the eligibility of graduates of osteopathic schools for hospital internship. D.O.'s are now accepted for full active membership in the AMA and for residency training by many American Specialty Boards, but the AOA frowns upon both these practices.

The AMA temporarily achieved its merger goal in California in 1962 when the osteopaths, acting in violation of the AOA, voted to join the ranks of the M.D.'s. The Los Angeles College of Osteopathic Physicians and Surgeons was renamed the University of California College of Medicine, Los Angeles, and an M.D. was inaugurated as dean. The faculty at the college received M.D. degrees and, within a year, the new medical school received the approval of the American Medical Colleges and the AMA. The merger plan enabled the D.O.'s to write in, enclose a fee of $65, and automatically receive an M.D. degree from the new school.[7] Approximately 2000 osteopaths chose to become M.D.'s under this option,[8] leaving around 150 D.O.'s still practicing in the state. This condition existed for twelve years until, in 1974, the California Supreme Court ruled as unconstitutional the law that had prohibited licensure of new osteopathic physicians. The court stated that the law violated the equal protection provisions of both state and federal constitutions. It had earlier determined that osteopathy has evolved into a complete school of medicine and surgery.

Osteopaths, in their training and practice, are becoming more closely allied with the view of orthodox medicine, a trend which the AMA sees as "an inevitable evolutionary process which should be expedited." According to the AMA, the appropriateness of osteopathic treatment should meet the following test: "Does the individual doctor of osteopathy practice osteopathy, or does he practice a method of healing founded on a scientific basis?"[9] At this point, the question seems to have been answered, since the AMA is now willing to take the osteopath into the fold.

CHIROPRACTIC

Chiropractic began in 1895 when Daniel D. Palmer "adjusted" the back of his janitor who had been deaf for almost seventeen years. This adjustment restored full hearing and the recovery was attested to by the patient's own physician. Palmer then went on to establish chiropractic (from the Greek *chier:* "hand" and *praktikos:* "practical," or "efficient hands"). According to Palmer, the roots of chiropractic go back to Hippocrates, the father of medicine, who admonished us to "look well to the spine for the cause of disease." Chiropractic, like osteopathy, stressed structural integrity and, in addition, claimed that mechanical pressure or irritation of a nerve caused inflammation and destruction of tissues served by that nerve. Palmer claimed that orthodox medicine was often treating the symptom and not the cause (spinal pressure).[10] Chiropractic is defined as "a system of mechanical therapeutics based on the principle that the nervous system largely determines the state of health and that any interference with this system impairs normal functions and lowers the body's resistance to disease."[11] "Subluxations" or minor displacements of the spine cause irritability of the nerves and are associated with disease. Chiropractic treatment consists primarily of "adjustment" (or manipulation) to align the spine properly and remove the subluxation. Other treatment approaches by chiropractors include: proper diet, physical therapy, and psychosomatic counseling.

Chiropractors receive their training in one of the thirteen chiropractic colleges in the United States which grant the degree of D.C. (Doctor of Chiropractic).* Approximately 650 are graduated each year and there are about 22,000 chiropractors in the United States (chiropractors like to point out that chiropractic is the second largest healing art). They are licensed in all states and in the District of Columbia. Most states require a four-year chiropractic course prior to licensing. In thirty-five states, two years of college are required before entry into a chiropractic college. A one-year internship after graduation is mandatory in four states. In eighteen states, a basic science certificate, obtained by examination, is prerequisite to taking the licensing examinations.[12,13] Approximately 45 percent of the chiropractors in the United States are located in five states: California has 20 percent, New York, 7 percent, Texas and Missouri each have 6 percent, and Pennsylvania has 5 percent. On a nationwide basis there are eight chiropractors for every 100,000 people in the United States. This compares to 174 physicians (M.D.'s and D.O.'s) per 100,000.[14] There are two national chiropractic organizations, the American Chiroprac-

---

* There are two additional chiropractic colleges: one in England, the other in Canada.

tic Association and the International Chiropractic Association.

Orthodox medicine has been violently opposed to the practice of chiropractic and has dismissed it as a cult. Around 1920, in California, the medical profession harassed the chiropractors in earnest and had about 75 percent of them convicted of practicing medicine without a license. The results of this campaign were not quite what the physicians had expected. Many of the chiropractors, instead of paying their fines, went to jail. This created considerable public sympathy for them and, in 1922, when Californians had a chance to vote on a bill to license chiropractors, they approved it by a considerable majority.[15] Since that experience, organized medicine has avoided the courts in its fight against the chiropractor and has concentrated upon attacking him through the press and in its own *Journal of the American Medical Association* and in *Today's Health*. One of the criticisms that has been leveled at the chiropractic approach to healing is the claim that there is no scientific basis for chiropractic (in 1967 the National Advisory Commission on Health Manpower referred to chiropractic as "cultism").[16] Others claim that chiropractic colleges have low admission standards and that the faculty members of these colleges are not well prepared.[17] The American Medical Association claims that chiropractors are licensed to practice today, not because of the scientific basis of their approach, but because of political influence.[18]

In spite of this opposition, chiropractic has continued to attract large numbers of patients and has gained acceptance and recognition in many ways. The U.S. Office of Education recognizes the Council on Chiropractic Education as a national accrediting agency for chiropractic colleges. Chiropractic services are provided for under Medicare and Medicaid. In all states except Kentucky, chiropractic coverage is included under Workman's Compensation laws (all federal workers are also covered under the Federal Employees Compensation Act). Over 600 insurance companies accept chiropractors' certification on claims. Chiropractors can also sign birth and death certificates in some states.

Chiropractors, because of their philosophy and because of certain limitations placed upon them, practice a very conservative brand of healing. When their patients need hospitalization, they must pass them on to orthodox medicine because they are not granted hospital privileges. Chiropractors cannot prescribe drugs or perform surgery, a fact that may discourage many would-be patients who are looking for the quick results that these two approaches may bring. Chiropractors point out that they have a very low incidence of malpractice claims brought against them because of their more conservative approach to healing.

It has been pointed out, in defense of chiropractors, that, like physicians, they are trying to improve standards within their own ranks; they are legally recognized to practice in all states; thousands of people find satisfaction in their treatment; and that "for certain muscular or skeletal problems, . . . chiropractors have as much, and perhaps more, to offer than most doctors . . . ."[19]

Chiropractors maintain that orthodox medicine has turned to physiotherapists for the same kind of manipulative procedures that chiropractors perform. Physiotherapists, however, are considered as health auxiliaries with the same relationship to the physician as nurses; that is, they remain under the formal supervision of the physician. Chiropractors claim that they have the competence to both diagnose and treat their patients.

PODIATRY

Podiatry is the profession that "deals with the examination, diagnosis, treatment, and prevention of diseases and disorders of the human foot."[20] This treatment may be made by medical, surgical, mechanical, and physical means. Podiatrists were known as chiropodists until 1958. The national professional organization is the American Podiatry Association and is the official voice of the more than 9,000 practicing podiatrists in the United States.

Podiatrists are licensed to practice in all fifty states and in the District of Columbia. Before they are licensed, they must have graduated from a college of podiatry (four-year course) and must have passed a state board (or the national board) examination. Three states also require a period of internship or practice before granting a license. Before admission to one of the five colleges of podiatry* in the United States, applicants must have completed at least two years of college. The first two years of podiatry training stress lecture and laboratory work in such basic sciences as anatomy, bacteriology, chemistry, and physiology. During the last two years students obtain their clinical experience. Upon graduation from a college of podiatry, a person receives a degree of Doctor of Podiatric Medicine (D.P.M.). Podiatric specialties include Foot Orthopedics, Foot Roentgenology, Foot Surgery, Podiatric Dermatology, and Podiatric Medicine.[21]

Most podiatrists (94 percent) are in private practice; the remainder hold salaried positions on staffs of hospitals around the nation, including Veterans Administration and Armed Forces hospitals. The podiatrist performs a variety of procedures in his practice. He may fit corrective and supportive devices or perform surgical and other operative procedures on the foot. He may also prescribe proper footwear, prescribe and administer drugs, and prescribe physical therapy for patient care. He can write prescriptions and admit patients to hospitals just as M.D.'s do.

A podiatric surgeon may perform surgery in his office if it is properly equipped or he may do his surgery at various hospitals where he has staff privileges. Usually, hospital surgery is more costly but most insurance companies do not cover out-of-hospital surgery.

---

* Colleges of podiatric medicine are located in Chicago, Cleveland, New York, Philadelphia, and San Francisco.

In recent years, the need for podiatric services has increased dramatically. Several factors have been responsible for this increased demand. To begin with, Medicare, Medicaid, Workman's Compensation, and most insurance companies include podiatric services. Also, the Armed Forces offer scholarships for podiatry students and commissions for podiatrists. A third factor is the increase in the proportion of older people in the U.S. population. Approximately ten million are now over sixty-five years of age and this age group requires more podiatric care than those under sixty-five. Fourth, the supply of podiatrists has not kept pace with population growth in the nation. Since 1950 the U.S. population has increased 35 percent; the number of podiatrists only 10 percent. By 1980, only 10,000 podiatrists will be available and the country will need nearly twice that number. Fifth, more and more people are afflicted with chronic diseases, such as heart disease and diabetes, that have related foot problems requiring the care of a podiatrist. Lastly, in recent years, there has been a considerable increase in public awareness of health matters and a better understanding of the role of the podiatrist.[22]

With the current and predicted shortage of podiatrists, it is essential that the profession explore the use of allied health personnel which could greatly increase the treatment capacity of the podiatrist. Such ancillary personnel are usually available in a well-organized health maintenance organization (see Chapter Seven). For example, "many of the technical tasks now being performed by the podiatrist could be taught to less-trained personnel who could function under professional supervision. The podiatrist could also be relieved from any purely administrative functions and related tasks by assigning these to other personnel. Furthermore, much of the time now required to obtain a patient's complete medical background could be saved, since most of this information would be available from the patient's record."[23] Since health manpower is a valuable resource, it should not be wasted by having the podiatrist function at a level lower than that for which he is prepared by education, experience, and licensure.

CHRISTIAN SCIENCE

"Christian Science is a religion based on the words and works of Christ Jesus. It draws its authority from the *Bible* and its teachings are set forth in *Science and Health with Key to the Scriptures,* by Mary Baker Eddy, the discoverer and founder of Christian Science."[24]

One part of Christian Science deals with the healing of physical disease by spiritual means alone. This is very difficult for a non–Christian Scientist to understand, especially when he has been raised on the germ theory of disease.

Science and Health was first published in 1875. It suggests that Christ's methods of healing are still applicable today, and man can heal himself and others if he has the right "Christ-consciousness."[25]

Healing is not the main purpose of Christian Science; it is merely a byproduct of a way of life. Christian Scientists believe that if a man has the proper view of life, he will be truly in God's image and will be healthy. Wrong thinking, such as fear, ignorance, or sin, is the cause of many physical problems from which man suffers. Christian Scientists may seek the help of a Christian Science practitioner when they have health problems.

Christian Science Practitioners

Christian Science practitioners are recognized in all states. You can find them listed in the Yellow Pages of your telephone book under "Christian Science practitioners." There are approximately 5,000 Christian Science practitioners in the United States, and a Directory of these is available in *The Christian Science Journal,* published monthly. To become a Christian Science practitioner, a person has to be a member of the church in good standing, have class instruction by an authorized teacher, and provide evidence of effectiveness in healing, usually in the form of testimonials. The Mother Church decides what constitutes evidence of effectiveness; it may be the healing of one or two serious disorders or several minor disorders. An aspiring Christian Science practitioner must also agree to be a full-time practitioner in order to be listed in *The Christian Science Journal*.

Healing, as Christian Scientists view it, is a process of spiritual awakening, and the practitioner's part is to help another discover more of his identity as a son of God. This involves the healing of the "whole man" and may concern family problems, moral problems, unhappiness, and questions of employment, as well as the healing of a physical disease. The practitioner provides no medical treatment or diagnosis. His is a spiritual ministry of prayer. The practitioner does not have to be near the patient to heal him. On this point, one of the instructional manuals states: "In Christian Science there is no thought transference, for mortal mind is not a factor in the healing. The Divine Mind, being omnipresent, the human knowing of the truth regarding the sick man at a distance brings truth to bear on the case the same as if he were nearby."[26]

The whole concept of healing through Christian Science is difficult enough for a non–Christian Scientist, but the idea of absent healing is almost impossible for many to accept. How effective are these attempts at healing? The only comparative study that we were able to find was done by Dr. Gale E. Wilson of Seattle, Washington, in 1965. He studied the causes of death of more than 1,000 Christian Scientists over a twenty-year period in the State of Washington. Although his study showed that there was no appreciable difference in the average age at death between Christian Scientists and the public at large in Washington, the causes of death brought out some interesting information. In some categories, Christian Scientists fared better than others. For example, no deaths from homicide or suicide were recorded, and deaths from automobile accidents and falls were almost nonexistent. (There are many who believe that fatal accidents, particularly those involving one person, are often the fulfillment of a death wish.) Pneumonia deaths were the same in both groups. As you might expect, Christian Scientists had distinctly higher death rates from cancer and heart disease, and death was also more frequent from diabetes and tuberculosis. Dr. Wilson concluded that 6 percent of all deaths of Christian Scientists were preventable.[27]

When discussing such comparative figures, certain points should be kept in mind. First of all, many diseases improve even without medical care; secondly, even the best medical care cannot cure many diseases. Also, improvements in public health have prevented many illnesses, to the benefit of both Christian Scientists and non–Christian Scientists. Lastly, ". . . if there is any truth in the notion that an excessive preoccupation with bodily functions and with emotional problems predisposes to disease, it may well be that Christian Scientists are protected from a number of illnesses to which they may otherwise be prone."[28]

Although Christian Scientists state that Christian Science cannot be combined with reliance on medical aid, they do allow a few exceptions. "As required by law, a doctor or qualified mid-wife is employed in childbirth."[29] A surgeon may also be employed to set broken bones, since no medication is involved. Christian Scientists cooperate with the proper authorities in reporting contagious or infectious diseases as required by law. They prefer, however, to depend solely on spiritual means for healing these cases.

The effect of emotions on the body is generally acknowledged and accepted. Such obvious examples as blushing, breaking out in a cold sweat, and increased heart rate, to the more complicated syndromes such as ulcers and some allergic reactions, have been linked to the emotions. If, through their religion, Christian Scientists can develop a positive emotional state, they may well provide a better environment for recovery. The autonomic nervous system, which controls the bodily processes such as heart rate and digestion, was for some time considered to be independent of our thought processes. It has now been shown that people can, by concentrating, slow their heart rate and change certain other bodily processes. Consider the effect of the "hex" by the witch doctor or shaman in some societies. Such persons can literally cause death. If such negative expectations have this power, what would happen if we stressed the positive expectations? The symptoms that drive people to physicians often have emotional overtones which have aggravated the situation. In such cases, the power of positive thinking would be very beneficial. Christian Scientists use this positive approach. Another advantage the Christian Scientists have in their approach to healing is the avoidance of so-called "drug reactions."

Christian Scientists, when they find that their own approach is not working, sometimes turn to orthodox medicine for help. It may be too late, as in the case of cancer which has metastasized (spread to other parts of the body), but if they are not too late, they are enjoying the best of both approaches. Their Christian Science practitioner can help them with the emotional or psychosomatic aspect, and the orthodox physician can treat the other components. Christian Science practitioners certainly do not cure all of their patients, any more than M.D.'s cure all of theirs, but faith can play a part—whether it's faith in yourself, in a higher power, or faith in your physician. For this reason, we suggested in Chapter Two that it is important that you should like your physician and have faith in him. You will probably be healthier for it!

HOMEOPATHY

Approximately 150 years ago, Samuel Hahnemann, a German physician, became dissatisfied with the then current practices of medicine which consisted mainly of bleeding, purging, and blistering. Using himself as a subject, he experimented with various drugs and developed the principle of "like cures like," which he named the "Law of Similars." "If a medicine administered to a healthy person causes a certain syndrome of symptoms, that medicine will cure a sick person who presents similar symptoms."[30] Homeopaths classify diseases by the symptoms they present rather than by the bacteria that are supposed to cause them. They believe that disease should be treated by drugs that produce in normal subjects symptoms similar to those of the disease being treated. Like should cure like—hence the name *homeopathy** ("like-disease").

In his treatment of patients, Hahnemann first used solutions that were quite potent, and as a result, noted "physiological aggravations." He reduced his concentrations and found that a small dose of a very dilute solution was able to create emotional, mental, and physical changes in healthy persons; these changes seemed to be reversible—they could be removed when they arose spontaneously in ill persons. Hahnemann used substances from the mineral, animal, and vegetable kingdoms. Homeopaths claim to have first proven many of the remedies now used by orthodox medicine; these include digitalis, quinine, belladonna, atropine, and ipecac.

The guiding principle of homeopathy is that "disease is primarily a disturbance in the vital force, or guiding energy which governs and regulates all of the organs and parts of the body."[31] This vital force maintains normal growth coordination of all organic functions. When this force is disturbed by some disease-producing cause, disharmony results. Disturbances may be caused by infections, injuries, or numerous other things.

To become a homeopathic physician, a person must first complete his regular M.D. training. Then he takes courses in homeopathy, during which time he intensively studies the actions of drugs on humans—rather than on laboratory animals—in order to apply them to his curative action in disease.

Whereas orthodox physicians often need the results of laboratory and pathology studies before they prescribe a medication, homeopaths claim that they can prescribe at once on the basis of "like cures like." They attempt to pro-

* Also spelled "homoeopathy."

vide a remedy that will stimulate the body's vital force to heal itself. Homeopaths state that they treat the patient, helping his body to cure itself, while orthodox medicine treats the disease or attacks the offending germ causing the disease. Homeopaths claim to use every technique of diagnosis that is available to the pathologist and radiologist to find the body's weak link and then correct it. They stress the importance of diet. Homeopathy does not claim to be a separate school of medicine, but rather "a specialized, intensive study of drugs in their action on the human body." Homeopathy does not eliminate surgery, but attempts to reduce the number of cases that require surgical correction.

At the present time there are only about 300 homeopaths in the United States who practice homeopathy exclusively, that is, prescribe only homeopathic remedies. There are about 7,000 physicians who call themselves homeopaths but actually practice what they consider the best of both branches of therapeutics.[32]

NATUROPATHY

Naturopathic Medicine has been defined as the "prevention and treatment of disease by using biochemical, psychological, and physical methods that assist the resident healing processes of the body."[33] It does not include the use of major surgery, x-rays, and radium for therapeutic purposes, or drugs (except for certain naturally occurring ones).

Naturopathic Medicine is physiologic in nature—"treatment assists the inherent physiologic processes as they relate to healing and normal biochemistry. Any method or form of treatment that violates natural or physiological laws is considered *unnatural* especially if such 'treatment' causes a new or different illness (iatrogenic disease) or complicates the existing disease process."[34]

The philosophy of naturopathy is based upon the premise that man is subject to natural laws that apply to all living things in both health and disease. These laws involve the mechanical, mental, and physiological principles of life and they establish a balance within the body. When this balance is upset, the result is ill health or disease. By applying natural agencies in conformance with these natural laws, the naturopath attempts to assist the body to maintain its health and to live by adaptation or by restoration of normal function.[35]

The treatment by naturopathic medicine of pathogenic abnormalities or injuries includes four fields of practice, correlated and administered in combination to produce the desired effects. The four fields of practice are:[36]

1. *Corrective nutrition:* dietetics, food supplements, botanicals, vitamins, minerals, and other natural preparations.
2. *Body mechanics:* anatomical manipulations, remedial exercises, and prosthetics.
3. *Physiotherapy:* natural physical agents including electricity, ultra sound, water, light, and heat.
4. *Remedial psychology:* psychosomatics and suggestive therapeutics.

Naturopaths state that they are trained to diagnose and utilize diagnostic methods common to medical doctors in routine office practice. Naturopathic physicians claim that they are qualified to treat any and all conditions that come under the realm of general practice.

A student wishing to become a naturopath must have completed two years of college before he can be admitted into the four-year program of the National College of Naturopathic Medicine in Seattle, Washington. At present it is the only institution granting the degree Doctor of Naturopathy (D.N.). The course of study includes the usual basic science classes of anatomy, physiology, chemistry, microbiology, and pathology as well as clinical courses in diagnosis and naturopathic therapeutic principles and practice.

Students must complete at least six months as externs in an out-patient clinic where they work with naturopathic physicians.[37]

Naturopaths are specifically licensed in ten states and in the District of Columbia as well as in five Canadian provinces.*[38] They may also be licensed to practice in other states although they may not be licensed specifically as naturopaths. For example, in Illinois, naturopaths may be covered by the Medical Practices Act. In most states, naturopathic physicians are confined by statute to the use of natural remedies, although Florida and Utah give licenses that are virtually unlimited. The National Association of Naturopathic Physicians reports that there are approximately 5,000 naturopathic practitioners in the United States and twenty-five to thirty are graduated each year.[39] There are no specifically naturopathic hospitals in the United States and naturopaths do not have hospital privileges. According to Inglis, naturopathy is the oldest medical system as well as the simplest. It represents the aim of all branches of medicine; that is, the prevention of all unnecessary disease. "Nobody disputes that if all citizens were to lead less unnatural lives, eat more sensibly, drink less, smoke less, and cultivate more serene dispositions, they would fall ill less often, and recover more rapidly from any illness they catch."[40]

* U.S.: Arizona, Connecticut, District of Columbia, Florida, Hawaii, Idaho, North Carolina, Oregon, Utah, Virginia, and Washington. Canada: Alberta, British Columbia, Manitoba, Ontario, and Saskatchewan.

ENDNOTES

1. Brian Inglis, *The Case for Unorthodox Medicine* (New York: G.P. Putnam's Sons, 1965), p. 135.
2. Martin L. Gross, *The Doctors* (New York: Random House, Inc., 1966), pp. 371–373.
3. "AOA Facts and Figures," *Journal of the American Osteopathic Association Education Annual,* Vol. 73 Supplement, 1974, p. 176.

4. U.S. Department of Health, Education, and Welfare, *Health Resources Statistics* (Washington, D.C.: U.S. Government Printing Office, 1974), p. 172.
5. *Journal of the American Osteopathic Association Education Annual* 73, p. 176.
6. American Osteopathic Association, *The Profession of Osteopathic Medicine* (Chicago, n.d.), p. 1.
7. Gross, *The Doctors*, pp. 458–459.
8. Arnold I. Kisch and Arthur J. Viseltear, *Doctors of Medicine and Doctors of Osteopathy in California* (Arlington, Va.: Public Health Service, 1967), p. 36.
9. Inglis, *The Case for Unorthodox Medicine*, pp. 128–129.
10. Dewey Anderson, *The Present Day Doctor of Chiropractic* (Washington, D.C.: Public Affairs Institute, 1956), pp. 5–6.
11. *Health Resources Statistics*, p. 47.
12. Ibid.
13. The Council on Chiropractic Education, *Educational Standards for Chiropractic Colleges* (Des Moines, Iowa, 1974).
14. *Health Resources Statistics*, pp. 48, 169.
15. Inglis, *The Case for Unorthodox Medicine*, p. 126.
16. U.S. Department of Health, Education, and Welfare, *Report of the National Advisory Commission on Health Manpower*, Vol. 2 (Washington, D.C.: U.S. Government Printing Office, 1967), p. 327.
17. H. Thomas Ballantine, Jr., "Will the Delivery of Health Care Be Improved by the Use of Chiropractic Services?," *The New England Journal of Medicine* 286; February 3, 1972, 237–242.
18. "Chiropractic Mounts Major Political Drive," *American Medical News* 15; January 24, 1972, 10–12.
19. Louis Lasagna, *The Doctors' Dilemmas* (New York: Harper & Row, Publishers, 1962), p. 38.
20. The American Podiatry Association, *Podiatry Education* (Washington, D.C., May, 1974), p. 1.
21. *Health Resources Statistics*, p. 263.
22. Leonard A. Levy, "The Potential of Podiatric Medicine in Comprehensive Health Care," *Public Health Reports* 89; September–October, 1974, 451–452.
23. Ibid., p. 455.
24. The Christian Science Publishing Company, *Facts About Christian Science* (Boston, 1959), p. 1.
25. Lasagna, *The Doctors' Dilemmas*, p. 72.

26. Inglis, *The Case for Unorthodox Medicine,* p. 223.
27. Ibid., p. 228.
28. Lasagna, *The Doctors' Dilemmas,* p. 76.
29. *Facts About Christian Science,* p. 10.
30. "Homeopathy—A Neglected Medical Art," *Prevention* 21; February, 1969, 59.
31. Ibid., p. 62.
32. Ralph Packman, Executive Director, National Center for Homeopathy, personal communication, November 13, 1974.
33. The Canadian Naturopathic Association, *Naturopathic Medicine in Canada* (Calgary, Alberta, 1966), p. 7.
34. Ibid.
35. The Canadian Naturopathic Association, *A Brief Respecting National Health Services* (Calgary, Alberta, n.d.), pp. 14–15.
36. Ibid., pp. 16–17.
37. National College of Naturopathic Medicine, *Catalog 74–75* (Seattle, 1974), pp. 16–22.
38. Ibid., p. 17.
39. John W. Noble, Secretary Treasurer, National Association of Naturopathic Physicians, personal communication, November 4, 1974.
40. Inglis, *The Case for Unorthodox Medicine,* p. 73.

Chapter Six

Allied Health

Since the 1940s, scientific breakthroughs and increased demand for medical services have greatly accelerated the specialization of labor in the health field. The traditional domain of the physician, dentist, and nurse have been invaded by a variety of health personnel with such titles as "physician's assistant," "inhalation therapist," and "biomedical technician." These new personnel, while more highly specialized, require less education and training than those functions usually identified with the health field. The term "allied health" is still relatively new in the health professions' vocabulary. "Allied health" can be defined as a term which "includes those individuals prepared at the technical and professional levels who work with physicians and dentists—aiding them in the prevention of disease, the maintenance of well-being, and the diagnosis and treatment of disease, including rehabilitation of individuals with residual defects and disabilities."[1] More simply, "allied health" can be defined as including "those individuals who support, aid, and increase the efficiency and effectiveness of the physician and dentist."[2] Although the education of allied health personnel tends to be of shorter duration, they have often developed knowledges and competencies in special areas which are beyond the competency held by the physician or dentist. Allied health personnel have increased in both numbers and types in recent years. Twenty-five years ago the ratio of supporting health workers to physicians was 4 to 1; today it is 25 to 1.

Since the field is changing so rapidly, we will limit our discussion to a very brief look at the major trends, the variety of occupations, licensure, and the problems of acceptance of allied health personnel by physicians and consumers.

TRENDS

In addition to the overall growth of personnel in the allied health field, several other trends are evident. In the past, allied health workers received their training in informal, on-the-job programs. The shift is now toward more formal education in community colleges and universities. This presents the problem of assessing health training requirements and priorities. When the worker was trained on the job, each institution decided what was necessary for him to know. There was no uniformity of training and no consensus on standards of performance. The workers had no specific credentials or organizations that set standards. With the shift to formal education, continuing in-depth studies are needed to assess the direction and training of the allied health professions.

There is no question that the most rapidly expanding segment of allied health is the semi-skilled worker. This phenomenon alters the way the total health delivery system operates because it changes the roles of the more traditional health care delivery personnel such as doctors and nurses. It also changes the relationship between the consumer and the provider. This relationship will become further fragmented as additional technological and scientific developments spawn even more specialized skills, new occupational titles and functions.

Health technology and occupational and physical therapy are also rapidly expanding areas. Many technologist and technician positions will double by 1985, and occupational and physical therapist positions will increase four times.[3]

Employment for allied health personnel is increasingly an urban phenomenon. Specialized skills are generally utilized in an institutional setting where specialized equipment is available and the supply of patients is more constant. Therefore, the trend seems to be to more centralization of health care in hospital settings. This may further impoverish the care available to rural areas.

The allied health field seems to attract and tends to have a labor force that is predominantly (over 70 percent) female.[4] This usually means lower than average wages and higher than average turnover and attrition; this puts more pressure on the educational institutions which are the source of supply for the allied health field.[5]

The above trends, combined with various studies in the allied health field, seem to indicate certain needs. First of all, the entire health training system needs to be coordinated. Planning to meet health personnel needs is an integral part of planning the overall health care program of an area. The need for coordination becomes even more evident when we examine the wide variety of career possibilities in allied health. Secondly, there is a need to increase greatly the number of persons trained for health careers. Obviously, technological advances require more skilled personnel; also, health care in the future should emphasize preventive, rather than merely curative, services. Such an approach will require the assistance of many more health workers. Thirdly, we must provide more opportunities for allied health training at the secondary school and junior college level. There is also a need to expand the vocational and/or technical school training of allied health personnel. Fourthly, we need to develop programs that are flexible enough to eliminate the "dead-end" nature of many health field jobs. Opportunity for upward mobility would not only attract more males into health-related job training but also encourage more women to remain in the labor market. Both vertical and lateral mobility must be available. Productivity, responsibility, and career mobility must increase along with salaries.[6] Lastly, since current training facilities and health-related employment opportunities are concentrated in urban areas, many rural areas are experiencing shortages of a variety of health workers. One possible solution to this problem would be to establish health training facilities in rural areas so that rural students might be drawn into the allied health professions and remain in rural areas.

CAREERS

Careers in allied health cover a wide spectrum of health categories. The box on pp. 108–128 illustrates some of these areas.* For those interested in more information about allied health careers, Appendix B contains the names and addresses of over 100 health organizations in the United States.

* This material was developed by the American Society of Allied Health Professions for specific and limited use in the compilation of a directory of educational programs within the allied health field.

SELECTED
ALLIED HEALTH CAREERS

ADMINISTRATION, PLANNING, AND OFFICE personnel function at various levels to maintain and operate clinical offices and institutions and to plan for improved health care and delivery.

Health Economist: Applies specialized knowledge of the laws of supply and demand, marketing, polling, econometrics, and motivation research to permit the efficient delivery of health services.

Health Care Administrator: Occupies top-level positions in a variety of health care settings: hospitals, official health agencies, long-term care facilities, social service agencies, voluntary and tax paying health agencies, and public health agencies. Policy development, activity coordination, procedural development, and planning are the primary functions of the position.

Health Care Assistant Administrator: Occupies middle management positions in a variety of clinical and health care settings: hospitals, public and private health agencies, long-term care facilities, social service agencies.

Health Planner: Works in state and areawide health planning agencies and related programs implementing community goals including planning and evaluating developmental policies.

Health Systems Analyst: Develops and applies the principles of industrial and systems engineering, operations research, and management to the design, evaluation, and implementation of improved health care.

Long-Term Care Administrator: Directs and coordinates all operations and activities of extended care facilities.

Medical/Dental Secretary: Assists physicians and/or dentists through the use of medical shorthand, typing, filing, accounting, appointment scheduling, receptionist duties, and office management.

Medical Office Assistant: Assumes responsibility for routine administrative, clerical, and record-keeping procedures in a physician's office, assists the physician in medical examinations and treatments, and cares for medical equipment and supplies.

Rehabilitation Administrator: Manages a rehabilitation agency's business aspects: Personnel, budget control, public relations work, training, programs planning, and services coordination.

Unit Clerk: Handles routine clerical and reception work in a floor nursing unit, receiving patients and visitors, scheduling appointments, and monitoring the location of all ward staff. (Ward Clerk)

BIOMEDICAL ENGINEERING personnel combine basic engineering and biomedical science in order to design, assemble, and adapt medical devices, instruments, and processes to improve the quality and cost in the delivery of medical health care.

Biomedical Engineer: Utilizes engineering ideas and techniques in the development of new instruments, equipment, processes, and systems for the medical care of patients and the improvement of health systems.
Biomedical Engineering Technician: Assembles, repairs, and adapts medical equipment to assist biomedical engineers, physicians, and scientists in the development and maintenance of medical equipment and systems for the delivery of medical and health care. (Biomedical Equipment Technician)

CLINICAL LABORATORY SERVICES personnel work in a clinical laboratory setting, collecting, mounting, processing, classifying and analyzing laboratory specimens.
Blood Bank Technologist: Medical technologist, working under the direction of a pathologist, physician, or laboratory director, prepared to collect, classify, store, and process blood, including preparation of components from whole blood, detection and identification of antibodies in patient and donor bloods, and selection and delivery of suitable blood for transfusion.
Chemistry Technologist: Works under the supervision of a pathologist, physician, or qualified scientist, in performing qualitative and quantitative chemical analyses of body fluids and exudates, utilizing quantitative equipment and a wide range of laboratory instruments, to provide information for diagnosing and treating diseases.
Cytotechnologist: Works under the supervision of a pathologist, physician or medical technologist, in handling, staining, mounting, and evaluating cells from the human body to determine cellular variations and abnormalities such as cancer and other physiologic changes.
Hematology Technologist: Works under the supervision of a hematologist, medical technologist, or laboratory director, in performing quantitative, qualitative,

and coagulation tests on cellular and plasma components of blood for use in the diagnosis and treatment of disease.

Histologic Technician: Works under supervision of a pathologist, physician, or medical technologist in sectioning, staining, and mounting human or animal tissues and fluid for microscopic study by pathologists or other qualified individuals.

Medical Laboratory Assistant: Works under the direct supervision of a medical technologist, pathologist, physician, or qualified scientist, in performing laboratory procedures requiring basic technical skills and minimal independent judgment, in chemistry, hematology, and microbiology. (Certified Laboratory Assistant)

Medical Laboratory Scientist: Performs clinical analysis procedures and research in the medical/clinical laboratories utilizing disciplines such as chemistry, biochemistry, bacteriology, and microbiology.

Medical Laboratory Technician: Works under the supervision of a medical technologist, pathologist, or physician, in performing more complex or specialized bacteriological, biological, and chemical tests, requiring limited independent judgment or correlation competency, to provide data for use in the diagnosis and evaluation of effective treatment of disease.

Medical Technologist: Performs a wide range of complex and specialized procedures in all general areas of the clinical laboratory, making independent and correlation judgment, and working in conjunction with pathologists, physicians, and qualified scientists. May supervise and/or teach laboratory personnel.

Microbiology Technologist: Works with a minimum of supervision by a pathologist, physician, or laboratory director, in performing many bacteriological, viral, parasitological, immunologic, and serologic procedures in a clinical laboratory setting.

Public Health Laboratory Scientist: Performs clinical laboratory procedures and research with specific public health focus or within a public health setting.

DENTAL SERVICES personnel render varieties of services to the dentist; they do general office work, laboratory work, and they assist the dentist at the chairside.

Dental Assistant: Assists dentist at the chairside in dental operatory, performs reception and clerical functions, and carries out dental radiography and selected dental laboratory work.

Dental Hygienist: Works under the supervision of dentist in providing services to dental patients, such as performing complete oral prophylaxis, applying medication, performing dental radiography, and providing dental education services both for chairside patients and in community health projects.

Dental Technician: Prepared to construct complete and partial dentures, make orthodontic appliances, fix bridgework, crowns, and other dental restorations and appliances, as authorized by dentists. (Dental Laboratory Technician)

DIETETIC AND NUTRITIONAL SERVICES personnel translate nutritional needs into the selection, purchasing, preparation, and service of appropriate foods; along with maintenance of equipment, sanitation, and cost control. They provide nutritional education to individuals and groups, and serve as nutritional consultants to health facilities and communities.

Dietetic Aide: Performs non-technical food preparation routines, as directed by a supervisor, serves meals to patients, and assists with food-related jobs in health care facilities.

Dietetic Technician: Functions as middle management and service personnel in the nutritional care of individuals in health care facilities, assisting with the planning, implementation, and evaluation of food programs, working with both the food service supervisor and the dietitian. (Food Service Manager, Food Service Assistant, Food Service Technician)

Dietitian: Applies the principles of nutrition and management in administering institutional food service programs, plans special diets at physician's requests, and instructs individuals and groups in the application of nutrition principles of the selection of food.

Dietitian/Nutritionist: Applies the principles of nutrition and management in administering institutional food service programs, instructs individuals and groups about nutritional requirements and food selection, and performs nutrition research.

Dietetic Assistant: Writes food menus following dietetic specifications, coordinates food service to patients, orders supplies, maintains sanitation, and oversees the work of food service employees in health care facilities. (Food Service Supervisor)

Nutritionist: Adapts and applies food and nutrient information to the solution of food problems, the control of disease, and the promotion of health, performs nutrition research, instructs groups and individuals about nutritional requirements, and helps people develop meal patterns to meet their nutritional needs.

EMERGENCY SERVICES personnel administer temporary medical help by responding to, evaluating, and assisting in emergency conditions.

Ambulance Attendant: Provides first aid and assistance in the transportation of critically ill and injured persons to a medical facility.

Emergency and/or Disaster Specialist: Develops and implements hospital-wide procedures for dealing with in-house and community emergencies and disasters.

Emergency Medical Technician: Responds to medical emergency calls, evaluates the nature of the emergency, and carries out specified diagnostic and emergency treatment procedures under standing orders or the specific directions of a physician.

ENVIRONMENTAL SERVICES personnel inspect, evaluate, and gather data for their use in the design,

operation, and control of systems for prevention and elimination of environmental hazards.

Environmental Engineer: Applies engineering principles to the control, elimination, and prevention of environmental hazards such as air pollution, water pollution, solids pollution, and noise pollution. (Sanitary Engineer)

Environmental Engineering Assistant: Works with and assists the environmental engineer in his tasks of designing and controlling systems to eliminate and control environmental health hazards.

Environmental Health Technician: Assists in the survey of environmental hazards and performs technical duties under professional supervision in many areas of environmental health such as pollution control, radiation protection, and sanitation protection. (Sanitarian Technician)

Environmentalist: Plans, develops, and implements standards and systems to improve the quality of air, water, food, shelter, and other environmental factors, manages comprehensive environmental health programs, and promotes public awareness of the need to prevent and eliminate environmental health hazards. (Sanitarian)

Industrial Hygienist: Conducts programs in industry to measure, and help control, eliminate, and prevent occupational hazards and diseases.

Sanitarian Aide: Collects and measures environmental sanitation conditions and implements corrective action on health hazards for which specific guidelines exists.

HEALTH EDUCATION personnel acquaint groups and individuals with the standards of optimum health and the principles of achieving and maintaining optimum health.

Community/Public Health Educator: Alerts community groups and individuals to changing patterns of health care, to health hazards, and to activities which will promote community health and safety.

School Health Educator: Teaches elementary, secondary, and college students principles of personal health sciences, total fitness, family living, consumer and environmental health, and community health trends and resources.

HEALTH-RELATED TEACHER PREPARATION combines teaching skills and health expertise in preparing: (1) Instructors of individuals who are physically disabled, emotionally disturbed, or mentally retarded; and (2) Allied Health Professionals who desire to teach within their specialty area.

Allied Health Educator: Teaches the specialty in which he was trained to students being prepared in the discipline. May also supervise other individuals in his occupation.

Teacher of the Deaf: Adapts methods and curricula in the teaching of special skills, elementary, and secondary school subjects to deaf and hard-of-hearing pupils.

Teacher of the Emotionally Disturbed: Conducts educational programs for emotionally disturbed pupils.

Teacher of the Learning Disabled: Develops and implements educational programs to assist children in overcoming or compensating for learning disabilities such as aphasia, dyslexia, or other related problems.

Teacher of the Mentally Retarded: Develops and implements educational programs for trainable or educable mentally retarded persons according to the pupil's level of learning.

Teacher of the Physically Handicapped: Develops and implements academic and recreational programs for handicapped persons after evaluating the physical limitations, abilities, and needs of the individuals.

Teacher of Special Education-Not Elsewhere Classified: Develops and implements educational programs suited to the needs of students with physical disabilities, mental retardation, or emotional disturbances.

Teacher of the Visually Handicapped: Teaches academic and practical skills to the blind or visually handicapped through the use of braille and other specialized methods.

INFORMATION AND COMMUNICATION personnel apply a communications orientation to the development, presentation, organization, and recording of medical facts and material for the benefit of medical personnel and the general public.

Health Writer: Specializes in the writing of health or medical materials.

Medical Communicator: Knows the properties and capabilities of communication media and applies this knowledge to the design and improvement of communication processes in the health field.

Medical Computer Specialist: Combines a knowledge of computer science and health science to provide systems and programming support in the medical field.

Medical Illustrator: Demonstrates medical facts by the creation of illustrations, models, and teaching films; serves as a consultant, advisor, and administrator in the field of medical illustration.

Medical Librarian: Combines a degree in library science with specialized knowledge of medical librarianship and bibliography, to acquire, organize, catalog, retrieve, and disseminate medical information.

Medical Library Assistant: Combines training in library technology and health subjects to assist medical librarians in the process of acquiring, organizing, cataloging, retrieving, and disseminating medical information.

Medical Photographer: Visually presents medical facts by means of lantern slides, motion pictures, photographs of patients, reproduction of x-rays, and photomicrographs.

MEDICAL INSTRUMENTATION AND MACHINE OPERATION personnel maintain and/or operate equipment and instruments which supplement and support body functions or which provide diagnostic or therapeutic services.

Cardiopulmonary Technician: Performs a wide range of tests related to the functions and therapeutic care of the heart-lung system, assists in cardiac catherization and cardiac resuscitation, and assists in the post-operative monitoring, care, and treatment of heart-lung patients.

Cardiovascular Technician: Monitors and records physiologic data in cardiac catherization, performs specific tests during procedures, and assists in patient care.

Circulation Technologist: Operates and designs heart-lung machines, dialysis machines, artificial organs, and similar circulation devices and monitoring instruments to provide circulatory support to patients.

Dialysis Technician: Operates and maintains an artificial kidney machine following approved methods and techniques to provide dialysis treatment for patients with kidney disorders or failures.

Electrocardiograph Technician: Operates and maintains electrocardiograph machines, records electromotive variation in heart muscle action, and provides data for diagnosis and treatment of heart ailments by physicians.

Electroencephalographic/Electrocardiographic Technician: Operates and maintains both electroencephalographic and electrocardiographic machines.

Electroencephalographic Technician: Operates and maintains electroencephalographic machines, recording brain waves on a graph to be used by physicians in the diagnosis of brain disorders.

Electromyographic Technician: Assists physicians in recording and analyzing bioelectric potentials which originate in muscle tissue, including the operation of various electronic devices, maintenance of electronic equipment, assisting with patient care, and record-keeping.

Respiratory Therapist: Administers respiratory care under the direction of a physician, evaluating the patient's progress, and making recommendations for respiratory therapy. His proficiencies include ventilatory therapy, cardio-respiratory rehabilitation, microenvironmental control, and diagnostic testing of the respiratory system. (Inhalation Therapist)

Respiratory Therapy Technician: Routinely treats patients requiring non-critical respiratory care, recognizes and responds to a limited number of specified patient respiratory emergencies.

MEDICAL RECORD personnel plan, organize and manage patient information systems and statistical reports for medical and administrative staff use and health care research.

Medical Record Administrator: Plans, designs, develops, and manages systems of patient information, administrative and clinical statistical data, and patient medical records, in all types of health care institutions.

Medical Record Technician: Serves as the skilled assistant to the medical record administrator, carrying out the technical work of coding, analyzing, and preserving patients' medical records, and compiling reports, disease indices, and statistics in health care institutions.

Medical Transcriptionist: Skilled in typing, medical spelling, medical terminology, and the proper format of medical records and reports; prepared to transcribe medical dictation using mechanical dictating equipment.

MENTAL HEALTH personnel assist the health professionals in the prevention and treatment of mental disorders through recreational, occupational, and educational programs.

Mental Health Associate/Technician/Assistant: Works under the supervision of professional personnel in supplementing physical care for persons with emotional problems through recreational, occupational, and readjustment activities, including participation in group therapy with clients and families; refers patients to community agencies, and visits patients after their release from an institution.

Mental Health Technologist: Works with other mental health professionals in diagnosing psychiatric disorders, counseling, and planning treatment for the emotionally disturbed or mentally retarded.

Mental Retardation Aide: Works under the supervision of a professional staff in attending to the physical needs and well-being of mentally retarded patients and in assisting with teaching and recreation processes.

Psychiatric Aide: Works under the supervision of professional personnel in caring for mentally ill patients in a psychiatric medical care facility; assists in carrying out the prescribed treatment plan for the patient; maintains consistent attitudes in communicating with the patient in keeping with the treatment plan; and carries out assigned individual and group activities with patients.

NUCLEAR MEDICINE personnel prepare or use radioactive nuclides in laboratory procedures, scanning-imaging, and function studies for diagnostic, therapeutic, and research purposes.

Nuclear Medicine Technologist/Technician: Works under the supervision of a physician in administering and measuring radioactive nuclides in diagnostic and therapeutic applications utilizing a variety of techniques and equipment.

Radiopharmacist: Prepares, stores, handles, dilutes, and pharmaceutically formulates products labeled with radioactive nuclides and develops new radiopharmaceuticals.

NURSING-RELATED services personnel assist the physician in bedside patient care, and provide specialty services as required by institutional and community needs.

Nurse Aide: Performs tasks delegated or assigned by the professional nursing staff, including making beds, bathing patients, delivering messages, counting linens, and escorting patients to other departments in the hospital. (Nursing Assistant)

Nurse Anesthetist: Registered nurse prepared to work under an anesthesiologist or physician in administering anesthetic agents to patients before, and after, surgical and obstetrical operations and other medical procedures.

Nurse-Midwife: Assumes responsibility for the care of apparently normal obstetrical patients during pregnancy, labor, delivery, and postnatal period.

Nurse Practitioner: Registered nurse prepared to carry out functions previously performed by the general practitioner or physician specialist; collaborates with other health professionals in planning and instituting programs for the delivery of primary, acute, or chronic care; provides direct care to clients by making independent decisions about nursing care needs.

Obstetrical Technician: Assists in the care of mothers in labor and delivery rooms before, during, and after delivery under supervision of professional personnel, including hygienic procedures, routine laboratory work, and sterilization of equipment and supplies.

Operating Room Technician: Works as general technical assistant on the surgical team by arranging supplies and instruments in the operating room, maintaining antiseptic conditions, preparing patients for surgery, and assisting the surgeon during the operation.

Orderly: Assists the nursing staff in providing care for patients, performs the heavier work in the nursing unit, maintains equipment, and administers simple treatment. (Hospital Attendant; Nurse Attendant)

VISION CARE personnel work with or carry out the prescriptions of the ophthalmologist and optometrist. Their duties include ophthalmic examinations, treat-

ment, and correction of ophthalmic disorders by physical or mechanical measures.

Ophthalmic Assistant/Technician: Assists the ophthalmologist in eye examinations and in the treatment of eye diseases and disorders.

Ophthalmic Dispenser: Adapts and fits corrective eyewear as prescribed by the ophthalmologist or optometrist.

Ophthalmic Laboratory Technician: Operates machines to grind lenses and fabricate eyewear to prescription.

Optometric Assistant/Technician: Assists an optometrist in diversified ways, including general office duties, vision testing patients, administering eye exercises, preparing and fitting corrective lenses, and styling eyewear.

Orthoptist: Works under supervision of an ophthalmologist in testing for certain eye muscle imbalances and teaching the patient exercises to correct eye-coordination defects.

PHARMACY SERVICES personnel assist the pharmacist with selected activities in pharmacy departments to provide pharmaceutical services to patients, nurses, and physicians.

Pharmacy Technician: Assists the pharmacist with selected activities including medication profile reviews for drug incompatibilities, typing prescription labels and prescription packaging, handling of purchase records, and inventory control.

PHYSICIAN EXTENDER personnel render direct and specific assistance to the physician specialist and general practitioner in clinical and research endeavors, taking medical histories, performing detailed physical examinations, and conducting visual, auditory, developmental, and laboratory tests.

Physician Assistant-Primary Care: Performs physician-delegated functions in the areas of general practice, including family medicine, internal medicine, pediatrics, obstetrics, and emergency medicine.

Physician Assistant-Specialist: Performs functions delegated by the clinical specialist in specific areas of patient care: urology, surgery, pathology, orthopedics, etc.

PODIATRIC SERVICES personnel work under the direct supervision of the podiatrist, performing supplementary duties for the foot specialist.

Podiatric Assistant: Supports the podiatrist in his service to patients by preparing patients for treatment, sterilizing the instruments, performing general office duties, and assisting the podiatrist in preparing dressings, administering treatments, and developing x-rays.

RADIOLOGICAL SERVICES personnel use ionizing radiation for diagnostic, therapeutic, and research purpose.

Medical Radiation Dosimetrist: Calculates radiation dosage in the treatment of malignant disease and plans the direction of radiation to its target in the safest way.

Radiation Therapy Technologist/Technician: Administers x-rays and electron beam equipment in order to treat disease in patients, and assist in preparing and handling radioactive materials for therapy purposes.

Radiologic Technologist/Technician: Maintains and safely uses equipment and supplies necessary to demonstrate portions of the human body on x-ray film or fluoroscopic screen for diagnostic purposes. May supervise and/or teach radiologic personnel. (X-Ray Technician)

REHABILITATION-OCCUPATIONAL personnel use work-related skills in treating or training patients who are physically or mentally ill, in preventing disability, in evaluating behavior, and in restoring disabled persons to health and social or economic independence.

Manual Arts Therapist: Uses industrial arts, workshops, and agricultural activities to assist in the rehabilitation of patients.

Occupational Therapist: Evaluates the self care, work, and play/leisure time task performance skills of well and disabled clients of all age ranges; plans and implements programs, and social and inter-personal activities designed to restore, develop and/or maintain the client's ability to satisfactorily accomplish those daily living tasks required of his specific age and necessary to his particular occupational role adjustment.

Occupational Therapy Assistant: Works under the supervision of an occupational therapist in evaluating clients and planning and implementing programs, and is prepared to function independently when working directly with clients who require an occupational therapy program.

Rehabilitation Homemaking Specialist: Trains disabled homemakers to perform normal household activities in spite of their disability.

REHABILITATION-PHYSICAL personnel use physical agents, assistive devices, and therapeutic exercise for the prevention of disease and disability, and toward restoration of function to disabled persons.

Corrective Therapist/Adapted Physical Education Director: Provides medically prescribed programs of therapeutic exercise to physically and mentally ill patients to prevent muscular deconditioning resulting from inactivity and to attain resocialization and specific psychiatric objectives.

Exercise Physiologist: Works with clinicians in hospitals with rehabilitation programs to provide exercise stress testing and cardiovascular rehabilitation for patients.

Orthotic/Prosthetic Assistant: Assists the orthotist/prosthetist in caring for patients by making casts, measurements, and model specifications and fitting supportive appliances and/or artificial limbs.

Orthotic/Prosthetic Technician: Fabricates and repairs supportive appliances and/or artificial limbs under the guidance of the orthotist/prosthetist and his assistant.
Orthotist/Prosthetist: Writes specifications for and makes and fits braces and appliances and/or artificial limbs following the prescription of physicians.
Physical Therapist: Uses physical agents, biomechanical and neurophysiological principles, and assistive devices in relieving pain, restoring maximum function, and preventing disability following disease, injury, or loss of bodily part.
Physical Therapy Assistant: Assists the physical therapist by assembling equipment, carrying out specified treatment programs, and helping with complex treatment procedures. Other duties include responsibility for the personal care of patients, safety precautions, routine clerical and maintenance work.

REHABILITATION NOT ELSEWHERE CLASSIFIED personnel apply the principles of rehabilitation to diversified areas of therapeutic technique, such as education, fine arts, and recreation.
Art Therapist: Applies the principles and techniques of art to the rehabilitation of physically and mentally ill patients.
Dance Therapist: Applies the principles and techniques of dance to the rehabilitation of physically and mentally ill patients.
Educational Therapist: Instructs patients in academic and vocational subjects to further their medical recovery and prevent mental deconditioning.
Music Therapist: Uses individual and group musical activities with physically and mentally ill patients to accomplish therapeutic aims, to create an environment conducive to treatment, or to influence behavior.
Recreational Therapist: Plans, organizes, and directs medically approved recreation programs such as sports, trips, dramatics, arts and crafts, either to help

clients in recovery from illness or in coping with temporary or permanent disability.

Recreational Therapy Technician: Assists the recreational therapist in conducting medically approved recreation programs such as sports, trips, dramatics, arts and crafts.

Rehabilitation Therapy Assistant: Prepared by a general orientation to various rehabilitation specialties, to assist the professional therapist in carrying out rehabilitation programs.

SOCIAL SERVICES AND COUNSELING personnel use individual or group counseling techniques or provide services offered by social agencies to assist individuals in personal and/or social adjustment.

Alcohol/Drug Abuse Specialist: Advises and assists people in their efforts to overcome personal, family, and social problems that are manifested in alcoholism and drug addiction.

Clinical Pastoral Counselor: Combines a knowledge of health and religion in counseling the confined ill and disabled.

Community Health Worker: Assists people in the community with medical, social, or mental health problems in finding and utilizing sources of available help.

Genetic Assistant: Obtains complete genetic case histories from families of patients with inherited diseases and birth defects to be used in genetic counseling.

Genetic Counselor: Counsels clients as to the origin, transmission, and development of hereditary characteristics and their relations to birth abnormalities.

Homemaker/Home Health Aide: Assists with meals, shopping, household chores, bathing, and the other daily living needs, both physical and emotional, of elderly, ill, or disabled persons, working under professional supervision required by the situation.

Medical Social Worker: Prepared to identify and understand the social and emotional factors underlying patients' illness and to communicate these factors to the health team; to assist patients and their families in understanding and accepting the treatment necessary to maximum medical benefits and their adjustment to permanent and temporary effects of illness; to utilize resources, such as family and community agencies, in assisting patients to recovery.

Psychiatric Social Worker: Serves as a liaison between the psychiatrist, patient, and patient's family, to provide counseling and emotional support to the patient, and to contribute to the evaluation and diagnosis of mental disorders as a member of the psychiatric team.

Rehabilitation Counselor: Helps disabled individuals become aware of and secure rehabilitation services designed to fit the disabled person for gainful employment, assists in job placement, and checks on job satisfaction after employment.

Rehabilitation Counselor Aide: Aides the rehabilitation counselor in developing and implementing a rehabilitation plan for an individual; under supervision, he may conduct client interviews, locate and file data about employment opportunities, match clients with jobs available, and locate additional individuals in need of counseling or rehabilitation services.

School Health Aide: Assists the physician or nurse with physical examinations and programs to improve or maintain students' health.

SPEECH AND HEARING SERVICES personnel evaluate, record, habilitate, and research speech and hearing disorders in children and adults.

Audiologist: Evaluates hearing function and performs research related to hearing; plans, directs, and conducts habilitative programs designed to improve the communication efficiency of individuals with impaired hearing.

Speech/Hearing Therapy Aide: Assists in testing, evaluating, and treating the problems of people with speech and hearing difficulties.

Speech Pathologist: Evaluates, habilitates, and performs research related to speech and language problems; plans, directs, and conducts remedial programs designed to restore or improve communication efficiency of individuals with language and speech impairments, whether arising from physiological neurological disturbances, defective articulation, or foreign dialect in children or adults.

Speech Pathologist/Audiologist: Evaluates and habilitates hearing, speech, and language disorders, such as neurological disturbances, defective articulation, or foreign dialect in children or adults.

VETERINARY SERVICES personnel work with the care, use, production, and husbandry of animals in a medical setting.

Laboratory Animal Specialist: Manages the husbandry, production, and use of laboratory animals including responsibility for the sanitation, caging, safety, and nutrition of animals and the business management of the animal laboratory.

Laboratory Animal Worker: Cares for the health of laboratory animals used in research by feeding the animals, cleaning cages, preparing the animals for experiments, administering medications, and keeping records on laboratory procedures.

HEALTH PROFESSIONALS NOT ELSEWHERE CLASSIFIED

Biostatistician: Uses statistical theory, techniques, and methods to determine useful measurements or meaningful relationships of information relating to health or disease.

Epidemiologist: Concerned with determining the distribution and causal factors of health problems, encompassing areas such as acute and chronic illness, communicable diseases, behavioral disorders, alcoholism, and drug abuse.

Health Physicist: Directs research, training, and monitoring programs to protect hospital patients and laboratory personnel from radiation hazards, inspects and evaluates standards and decontamination procedures, and develops new methods to safeguard man and his environment against unnecessary radiation exposure.

Health Physics Technician: Monitors radiation levels, gives instructions in radiation safety, labels radioactive materials, and assists the health physicist in conducting experimental studies in radiation.

Population and Family Planning Specialist: Uses demography, demographic techniques, and reproductive physiology to plan, conduct, and evaluate family planning programs.

Public Health Practitioner—Not Elsewhere Classified: Professional trained to work in a public health capacity not specifically defined elsewhere in this glossary.

Toxiocologist: Concerned with the nature and extent of the injurious response to the ingestion of chemical compounds, and the determination of safe levels of exposure or ingestion in man and other species.

Source: Courtesy the American Society of Allied Health Professions.

PHYSICIAN ACCEPTANCE OF ALLIED HEALTH PERSONNEL

It is common knowledge that much of the physician's activity could be performed as well or better by allied health personnel, but the transfer of traditional medical functions to others has often been resisted by physicians. Several factors appear to be involved.[7] First of all, physicians are generally conservative and, in the past, have opposed new ideas related to the practice of medicine. Secondly, since they are usually self-employed, they are concerned about economic factors and tend to view allied health personnel as competitors for the health care dollar. Thirdly, when duties taken over by another are seen as a surrender of function rather than a delegation of function, physician resistance is greater. If a function is viewed by physicians as "nonmedical," they are more likely to allow someone else to do it. Physicians view nonmedical functions as those not concerned with life and death matters; for example, care of the feet, or those functions that become so routine that human judgment is minimized, such as eye refractions. Lastly, the more comprehensive the function (chiropractors and osteopaths), the greater the resistance by physicians. Those who offer limited care, such as psychologists, podiatrists, and optometrists are accepted because they present no danger to the role of the physician.

Resistance to allied health personnel should decrease as more medical students are accepted from workingclass backgrounds. These students are expected to challenge many of the traditional objections held by physicians. Another trend that should encourage acceptance is the increase in group practice, where physicians are on salary and do not view allied health workers as economic threats. Finally, if the team approach can be developed in health care to the point where there is a sense of shared medical responsibility, it will be easier for physicians to delegate certain functions with less anxiety.[8]

Nurse Practitioners and Physician Assistants

Two examples of allied health personnel who work very closely with physicians are nurse practitioners and physician assistants. In many states, laws have been passed and medical practice acts changed to facilitate their utilization as vital members of the health care team. More legislation is needed, however, before optimal use of their abilities is realized. Also, national agencies will have to approve teaching programs and test the graduates, and professional organizations will have to monitor accreditation and certification procedures. Hopefully, future education programs for these personnel will be scheduled so that if they wish to continue training to obtain an M.D. degree, progression would be logical and smooth. Uncertainty about roles and responsibility will have to be worked out as the use and availability of nurse practitioners and physician assistants increases.[9]

"Throughout the history of medicine, male-female antagonism or dominance-submissiveness was brought to the bedside, and the demarcation of territory between the sexes was extended to territorial barriers in the healing arts. . . . New efforts for health manpower have continued this division—physician assistants are ex-corpsmen and male; nurse practitioners are female."[10] This problem has been recognized and efforts are being made to recruit both men and women into allied health programs, hopefully eliminating the sex-linked identification of a particular role.

Patients' acceptance of nurse practitioners and physician assistants has been very good. The main problem has been the lack of acceptance by physicians who appear to want to maintain absolute control of patient care. The optimum use of nurse practitioners and physician assistants requires the physician's ability to work cooperatively with others. Medical schools have traditionally fostered and selected students who were self-reliant, competitive, and authoritarian. Medical students have been trained to give orders rather than work cooperatively with other health providers. New roles will have to be defined by patient-oriented functions rather than by traditional professional or sex images.[11]

Studies indicate that any reservation on the part of physicians to nurse practitioners and physician assistants will likely stimulate public resistance to their employment. This presents an obvious problem. If they are to be integrated successfully into the health care delivery system, they must be accepted by both physicians and patients, and also be able to increase the physician's productivity without sacrificing quality.[12,13] Physicians who have had first-hand experience with nurse practitioners and physician assistants accept them much more readily than those physicians who have not had such experience.

LICENSURE

Licensure of the new categories of health personnel can be a barrier to effective and innovative use of their skills. What was intended as a guarantee of quality can become only an indication of whether certain functions can be performed legally. Some legislatures have incorporated into their medical practice acts procedures for review of qualifications and job functions of allied health personnel. This gives legitimation to their functions, some assurance of quality control, guidelines for appropriate functions to be delegated, plus a certain flexibility.[14]

THE AMERICAN SOCIETY OF ALLIED HEALTH PROFESSIONS

The organization representing the diverse fields of allied health is the American Society of Allied Health Professions (ASAHP).* Through its three councils (Educational Institutions, Professional Organizations, and Individual Members), ASAHP attempts to provide:

(a) leadership on topics of general concern to the allied health field;

(b) unity in allied health;

* Address: One Dupont Circle, N.W., Washington, D.C. 20036.

(c) a mechanism for orderly change and progress;

(d) representation at the national level on matters affecting allied health;

(e) a vehicle for joint planning with other health associations in matters of vital concern to the health care system that affects the well-being of all citizens.

CONCLUSION

The use of allied health personnel has created additional dimensions and additional problems in the delivery of health care. The problems of training, utilization, licensing, flexibility, and acceptance are going to be difficult to solve. "Allied health manpower can be improved and reshaped to add to the total efficiency of the industry. It can and probably will help make health care more efficient if its own inherent rigidity is overcome. But it is not a solution to the problem of redirecting this enormous industry to a new social responsibility. It alone will not create a health industry whose primary concern is the health of the people."[15]

ENDNOTES

1. Aaron L. Andrews, "Current Status of Allied Health Programs," in *Technician Education Yearbook, 1973–1974* (Ann Arbor, Michigan: Prakken Publications, Inc., 1974).

2. Ibid.

3. Thomas N. Chirikos, *Allied Health Manpower in Ohio* (Columbus, Ohio: Ohio Advisory Council for Vocational Education, 1972), p. 68.

4. Anthony Robbins, "Allied Health Manpower—Solution or Problem?" *The New England Journal of Medicine* 286; April 27, 1972, 918.

5. Chirikos, *Allied Health Manpower in Ohio,* p. 24.

6. American Medical Association, *A Report on Education and Utilization of Allied Health Manpower* (Chicago, 1972), p. 10.

7. Leo Levy, "Factors Which Facilitate or Impede Transfer of Medical Functions from Physicians to Paramedical Personnel," *Journal of Health and Human Behavior* 7; Spring, 1966, 50–54.

8. Ibid.

9. Len Hughes Andrus and Mary Fenley, "Assistants to Primary Physicians in California," *The Western Journal of Medicine* 122; January, 1975, 80–86.

10. *Internal Medicine News* 5; January 1, 1972, 5.

11. Andrus and Fenley, "Assistants to Primary Physicians in California," pp. 80–86.

12. Theodor J. Litman, "Public Perception of the Physicians' Assistant—A Survey of the Attitudes and Opinions of Rural Iowa and Minnesota Residents," *American Journal of Public Health* 62; March, 1972, 343–346.

13. Eugene C. Nelson et. al., "Patients' Acceptance of Physician's Assistants," *Journal of the American Medical Association* 228; April 1, 1974, 63–67.

14. Roger M. Barkin, "Need for Statutory Legitimation of the Roles of Physician's Assistants," *Health Service Reports* 89; January–February, 1974, 31–36.

15. Robbins, "Allied Health Manpower—Solution or Problem?" p. 923.

Chapter Seven

Health Maintenance Organizations

The traditional way of arranging for health care in the United States has been for the patient to select a doctor and to pay him for his services. The selection process is supposed to allow the consumer "unlimited free choice" of a physician. Having selected a doctor, the consumer pays him for each service that is rendered. This is called "fee-for-service" medicine and is the basis of most health care practiced in the United States. When hospitalization is needed, the doctor admits his patient, performs whatever treatment is required, and the patient's health insurance supposedly pays the bill. Let us look closely at these cornerstones of medicine in the United States.

THE THREE CORNERSTONES

Unlimited Free Choice of Physician

Most consumers are not able to judge a doctor's medical competence. One study conducted by the Columbia University School of Public Health and Administrative Medicine showed that when one group of consumers selected their own physicians in New York City, one-third of the doctors consulted had no hospital staff appointments. Yet 40 percent of these consumers felt they were getting "the best that modern medicine provides." The consumer obviously doesn't have free choice in his selection of a physician; in most areas, he must choose a solo practitioner. Nor does the consumer have his choice of prepayment plans or health maintenance organizations (HMOs); usually, he must select a Blue Shield plan at fee-for-service prices. Even assuming that a person is capable of choosing a competent physician, there are other limitations to the free choice concept. Geography often makes it inconvenient to visit a physician who is some distance away, either across town or in another city. Financial barriers also often prevent a patient from seeing the doctor who is best qualified to treat him.

Fee-for-service

The physician who practices fee-for-service medicine generally has a financial interest in sick persons (obstetrics is an obvious exception), and his practice might be better characterized as "sickness care" rather than "health care." Also, since patients must pay for each "service" they receive, they tend to wait until they are really sick before they visit their solo practitioner. Sometimes such delay allows a condition to become chronic and the opportunity for easy and early correction is lost.

If the fee-for-service practitioner performs an operation, he is paid according to a given scale, and although prices vary, surgery is still very lucrative. On the other hand, some physicians may hesitate to perform needed operations because their patients may not be able to pay for them. In either case, financial considerations may take precedence over sound medical practice.

Fee-for-service has been characterized as the most costly method of physicians' reimbursement. This traditional approach has also enabled a doctor to determine his fees and income unilaterally, except, of course, during a time when the government has imposed a price freeze. Any system that allows those providing a service to set their wages unilaterally is open to possible abuse. Before the telephone company or the airlines are allowed to raise their rates, they must show that the increase is justified.

The traditional fee-for-service principle is actually a piecework approach to health care. Industry has successfully used this approach to provide financial incentives for workers to produce more pieces. Many studies over the years have shown that this piecework approach to medical care has had an inflationary effect. One study showed that surgery varied with the ability of the patient (or his insurance company) to pay: "the appendectomy rate for insured persons in the age group 6–54 was 11 per 1,000; for those without insurance, 5; the hospitalized tonsillectomy rate for those under 17 years of age was 30 per 1,000; for those without insurance, 9."[1] Another study found that the rate of surgery dropped 50 percent when salaried physicians replaced solo practitioners who had been paid on a fee-for-service basis.

Under our present system, the doctor views himself as an independent businessman. Consequently, he practices where he can make the most money, not necessarily where his services are most needed. If we plot the locations of physicians' offices in any large city in the United States, we will find that doctors are most numerous in the more affluent sections, and that sick persons in poverty areas usually have to travel many miles (often by public transportation) and spend hours to get to a doctor or to needed health facilities. One health care expert observed, "It is time we took health care out of the marketplace and by so doing we will be doing a favor for the doctor. We will be saving his professional soul from the corrupting influence of the marketplace."[2]

Insurance Pays the Bill

Many years ago, the rich were charged more for their medical care and the poor received their care free of charge. Now, with Medicaid, Medicare,* and health insurance, the assumption is that people's health care bills are no longer a problem. Approximately 90 percent of the civilian population under 65 have some form of health insurance. However, of all consumer expenditures for health services in a recent year, only one-third of the amount was covered by insurance benefits! These figures, of course, included the 10 percent who had no health insurance at all as well as those who had inadequate health insurance. However, many who have insurance still must pay a considerable sum when they are hospitalized.

The above discussion illustrates some of the problems with our traditional approach to medical care. It tends to be sickness, rather than preventive, care. Many people have to travel to various locations in a city to obtain appropriate care, and when they do, their medical records are often left scattered in several offices and perhaps the hospital. This does not encourage a comprehensive view of patient care. There is also the concern, borne out by various studies, that much health insurance provides the wrong kinds of incentives. It encourages costly hospitalization while discouraging out-patient and preventive services, and because it pays doctors for each service they perform, it encourages them to provide unnecessary or questionable services. Is there a suitable alternative to this traditional approach to medicine? Many persons feel that health maintenance organizations will answer some of the above problems.

HEALTH MAINTENANCE ORGANIZATIONS

The term "Health Maintenance Organizations" (HMOs) is almost certain to stir up strong feelings among physicians. Because the typical HMO pays doctors a salary, instead of

---

* For a detailed discussion of Medicaid and Medicare, see Chapter Eleven.

a fee for each service performed, some physicians feel that HMOs are a threat to the private practice of medicine. They claim that putting doctors on a salary destroys incentive and will result in a deterioration of the quality of patient care. Proponents of HMOs point out that the "incentives" of fee-for-service have resulted in over-servicing, which includes too much hospitalization and too much surgery for patients.

Briefly, an HMO "assembles a number of health services under one roof for its enrolled members. Instead of charging a fee for each service, the HMO collects a lump sum in advance from subscribers (or their employers). That sum is supposed to pay for comprehensive health care by the HMO's physicians. HMO, in short, is another name for prepaid group practice or group health."[3]

Although the HMO concept may stimulate heated discussion today, this response is mild compared to the controversy it caused when it was first introduced as prepaid group practice in the 1930s. At that time, medical societies promoted the passage of laws that discouraged the establishment of prepaid medical practice. Also, physicians who chose to practice this kind of medicine were refused membership in county medical societies, prevented from obtaining admission privileges at hospitals, and were denied access for specialty board examinations![4] This harassment might still be evident today were it not for the 1941 landmark case of the *United States* v. *the American Medical Association* (AMA), held in the District of Columbia. The verdict: "The AMA and the District of Columbia Medical Society had engaged in an unlawful combination in restraint of trade in violation of Section III of the Sherman Anti-Trust Act."[5]

After a study of various medical care plans in 1959, the AMA decided that there was no legitimate basis for opposing prepaid group practice as either unethical or incompetent. In spite of this pronouncement, some states still have restrictive laws which require prepaid group practices to be approved by medical societies and governed by physicians.

In 1973, Congress enacted a Health Maintenance Organization (HMO) Act which overrides restrictive state laws for any HMO which meets federal standards. The act requires any employer with twenty-five or more employees to offer its workers a federally approved HMO if conventional health insurance is provided as a fringe benefit.[6]

In the remainder of this chapter, we will concentrate on three HMOs: the Health Insurance Plan of Greater New York, the Group Health Cooperative of Puget Sound, and the Kaiser Foundation Medical Care Program.

Health Insurance Plan of Greater New York

The Health Insurance Plan of Greater New York (HIP) began in 1947 and now enrolls nearly a million members who receive comprehensive health care provided by forty-five affiliated medical group centers located throughout the greater New York area. The medical group is the foundation of health care in HIP. Each medical group consists of family doctors, pediatricians, gynecologists, and teams of medical specialists in fourteen fields of medicine. HIP members have their own family doctor in their medical group who looks after their medical needs. Medical, surgical, specialist, maternity, and preventive care is provided as long as there is medical need. There are no deductibles, no co-insurance, no claim forms, and no out-of-pocket payments. HIP members may change to another medical group or change family doctors within a medical group. The fee-for-service method of payment is not used. Instead, a capitation system is used, in which each of the medical groups is paid for each member enrolled. Coverage under this plan includes *unlimited* doctor's office visits, hospital visits, hospitalization, maternity care, eye examinations, and x-ray and laboratory procedures. Also completely covered are physical examinations, physical therapy, immunizations, injectable drugs, ambulance service, and visiting nurse services.[7]

Exclusions: not included are dental care, prescribed drugs, eyeglasses, artificial limbs, cosmetic surgery, treatment for alcoholism and drug addiction, or treatment by a psychiatrist after diagnosis.

HIP utilizes full-time professional health educators to assist the physicians in their role as teachers of sound health information and attitudes. The health educators guide the development of a wide variety of educational activities, all with the sponsorship and participation of the physicians, including periodic bulletins, a variety of subscriber-physician meetings, pamphlets, films, and intimate discussion groups.

The School of Public Health at Columbia University conducted a four-year study of nonprofit medical and dental prepayment plans and concluded that HIP:[8]

1. Offered the most complete contract for medical care in New York State.

2. Had high standards of care. Eighty-three percent of the surgical procedures at HIP were performed by Board-Certified surgeons. This compared with 57 percent for surgical operations under the Group Health Insurance Plan and 62 percent under Blue Shield.

3. Provided greater financial protection. Over a third of patients in a competing plan were charged supplemental fees, so they incurred out-of-pocket expenses.

4. Provided high-quality physicians.

5. Had lower hospital admission rates than for subscribers of other plans.

Group Health Cooperative

The Group Health Cooperative (GHC) of Puget Sound was also formed in 1947. Its purpose is to provide Seattle families with better medical care at a more equitable cost on a prepaid basis. GHC is a nonprofit medical care plan, classified under Washington state law as a "welfare organization." This means that its hospital and central facilities are tax-free. There is an initial capital investment of $100.00, which can be paid during the first year or at the rate of $1.00 per month for ten years. There are now approximately 200,000 GHC members.

The health care "package" completely covers the following: medical and surgical care; mental health care (ten visit per year); hemodialysis (up to $10,000 per year); family planning consultations; hospital care including room and board, drugs and medicines, dressings, nursing care, operating room, anesthesia, cast room, plaster casts, x-ray, laboratory examinations, and other services customary in modern hospital procedures. Also completely covered are special nurses and a private hospital room when deemed necessary; a group health physician; immunizations and vaccinations; out-of-area emergency care* (up to $10,000); ambulance service and home calls when considered necessary by group health physician.

Complete maternity care by Board-Certified obstetricians is covered for a flat fee of $230, which is a savings of more than $300 over average maternity costs in the area.

Services and procedures not covered are: eyeglasses, artificial limbs and appliances, cosmetic surgery, dental care, treatment for drug addiction and alcoholism, and care for pulmonary tuberculosis.

GHC members receive health care in various medical centers which are located throughout the Puget Sound area. These centers have laboratory, x-ray, and pharmacy facilities which enable GHC members to receive care close to home. If hospitalization is necessary, they are taken to a centrally located hospital.

A physician, appointed by an elected board, serves as director of the organization. He works closely with the superintendent of the hospital, who is also appointed by the board. Most of the more than 100 physicians in the GHC belong to the King County Medical Society. Physicians operating in a specialty are required to be Board-Certified as specialists in that field. To reduce drug costs, physicians

---

* Care administered when the member is unable to reach a Group Health Cooperative (GHC) physician or GHC hospital.

must use drugs which are on an approved drug formulary (list). Any doctor wishing to add a drug or medicine can apply to have it included in the formulary. The fact that applications are carefully reviewed tends to prevent the proliferation of identical or nearly identical drugs. The effect of the formulary, of course, is to reduce the cost of drugs without interfering with the doctor's practice of medicine.

There are no income limitations on joining GHC and no physical examination is required prior to membership. When treatment is received, there are no claim forms to complete.

GHC offers alternative plans for those who wish partial coverage and a special plan designed to supplement Parts A and B of Medicare.

Patients have free choice of medical care from among the physician members of GHC. If, for some reason, a patient is not satisfied with one doctor he can choose another. The doctor-patient relationship is not interfered with in any way.

GHC is interested in a preventive approach to health care. To this end, it provides information and advice on staying healthy through its bimonthly magazine, *View*. Also, new programs and classes are always being developed by GHC's Department of Health Education to help consumers deal with their individual health problems and questions.

GHC maintains a staff of well-trained physician assistants (PAs) and nurse practitioners who work under the direct supervision of doctors. PAs and nurse practitioners save physician time by handling minor problems such as sprains, burns, cuts that may require stitches, colds, and simple skin ailments; they also assist with routine checkups. If symptoms of serious problems appear, they are trained to consult with a physician.[9,10]

Kaiser Foundation Medical Care Program

The Kaiser Foundation Medical Care Program is the largest HMO in the United States. Through more than 2,100 licensed hospital beds and 1,500 physician offices, it serves the needs of nearly three million Americans located in California, Oregon, Hawaii, Colorado, and Ohio. The goal of Kaiser's program is to organize and provide comprehensive health care at costs that the average family can afford.

Kaiser traces its origin back to the Southern California desert in the depression years of the early 1930s. Construction workers on an aqueduct project were 200 miles away from the nearest doctor. At the request of the contractor, a surgeon named Dr. Sydney R. Garfield built a fifteen-bed hospital and organized a team of physicians to care for the desert workers. Fee-for-service payments were discontinued in favor of prepaid medical care. The cost was $1.50 per month for each employee.[11]

In 1938, when Henry Kaiser was building the Grand Cooley Dam in Washington, he wanted his workers to be happy—and to be happy, he reasoned, they must first be healthy. To arrange for this, he asked Dr. Garfield to set up a prepaid medical plan in which his workers paid fifty cents a week.[12] The plan was soon extended to cover dependents of the workers. Since this modest inception, the program has grown in size and coverage, and while Kaiser Industrial employees and their families still belong to the health plan, they now comprise less than 4 percent of the total membership.

The fundamental principles of the Kaiser Foundation Medical Care Program (hereafter called Kaiser) are group practice, prepayment, preventive medical care, integrated medical facilities, and voluntary enrollment. The plan is carried out by several separate entities working closely together for a common purpose. One entity, Kaiser Foundation Health Plan, contracts with groups and with individuals offering medical and hospital services on a prepaid basis. The health plan, in turn, contracts with the Permanente Medical Groups, which agree to provide medical services to health plan members in return for regular payment. Such payment is made on a capitation basis rather than in the form of a fee for each individual service which has been performed. The health plan also contracts with Kaiser Foundation hospitals, which agree to provide hospital services to health plan members, again without the traditional fee-for-service compensation. A fourth entity performs certain basic services of a housekeeping nature, such as purchasing and payroll for the other entities.

A comment about the integrated facilities: at the major centers, the offices of physicians are adjacent to or within the hospitals; common laboratory and x-ray facilities serve both in-patients and out-patients. In addition, in some areas, the major centers are ringed by outlying medical offices at which many families may receive much of their more routine medical care.

Various plans of coverage are available through Kaiser, according to the needs and wishes of the members. There are several individual group plans and a special plan for members over sixty-five who are covered by Medicare. To illustrate, let's look at a group plan in Southern California for members under sixty-five.[13] Members generally must be within a radius of thirty air miles from the plan's medical offices and hospitals. Coverage is as follows: *In the doctor's office,* there is no charge for office visits, eye examinations, physical therapy, laboratory tests, or x-rays. Drugs, medicines, injections, and allergy treatment materials are provided at reasonable rates. *In the hospital,* there is no charge for physicians' and surgeons' services, including operations and anesthesia. There is no charge for 125 days (approximately four months) each year for room and board, general nursing, and use of the operating room; for the remaining 240 days, these services are provided at one-half the prevailing rates. There is no charge for drugs and medicines, injections, special duty nursing, dressings and casts, x-rays, laboratory tests, and physical therapy. Blood transfusions are provided at no cost if the blood is replaced.

The plan also covers up to twenty psychiatric visits or short-term in-patient therapy. Full maternity care, with doctors' services, hospitalization, x-ray and laboratory services, and Caesarian section, if necessary, cost the patient $100. Ambulance service is also provided at no extra charge.

The plan does not cover drug addiction, self-inflicted

injuries, dental care, neuromuscular rehabilitation, organ transplants (other than kidney), or plastic surgery performed primarily for cosmetic purposes.

The regulations stipulate that members must use Kaiser Foundation doctors and hospitals. Out-of-area coverage is $3,000 per person.

As a member of Kaiser, you are urged to choose a family doctor and a pediatrician for your children from the doctors located at the office most convenient to you. Medical care is provided for prevention of disease as well as for treatment of illnesses. You are urged to have periodic checkups, seek medical advice, and get prompt attention at the first sign of illness.

Doctors at Kaiser are selected by other doctors. They work in teams and include personnel in all major specialties. About 75 percent of physicians at Kaiser are members of American Specialty Boards or are Board eligible.[14]

Successful comprehensive HMOs such as Kaiser, HIP, and GHC have provided needed information and have dispelled many fears about this method of practicing medicine. They have shown that even a plan which offers almost unlimited medical care will not collapse from overutilization, since very few tend to abuse the services. There is actually a much lower rate of hospitalization under these plans. Some reasons for this: stress is placed on preventive, rather than curative, care; patients do not have to be admitted to the hospital for their diagnostic work; and there is no financial incentive for a physician to perform unnecessary treatment, including surgery. These plans have also shown that the fee-for-service philosophy is not necessarily the only, or for that matter, the best approach to comprehensive health care. They have also shown that a good doctor-patient relationship can be developed within an HMO. Finally, such plans have shown that unlimited free choice of a physician is not that important to the consumer if he knows he is getting good-quality care.

ADVANTAGES AND
DISADVANTAGES
OF HMOs

Consumer Advantages

Studies have shown that the elements in HMOs which consumers particularly appreciate are the following:[15]

1. Most services are available under one roof.
2. You can select from physicians whose competence has been evaluated by other doctors.
3. Referral for consultation by specialists is easily done, and there is no threat to your personal physician of loss of prestige or income.
4. Services are available on a twenty-four-hour basis, every day of the year. If your personal physician is not available, a competent doctor from the same team will be, and he will have access to your medical records.
5. Your medical records will always be available, even if your physician moves to another locality.
6. Doctors caring for you can plan for treatment on the basis of their medical judgment—that is, independent of any monetary influence.
7. Your expenses are predictable and you can budget for health care just as you do for rent and utilities. Utilizing the insurance principle, the cost of each member's treatment is spread over a large number of persons, thus reducing individual expenses.
8. HMOs provide one of the most potent controls on the quality of medical care: the judgment by physicians of their colleague's skill. This surveillance is almost entirely lacking among solo physicians in their private offices.
9. Physicians are not motivated by financial gain to perform unnecessary treatment, including surgery.

10. HMOs encourage preventive care. Treatment is not put off until you can afford it, because you can always afford it.

11. No claim forms have to be filled out!

Consumer Disadvantages

In some HMOs, one of the main complaints is the delay in obtaining routine appointments with a personal physician. In order to alleviate this problem, Kaiser operates a "same day" appointment system. A member who wishes to see a doctor immediately, calls in and is given a specific appointment-time the same day. The result has been that patients who formerly sat in the waiting room of the clinic from 8:30 a.m. until their turn came, can now spend the time more profitably. Studies have shown that waiting time at Kaiser for appointments *and non-appointments* for all departments is twenty-one minutes. The average waiting time in a physician's reception room for the United States is thirty minutes for a patient with an appointment, and nearly forty-five minutes for a patient without an appointment.[16]

Another complaint is that HMOs encourage assembly-line medicine. However, some physicians will practice assembly-line medicine whether they are in HMOs or solo practice. The way a physician practices is determined by the physician himself, not the plan.

As we all realize, not everyone is going to be completely satisfied with group plans. Neither all physicians nor all consumers will find their greatest satisfaction in this sort of system. "It takes two to play the game successfully. As a stable marriage depends not only on finding the right partner, but also on being the right partner, contented membership in HMOs requires sympathetic cooperation on the part of the consumer and a willingness to live with some of the minor rules of conduct essential to any organized program."[17]

Consumers may say, "I have heard some terrible things about that group plan." Let's look at this kind of statement and see how it might have developed. Physicians are usually very careful to avoid criticism of their colleagues. However, because of a smoldering irritation with HMOs, some solo physicians make open comments such as the following: "That physician is on salary because he couldn't make it on his own" or "A doctor doesn't really care about his patients when he is practicing that kind of medicine; he has a captive audience."

Some patients are chronic complainers and they go from one doctor to another, seeking cures for their imaginary ills. If dissatisfaction develops, it will likely be directed against "Doctor X" or "Doctor Y." In an HMO, however, such dissatisfaction is usually not directed against the offending doctor, but against the HMO. In addition, since the HMO may be serving thousands or hundreds of thousands of patients in a city, such dissatisfaction usually receives wider dissemination than it would for a solo practitioner who would not have such a large number of patients.

Physician Advantages[18]

In the first place, beginning physicians are familiar with the HMO routine. As students in medical school, they functioned in a framework of a loose group, namely the faculty. The group structure was also present during their internship, residency, or duty in the armed services. Secondly, after a physician has finished four years of college, four years of medical school, internship, and three or more years of specialty training, he is usually married, with children, and in debt. The prospect of going further into debt to equip an office is not too appealing to him. Entry into an HMO avoids this added financial burden. Thirdly, no matter how many years he spent in his training, when a physician enters practice there is still much for him to learn. An HMO provides an excellent environment in which he can learn from other doctors who want to see him succeed. Fourthly, in spite of excellent training and cooperative colleagues, it is still necessary for a physician to partake of self-renewal through further postgraduate education. In the coming years, this will become even more important. Regular time off for further study or for other reasons can be arranged in an HMO, through the rotation of physicians. This arrangement also allows a doctor to have predictable free nights and weekends so that he may enjoy a reasonably normal and wholesome family life. When a dedicated solo practitioner assumes responsibility for a patient, he takes on a twenty-four-hour day, 7 days a week, for 365 days a year. This can be a staggering load and completely out of line with the diminishing work weeks being enjoyed by most other members of society.

Another advantage is that, during the many years of training, a physician has concentrated all his attention on medicine. He is not really prepared for the business aspects of operating a private practice. HMO membership enables him to devote his full time to practicing medicine as he was trained to do, leaving the business end of it to administrators who are trained in administrative aspects. For another thing, the beginning physician in private practice usually finds that business is slow not only for a few months, but often for years. As one surgical specialist who had been in practice said, ". . . it's virtually impossible for a well-trained, completely honest man to become successful before his skills deteriorate." When a doctor is taken into an HMO, there is always a supply of patients for him. Also, during the peak of specialty solo practice, incomes are generally high. HMO earnings, however, are still competitive because of three factors: they begin at a higher level, they are more predictable, and they do not fall off as rapidly in later years.

Finally, doctors associated with HMOs can plan for treatment in accordance with their medical judgment, secure in the knowledge that their patients will not suffer financially as a result.

Physician Disadvantages

The greatest deterrent to group practice still seems to be the "bitter opposition of organized medicine." In spite of the Larson report, published by the AMA in 1959, which gave a favorable analysis of group practice, there is still much resistance at the local (County Medical Society) level. Even though the AMA is not officially opposed to group practice, discrimination at the local level is devastatingly effective against physicians who practice in groups: denial of patient referral, denial of hospital privileges or no promotions on hospital staffs, and sometimes social ostracism.

Obviously, an HMO is not every doctor's choice, nor is this a reflection on the physician. Some physicians object to adhering to certain regulations, intragroup medical audits, limitation to certain formularies, and other procedures which are necessary in any properly supervised HMO.

Some physicians object to the limitation of consultants in some of the smaller HMOs, and this is admittedly a serious shortcoming. Most HMOs, however, allow for consultation outside if HMO physicians feel such a consultation is necessary.

Another objection is that the physician in an HMO may feel less committed to his patients. This has been referred to as a "collusion of anonymity." It may occur when many doctors are caring for a patient, and no one physician takes the basic responsibility for the care of the *whole* patient. To prevent this from happening, most group plans encourage the consumer to select a personal physician who may guide the patient to the needed specialists but who takes ultimate responsibility for total patient care.

Some physicians still refer to group practice as "closed panel" medicine because the consumer is limited to a panel of physicians who are members of the plan. Actually, staffs of group plans can be compared to the staffs of voluntary hospitals. A consumer seeking care in any hospital is limited in his choice of physicians to those on the staff of that particular hospital. This is also true of group plans.

HMO RESULTS

What are the results when consumers select an HMO? Several studies have been done to compare group plans with the traditional approach to medicine. One study compared fee-for-service care with Kaiser. Under the Kaiser plan, "hospital admissions declined in this instance from 135 per 1,000 beneficiaries for those under the care of solo practitioners on a fee-for-service basis to 90 per 1,000; hospital days per 1,000 per annum from 1,032 to 570, and major surgical procedures per 1,000 from 69 to 33."[19]

A study which involved six-and-three-quarter million employees and their dependents showed similar trends. These consumers were members of the Federal Employees Health Benefits Program. Hospital utilization rates were compared among persons in a multiple-choice program who could elect Blue Cross/Blue Shield or an HMO. Hospital utilization under the HMO was 40 percent less than in the other plans. Those covered by the "blues" had two-and-one-half times the rate of tonsillectomies, and twice the rate of appendectomies.

Another study of eight states and the District of Columbia compared rates for members of Blue Cross with members of group practice plans (HMOs). The HMO members had half the hospitalization rate of that for Blue Cross members. The same study revealed that the surgery rate per 1,000 enrollees was 34 for the HMOs, and 75 for Blue Shield. Also, less than half the number of surgical procedures was performed in the HMO than in Blue Shield.[20]

Studies such as these have caused knowledgeable consumers to view the "unlimited-free-choice" concept with a more critical eye. They realize that it can be a serious disadvantage for an uninformed patient to select an unlabelled product. In the HMOs, other physicians do the screening and select those doctors who meet certain standards.

If physicians do not soon support group practice, they may find that the government will impose a system of medicine which may be even less attractive to the American doctor. Consumers are not likely to stand idly by and allow the present abuses to continue.

The HMOs provide care in an organized setting and physicians are not paid on a fee-for-service basis, so they do not have any incentive for unnecessary hospitalization or unnecessary surgery. "In contrast to the insurance concept which reimburses the patient after he gets sick, the pre-payment concept involves contracting with the medical group for all necessary services to keep the patient in good health. In short, if you get sick the plan loses, but if the plan keeps you well the plan stands to gain. The group practice plans emphasize preventive care and early diagnosis and treatment."[21]

The federal government has viewed with alarm the sky-rocketing cost of health care in this country. Since HMOs reduce costs and provide comparable or better health care, it is clear that these plans will continue to grow in importance and eventually become the dominant pattern of professional activity. In late 1975, the Department of Health, Education, and Welfare declared that if a firm employs 25 or more persons, and provides a health insurance plan, it must offer an HMO alternative to the traditional health insurance plans. This declaration affects the nation's 400,000 largest employers, and opens up the possibility of HMO membership to their employees, which make up 80 percent of the work force (over 52 million persons).[22]

ENDNOTES

1. Caldwell B. Esselstyn, "Group Practice as a Solution," in U.S. Department of Health, Education, and Welfare, *Public Health Service-Labor Seminar on Consumer Health Services* (Washington, D.C.: U.S. Government Printing Office, 1968), pp. 38–39.
2. Richard E. Shoemaker, "Health System Problems and Approaches," in U.S. Department of Health, Education, and Welfare, *Public Health Service-Labor Seminar on Consumer Health Services* (Washington, D.C.: U.S. Government Printing Office, 1968), p. 28.
3. "HMO's: Are They the Answer to Your Medical Needs?" *Consumer Reports* 39; October, 1974, 756.
4. Ibid.
5. "The Two Barriers to HMO Success: The Doctors and the Patients," *Modern Healthcare* 1; May, 1974, 49–50.
6. *Consumer Reports* 39, p. 760.

7. City of New York Health Services Division, *A Choice of Health Plans* (New York, 1973), pp. 34–37.

8. Health Insurance Plan of Greater New York, *What the Experts Said About HIP!* (New York, n.d.).

9. Group Health Cooperative of Puget Sound, *View* 17; July/August, 1974.

10. Group Health Cooperative of Puget Sound, *Members Agreement,* 1974.

11. Kaiser Foundation Health Plan, *Kaiser Foundation Medical Care Program, 1960* (Oakland, Cal., 1961), p. 10.

12. Paul De Kruif, *Kaiser Wakes the Doctors* (New York: Harcourt, Brace and Company, 1943), p. 18.

13. Daniel A. Scannell, Public Affairs Director, Kaiser Foundation Medical Care Program, personal communication, October 2, 1974.

14. Kaiser Foundation Health Plan, Inc., *Southern California Group-Practice Plan* (Oakland, Cal., 1974).

15. Esselstyn, *Public Health Service-Labor Seminar on Consumer Health Services,* p. 22.

16. Kaiser Foundation Medical Care Program, *Kaiser Foundation Medical Care Program, 1973* (Oakland, Cal., 1973), pp. 16–18.

17. Esselstyn, *Public Health Service-Labor Seminar on Consumer Health Services,* p. 33.

18. Ibid., pp. 33–35.

19. Ibid., p. 39.

20. George S. Perrott, *The Federal Employees' Health Benefits Program* (Washington, D.C.: U.S. Department of Health, Education, and Welfare, 1971), pp. 11–19.

21. Shoemaker, *Public Health Service-Labor Seminar on Consumer Health Services,* p. 16.

22. *Los Angeles Times,* October 25, 1975, Part I, p. 4.

Chapter Eight

Hospitals

In a recent year, there were nearly 7,200 hospitals in the United States registered by the American Hospital Association; they had close to 1.7 million beds and admitted nearly 37 million in-patients. These hospitals spent over $45 billion to provide services for in-patients and out-patients. There was one admission for every six persons in the United States, which meant an expenditure of $215 for each resident in the nation.[1] In short, hospitals are big business.

Have you ever wondered who owns hospitals? Who is responsible for their organization and operation? What are the various types of hospitals? What is involved in accrediting a hospital? How to choose a hospital? In this chapter, we shall explore the above questions as well as certain other issues and problems affecting our modern hospitals.

DEVELOPMENT OF THE HOSPITAL

Hospitals have moved through several stages in their development in America. They came into being as religious asylums, an expression of Christian concern for the poor, old, and homeless who were unlucky enough to become ill.

Custodial care was provided on a charity basis and the patients admitted under these conditions usually died. Understandably, most people dreaded the thought of going to the hospital.

Surgeons in the first half of the nineteenth century knew enough anatomy to enable them to perform many ordinary operations, but they did not attempt to keep the wounds clean. Pain, hemorrhage, infection, and gangrene were so common that over 90 percent of the surgical patients died. If patients did not have an infectious condition when they were admitted to the hospital, they soon acquired one from other patients. The hospital was a place of last resort.

During the middle and late nineteenth century, with the work of Semmelweiss (puerperal or childbed fever), Pasteur (germ theory), Lister (antisepsis), and the discovery of anaesthesia, doctors became interested in the possibilities of applying this new knowledge to benefit their rich patients. Doctors were allowed the privilege of admitting their own patients to the hospital for treatment, and in return they would provide charity care for the sick poor in the hospital. During this time, operations were done without the masks which we now take for granted in modern surgery, and yet there was some hope of a cure. According to Wilson,[2] doctors with their superior knowledge of treatment very frequently assumed control of the hospital setting. There was no resistance from the religiously oriented institutions, geared more to passive rather than to active care of the ill. The role of the physician has been likened to that of a guest who regulates the thermostat but doesn't pay the fuel bills. The physician was able to maintain the doctor-patient relationship and take advantage of whatever technical and therapeutic facilities the hospitals offered.

Custodial care was relatively easy to provide, but curative care needed trained personnel. During the late nineteenth century and the early part of the twentieth century, larger metropolitan hospitals took on the task of providing the training of nurses to assist the physician. Other skilled personnel were soon needed as more medical discoveries were made.

As hospitals developed, the physician assumed a major role in decisions that affected the operation of a hospital. A nurse was often appointed to order supplies and materials and to take care of certain other matters. When hospitals grew in size and complexity, it became clear that someone had to take responsibility for the organization and smooth operation of the many departments. At this point, the hospital administrator came on the scene. At first he was challenged by the physicians, who were accustomed to making most of the decisions affecting the operation of the hospital. When it became obvious that the administrator was here to stay, that he was generally well trained, and had an important job to do, a colleague relationship sometimes developed between him and the M.D.'s at the hospital. This, however, is not a universal development, and in many hospitals there is still a struggle for authority between the administrator and the staff physicians.

Perhaps because of their independent origins, hospital needs have been determined by religious, fraternal, or other civic-minded groups, without regard for the way they are used. The result has been duplication of some facilities and inadequate allowances for others. For example, empty pediatric and obstetrical beds are the general rule across the nation, while the chronically ill must stay in expensive acute hospital beds because of a shortage of less expensive nursing home beds.

One striking example of duplication in the state of New York came to light when the Governor's Committee on Hospital Costs found that thirty-eight hospitals had facilities to perform open heart surgery. The Committee noted that, in a one-year period, six of these hospitals did not perform a single open heart operation, seven did less than ten operations, and twelve did from ten to twenty-four operations. Only one of the thirty-eight hospitals met the requirement of one operation per week needed to maintain the proficiency of the heart surgery team![3] This is a shocking waste of the taxpayer's money and illustrates the dire need for state and local comprehensive planning for health facilities. Careful planning is needed if a business is going to succeed, and hospitals today are big business. However, since they have not been expected to "show a profit" as business must do, hospitals have rarely done any serious comprehensive planning. Traditionally, there has been no cost accounting, or careful projections of population and the usual signs of careful forecasting to anticipate needs.

In spite of these deficiencies, hospitals are becoming the nucleus of health care because of new techniques and the expensive equipment required for diagnosis and treatment. Private health insurance and Medicare-Medicaid help defray the costs, so people have been admitted to the hospitals in ever-increasing numbers. Unfortunately, there is now an overutilization of hospital facilities, encouraged by many private health insurance schemes, which do not pay for services which are rendered in out-patient departments, nursing homes, or physicians' offices. The public is now looking with some alarm at the soaring cost of hospital care and the obvious question comes to mind: How can we improve the efficiency of our hospitals without reducing quality? Unfortunately, the answer to this question is not so obvious and it will be of concern to hospital administrators and government officials for years to come.

FEDERAL SUPPORT OF
HOSPITALS

The Hill-Burton Program came into being in the mid-1940s under the Truman Administration to help ease the hospital shortage. By helping with funds, it encouraged local communities to build needed hospitals. If certain planning and construction standards were met, the federal government would appropriate money according to a formula based on population and relative per capita income.

In the early 1970s, the Hill-Burton program shifted from new buildings to an almost exclusive emphasis on renovation and/or replacement. The trend was also toward the

TABLE 8.1 Changes Under Hill-Burton

Mid-1940s	Early 1970s
New construction was greatest need. More than half of funds spent for new facilities—particularly in rural areas where none existed.	Modernization of old facilities, mainly in cities, was greatest need. Renovations and replacements received nearly 90 percent of funds.
No Statewide planning.	States required to develop plans.
Few planning agencies.	All metropolitan areas with 1 million population (24) have planning agencies. More than 70 agencies received Hill-Burton aid.
No National standards relating to functional relationship and efficiency of design.	Minimum standards, originally established in 1947, continually updated. Hill-Burton guide materials used internationally.
Separate-but-equal facilities.	Integration required in 1964—one year prior to implementation of Civil Rights law.
Only hospitals and public health centers eligible for aid.	Grants also aid long-term care facilities, outpatient facilities, rehabilitation facilities, State health laboratories, and emergency departments.
Few States had standards of maintenance and operation.	All States have standards. Most State standards follow closely those developed by Hill-Burton.
Little attention given to environmental control programs in hospitals.	Leadership given to developing guide materials and conducting conferences to promote improved hospital environment.
Grants were the main focus of Federal assistance under Hill-Burton.	The main thrust was the direct loans for public health facilities and loan guarantees with interest subsidies for private nonprofit health facilities. Grant funds were also authorized.

TABLE 8.1 (Continued)

Mid-1940s	Early 1970s
Federal aid for equipment purchase was possible only when associated with construction or modernization.	Equipment-only projects were aided when they provided a service not previously available in the community.
The primary focus was on inpatient care.	Ambulatory care, including outpatient and emergency service, was emphasized.
Outpatient facilities were required to be hospital-based to receive aid.	Freestanding outpatient facilities, including neighborhood health centers, can be aided.
Priority for rural areas was mandatory.	Priority was given to urban and rural poverty areas and Federal financing was, at State option, up to 90 percent.
Need for education and training programs for health facility personnel not recognized.	Organized education and training programs and workshops developed and gaining momentum.
Hospitals functioned completely independently.	Impetus given to sharing concept in facilities, services, manpower, and equipment. 1970 legislation authorized increasing the Federal share up to 90 percent (at the option of the State agency) for facilities that provided shared services.

Source: U.S. Department of Health, Education, and Welfare, *Hill-Burton Is* . . . (Washington, D.C.: U.S. Government Printing Office, 1972)

construction of ambulatory care facilities because in most urban areas, excess acute general care hospital beds were responsible for a large portion of accelerating hospital costs.[4] Table 8.1 illustrates some changes in the hospital field from the mid-1940s to the early 1970s.

As desirable as the Hill-Burton program was, its requirements for planning affected only those hospitals that applied for federal funds. Other hospitals did not have to show evidence of prior planning and need for building.

State approval is needed before a hospital can be built, but the state is mainly interested in construction standards and safety features, rather than a coordinated program on a regional basis. Fortunately, additional approval is now needed before hospitals can be built or can add beds. Other planning agencies now review applications for new facilities and decide whether the community needs the additional beds. If a new hospital is built without such approval, it will not be eligible to receive money for Medicare and Medicaid patients.

During its nearly thirty years of operation, the Hill-Burton Program aided approximately 11,000 projects throughout the nation.

The National Health Planning and Resources Development Act of 1974[5] replaced the Hill-Burton Program. The Act, known as Public Law (P.L.) 93–641, is administered by the Department of Health, Education, and Welfare, and authorizes $390 million over a three-year period for health facilities construction and modernization grants.

The funds are for projects to:

1. modernize medical facilties,
2. construct new outpatient medical facilities,
3. construct new inpatient medical facilities in areas which have experienced recent rapid population growth, and
4. convert existing medical facilities for providing new health services.*

In setting priorities among projects within a given state, special consideration is given to: (1) projects for medical facilities serving rural areas and those with relatively small financial resources; (2) the modernization of facilities serving densely populated areas; (3) the construction of outpatient facilities in rural and poverty areas; (4) projects to eliminate or prevent safety hazards and to assure compliance with state licensure and accreditation standards; and (5) medical facilities that will provide comprehensive care, in-

* Encouraging construction and modernization of health facilities is only one part of P.L. 93–641. Appendix C contains the priority items included in the law.

cluding outpatient and preventive care as well as hospitalization.

Grants under P.L. 93–641 may cover up to two-thirds of the cost of projects, except in rural or urban poverty areas, where they may cover 100 percent.

HEW will provide general standards of construction, modernization, and equipment for medical facilities assisted through this program. It will prescribe criteria for determining the need for medical facilities as well as the extent to which existing facilities need modernization. To receive grants under P.L. 93–641, a state must provide adequate medical facilities for all persons residing in the state, including those unable to pay.

CLASSIFICATION OF HOSPITALS

Hospitals are usually classified on the basis of type of patient treated (clinical) or on the basis of ownership and control. Actually, to be accurately described, a hospital must be classified according to both systems. For example, a general hospital may be classified in many ways on the basis of ownership, and a community hospital may fall into one of several clinical categories. The two classifications are listed in Table 8.2. A third classification can be made on the basis of length of stay: a short-term hospital is one that usually provides care for patients up to thirty days; long-term hospitals, for conditions such as chronic, mental, and neurological diseases, generally require longer periods of hospitalization. Short-term hospitals take care of 92 percent of all admissions in the United States.

ORGANIZATION OF HOSPITALS

Figure 8.1 shows the organization of the hospital. We will briefly discuss a few of the main areas in this organization.[6]

TABLE 8.2 Classification of Hospitals

Clinical	Ownership and Control
General	Governmental
Special	Federal
Medicine	Army
Internal Medicine	Navy
Nervous and Mental	Air Force
Tuberculosis	Veterans Administration
Children	U.S. Public Health Service
Communicable Diseases	State
Venereal Disease	County
Surgery	City
Eye, ear, nose, and throat	Nongovernmental
Orthopedic	Church
Diseases of women	Fraternal Order
Cancer	Community
Industrial	Private—not for profit
Maternity	Private—for profit
Chronic Diseases	
Convalescent	

Source: Malcolm T. MacEachern, *Hospital Organization and Management* (Berwyn, Ill.: Physicians' Record Company, 1962), pp. 34–35.

The Governing Board

The Governing Board is usually composed of eight to fifteen members selected from representative citizens in the community (normally, successful businessmen). It is reasoned that a man who has not been able to manage his own affairs should not be placed on the Board to direct a large and complicated institution such as a hospital. Board members are appointed for terms of three to five years, with three members retiring each year, so there is never a Board composed completely of new members. The Board is responsible for: a) establishing the policies of the hospital; b) providing equipment and facilities; c) establishing professional standards for the care of the sick; d) providing adequate financing and enforcing businesslike control of funds; e) keeping

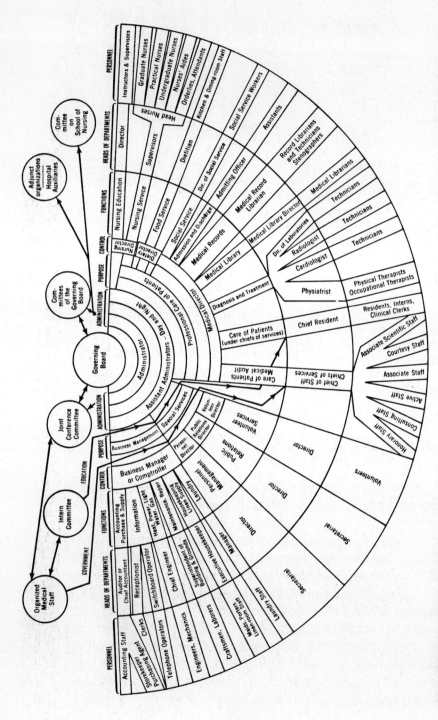

FIGURE 8.1 Organization of the Hospital: Trends of Responsibility and Authority. *Source:* Malcolm T. Mac-Eachern, *Hospital Organization and Management* (Berwyn, Ill.: Physicians' Record Company, 1962), p. 84.

adequate records of finances and activities, as well as a host of other items.

The Governing Board is the supreme authority in the hospital, the one to which everyone else in the organization, directly or indirectly, is responsible. In a proprietary (privately owned) hospital, the Board will usually be composed of the owners of the hospital.

The Administrator

The Governing Board appoints an Administrator (sometimes called a Director or Superintendent), who is responsible to the Board for the efficient management of the hospital. He coordinates the activities of the medical staff and the various personnel in the many departments of the hospital. Decisions about the treatment of patients are made by the attending physician, who relays orders to the medical staff, department heads, nurses, and others directly concerned with patient care. The Administrator has potential control over the hospital activities of the medical staff. He must see to it that the staff adheres to the rules and bylaws enacted by the Governing Board. He could, if necessary, suspend or cancel the appointment of a given physician who was obviously not performing adequately, but the Administrator usually follows the recommendations of the committees of the medical staff.

The Administrator selects all department heads and is responsible for the proper functioning of each department. Since he cannot be on duty at all times, nor can he personally take care of all details in a large institution, he may have one or more assistants.

Department Heads

Under "Functions" in Figure 8.1, there are many separate but interrelated departments. These range from accounting, information, and maintenance to services such as food, nursing, and medical care of patients. Each department has a director (see "Control") who is responsible to the Administrator.

HOSPITAL COSTS

Hospital costs can be defined as the expenses hospitals incur in the treatment of patients. These costs are usually listed as per diem and ancillary expenses. The per diem charges are for room and board which include "(1) fifty different diets of three meals a day served in bed . . . , (2) the salaries of three shifts of nurses per day, seven days a week, (3) the salaries of house staff (interns and residents) available to the patient 24 hours a day, and (4) the cost of supplies, medical records, and medical social workers."[7] Ancillary expenses include the use of operating rooms, drugs, radiology, and many other services and facilities which the patient does not see, such as laboratories, medical supplies, and anesthesiology.

Changing Product

Hospital patients today are receiving better care than they did years ago. To begin with, there are more personnel providing services. In short-term hospitals, the average number of employees per occupied bed, not counting doctors, has risen from 1.5 thirty years ago to 3.0 today. That is, for every 100 bed patients, a hospital has to have 300 employees to provide around-the-clock care. New occupational categories have been developed, such as inhalation therapists and biomedical technicians. Secondly, the more traditional categories of personnel have increased expertise because of better education and training. A third factor is the nonlabor aspect of care, such as more laboratory tests and a higher level of accuracy of these tests. There are now three times as many laboratory tests avaiiable as were available ten years ago. New equipment, such as nuclear scanning devices and sophisticated monitoring apparatus, is now being used for patient care. This sophisticated equipment is very costly and it becomes obsolete in a very short time. It enables hospitals to provide heart surgery and intensive care, but it also requires personnel who are trained in electronics to maintain it. These personnel are in great demand by industry and research centers, so hospitals must compete with these outside institutions for this high-priced expertise. More drugs are now available for patient care; 80 percent of the drugs used today had not been discovered fifteen years ago. We tend to concentrate on the changes in the per diem costs of basic care and forget about the changes in the levels of patient care.[8]

Other Factors

Other factors are related to the rise in hospital costs. Hospital wages have increased dramatically. In the early 1900s when the hospital was viewed as a charitable institution, it was accepted that employees worked for next to nothing. People who could not find employment anywhere else came to work at the hospital where meals, lodging, and medical care were provided instead of adequate wages. It was not until 1966, however, that the minimum wage provisions of the Fair Labor Standards Act were applied to hospital workers. There is a domino effect on wages throughout the hospital when workers covered by the minimum wage provisions receive a raise. When the lowest paid workers receive an increase, there must be increases in the wages of higher paid personnel so that wage differentiations based on skill are maintained. Since the Fair Labor Standards Act, salaries for hospital employees have increased at a faster rate than that for employees in other fields, but they are still somewhat lower than wages paid in other industries. Wages account for 55 percent of hospital costs.

Working conditions have improved. Twenty-five years ago, the twelve-hour day was an accepted practice. With the eight-hour day, three employees are now required to provide the same services that two employees provided in the past.

Since hospital employees are required to have new skills, there is a greater demand for these skills than can be met. This demand forces employers to offer better wages to attract the more skilled personnel. Hospitals, like other institutions, have to pay more for nonlabor items, such as equipment, supplies, and their physical plant. Supplies now account for approximately 45 percent of all nonlabor hospital items. The cost of capital for operation and expansion has also increased dramatically. Private grants (philanthropy) and government grants have been decreasing with the result that hospitals have been increasingly dependent on long-term commercial borrowing in the form of either mortgages or bonds.

Increased demand for hospital care for patients has resulted in higher costs. Our standard of living has increased and people expect better hospital care. These expectations are translated by attending physicians into greater numbers and types of tests, procedures, and treatments which they feel should be done. In response to these needs, hospitals increase their staffing, equipment, and facilities. Another facet of the increased demand for hospital care is the extent of public and private health insurance coverage, which encourages hospitalization by providing benefits for hospitalized patients only. Often diagnostic procedures could be done on an out-patient basis, but would not be covered by insurance. While hospital insurance lowers the actual amount that an individual has to pay out-of-pocket at the time of service, he tends to forget that he has already paid a substantial amount to the insurance company. Most patients are concerned only with this out-of-pocket expense and it has not increased as rapidly as hospital costs in general. Medicare and Medicaid have also had an effect on hospital demands since both of these programs have provided easier access for two large groups—the elderly and the poor.[9]

Several suggestions have been made to contain the costs:[10]

- Promote regional planning to avoid duplication of costly equipment and services.
- Encourage changes in health insurance that will promote more ambulatory care, health education, and preventive approaches.
- Develop more Health Maintenance Organizations.
- Properly utilize hospital beds.
- Improve cost accounting (costs need to be clearly identified).
- Reduce turnover rates of hospital employees (now as high as 70 percent).
- Utilize labor-saving devices, such as automated machines and computers.

HOSPITAL ACCREDITATION

Accreditation is a stamp of approval which signifies that a hospital has achieved certain minimum standards of service to patients. Hospitals in the United States are accredited by the Joint Commission on Accreditation of Hospitals (JCAH), composed of the American College of Surgeons, the American College of Physicians, the American Hospital Association, and the American Medical Association. These accrediting bodies are set up as independent voluntary non-profit organizations, which are supported by their member associations. The accreditation procedure is voluntary and some hospitals choose not to seek accreditation. This does not necessarily mean that they are not providing good care. To apply for accreditation, a hospital must be registered with the American Hospital Association, have at least twenty-five beds, and have been in operation for at least twenty-one months.

The Joint Commission on Accreditation of Hospitals does not evaluate the quality of care provided in a hospital by a doctor or nurse. It does evaluate the physical and organizational structure, processes, and documentation of action taken by a hospital to provide the best possible care. A JCAH director stated: "If I pick up a chart of a woman who was admitted for a hysterectomy, I don't examine it to see if I think it was justified that a particular diagnosis was made or procedure proposed. I'm not a gynecologist, I'm not on the hospital staff, and I don't have privileges. I do see that the woman had the proper workup before she went to surgery. Does the record show that the hospital followed its own rules about the justification of admission and workup? Was there an operative report written? Did the anesthesiologist visit the case? Did all the artifacts of practice (proper record keeping) take place?"[11]

The requirements for accreditation are quite detailed, and all cannot be listed here, but the main items are as follows:[12]

I.   Administration
   A)   The hospital must have a governing body that is able to assume legal and moral responsibility for the conduct of the institution—a responsibility toward the patient, the community, and the sponsoring organization.

   B)   The physical plant of the hospital—the buildings—must be constructed, arranged, and maintained to ensure the safety of the patients, and provide adequate facilities for diagnosis and treatment, and for special hospital service appropriate to the needs of the community.

   C)   It must maintain such facilities and services as:
      1)   A dietary staff
      2)   Medical records

3) Pharmacy or drug room
4) Clinical—pathology and pathologic—anatomy department
5) Radiology department
6) Emergency care for mass casualties
7) Medical library

II. Medical Staff
The hospital must have a medical staff that is properly organized, that is responsible to the patient and the governing body of the hospital for the quality of all medical care provided in the hospital and for the ethical and professional practices of its members.

III. Nursing Staff
The hospital must provide nursing facilities that guarantee a licensed graduate registered nurse on duty at all times, and a graduate nursing service that is available for all patients.

In addition to the above, patients with communicable diseases must be isolated; an emergency lighting system must be available in the operating room, delivery room, and stairwells; a minimum of 20 to 25 percent of all hospital deaths must be autopsied; consultations are required for Caesarean sections, curettages (scraping and removing the contents of the uterus), sterility operations, and certain others.

Accreditation also requires that there be certain functioning committees such as: *Credentials Committee,* for appointment and annual reappointment of medical staff members; *Joint Conference Committee,* for liaison between the administrator, the governing body, and the medical staff; and the *Medical Records, Tissue, and Medical Audit Committees,* which evaluate the quality of care the patients receive. For example, pathologists examine all tissue removed from patients, and, as noted previously, if more than 10 percent is healthy, the matter is investigated. Other committees include the *Utilization Review Committee,* which checks on the need for and length of hospitalization; the *Infection Review Committee;* and the *Pharmaceutical and Therapeutic Committee.*

Approximately 70 percent of the nation's hospitals are accredited by the JCAH. Most of the hospitals not accredited by the JCAH are certified by a state inspection team. There is concern about state certification standards because some states' standards are even lower than those of the JCAH. If a hospital loses its accreditation, it could also lose its internship and residency program, if the AMA's Council on Medical Education felt that the deficiencies found by the JCAH would adversely affect training programs. At one time, JCAH approval meant that hospitals were automatically eligible to receive Medicare patients. Recent legislation, however, has authorized the Secretary of Health, Education, and Welfare (HEW) to make validation surveys, either on a sample basis or on the basis of complaints. If HEW finds any significant deficiencies which it considers potentially detrimental to the "health and safety" of patients, it can rule the hospital ineligible for Medicare participation—in spite of JCAH accreditation. As of 1976, hospitals must conduct their own quality assurance programs, or be subject to external (government) controls.

Most JCAH survey teams are composed of two people, sometimes three—a physician and either a hospital administrator or a nurse, or both. About three months before the onsite visit, the hospital requesting the survey sends the JCAH a completed questionnaire which provides information on facilities and services. This information is analyzed by a computer and the survey team has the results before they visit the hospital. The survey team may spend two days at the hospital reviewing various departments and examining hospital records, bylaws, and regulations. At the end of the survey, a conference is held with the hospital administrator and department heads and the results of the onsite visit are discussed. The recommendations of the survey team are forwarded to Chicago where they are reviewed by the Accreditation Committee of the JCAH. It may decide to deny accreditation, or accredit the hospital for a one-year, or a two-year period.

Approximately 5 percent of hospitals that apply for accreditation fail to meet JCAH standards, and it appears that these standards will become more stringent in the future.[13,14]

Many experts in the hospital field view the JCAH requirements as minimal and claim that a good hospital will provide facilities, services, and records which far surpass the conditions of JCAH. The hospital to which you are admitted should be accredited. To make certain, you may phone the hospital or write to the Joint Committee on Accreditation of Hospitals.*

If your doctor suggests hospitalization, make sure that it is necessary; ask him if there is any possibility of the services being provided at home, in his office, or on an outpatient basis at the hospital. Not only is hospitalization expensive, but there is also the chance of acquiring a hospital-induced (nosocomial) infection.

CHOOSING A HOSPITAL

How would you choose a hospital? Some consumers' judgments about hospitals are based on items that have very little to do with quality of care. These items include the quality of coffee served, the type of paintings in patient rooms, the quality of television reception, the provision of newspapers in the lobby, and the adequacy of parking facilities.[15] While these things can be sources of pleasure or annoyance to a hospitalized patient, they are not good ways to determine quality of care. What are the best criteria for choosing a superior hospital? When a group of hospital administrators, doctors, health care consumer advocates, and nurses were asked that question, they gave the following suggestions.[16,17]

* Address: 875 N. Michigan Ave., Chicago, Ill. 60611.

Is It Accredited?

As described earlier, accreditation means that the hospital meets certain minimum standards of facilities and services. Try to avoid nonaccredited hospitals.

What Affiliations Does It Have?

Is it affiliated with a medical school and/or nursing school? Is it approved by the American Medical Association and specialty boards for intern and resident training? A "yes" to these questions usually means a high quality of care because at these institutions you are more likely to have student eagerness, an interest in research, and competent medical school faculty who keep abreast of the latest medical developments. However, since there are only 114 medical schools in the United States, not all hospitals can have such affiliation. And not everyone wants to be admitted to a university hospital since it means that the patient must accept medical students as observers of his treatment. Often medical students do more than observe; they may feel an enlarged liver, listen to an unusual heartbeat, or probe body openings. This participation is necessary for them to become proficient in diagnostic techniques, but not all patients want to be "used" in this way.

Who Owns the Hospital?

Table 8.2 lists various types of hospital ownership. Although it is dangerous to generalize about the quality of care based on the type of ownership, some comment should be made. In good community hospitals, there is strict adherence to the inspection, evaluation, and control of the medical activities of staff physicians. Government-sponsored hospitals also tend to have high standards. Proprietary hospitals, however, do not seem to be as careful and may, for example, allow major surgery by general practitioners. Also, proprietary hospitals may tend to concentrate on diseases and disorders that can be treated without elaborate equipment or highly specialized technical support. They are more likely to emphasize relatively simple operations such as appendectomies and tonsillectomies, rather than the complex surgical procedures like heart surgery. Proprietary hospitals also tend to have fewer facilities such as blood banks, medical libraries, postoperative recovery rooms and therapeutic x-ray services.

What Is the Size of the Hospital?

The current trend is toward larger hospitals. From 1963 to 1973, hospitals with less than fifty beds decreased, while those with fifty or more beds increased. (See Table 8.3.)

TABLE 8.3 Distribution of Community Hospitals by Bed-Size Category, 1963 and 1973

Bed-size category	Number of beds		Percent change
	1963	1973	
6– 24	627	327	−47.8
25– 49	1,464	1,187	−18.9
50– 99	1,466	1,511	3.1
100–199	1,058	1,269	19.9
200–299	540	641	18.7
300–399	262	372	42.0
400–499	124	213	71.8
500 and over	143	269	88.1

Source: American Hospital Association, Hospital Statistics, 1974.

"Bigness" doesn't necessarily mean "goodness," but the larger the hospital, the better the chances that it will be equipped to offer more comprehensive care. Most authorities agree that a university hospital that is part of a medical school should be your first choice; next comes the regional hospital, which is usually interested in physician education and is above average size. The third choice is the community hospital, which is usually smaller than the first two. Generally, it does not attract the medical specialists that so many people want. Why? Because most specialists want to be where there are other specialists—at university and teaching hospitals. Also, in outlying areas, there are usually not enough specialty-related problems to keep a specialist busy. Not everyone agrees with the above view. William A. Nolen, a physician at the Litchfield Clinic in Litchfield, Minnesota, and author of two best sellers, *The Making of a Surgeon* and *A Surgeon's World,* has a different opinion. He feels that a good doctor will not "feel locked into a given hospital and become defensive about it," but will refer you to a larger facility if he thinks you need more sophisticated care. Nolen states that many physicians and patients have a "fixation on equipment." He estimates that 98 percent of the ailments of 98 percent of all patients can be treated perfectly well by a doctor working with the basic equipment all hospitals have. The important thing, according to Nolen, is that your doctor "knows enough to know when he doesn't know." Most authorities agree that it requires a team effort to help patients recover. If you find a lot of dissension and dissatisfaction among hospital employees, you will likely be the one who suffers.

Answers to questions about accreditation, affiliation, size, and ownership are rather easily obtained from a hospital because they do not require any research, but they may cause some hospital personnel to ask why you want the information. Answers to the following questions will be more difficult to obtain and may require some persistence on your part. If you are told that the hospital does not give out the information, ask where you can obtain it.

What Is the Nurse/Patient Ratio?

There should be at least one registered nurse (R.N.) for every six on-the-job personnel. What is the R.N. coverage at night? Patients often become fearful after dark and may have more symptoms than during the day. At night, there should be at least one R.N. for every ten to fifteen patients. The auxiliary personnel (licensed vocational nurses, practical nurses, orderlies) should have quality training so that they are able to report anything unusual to the R.N. The auxiliary personnel spend more time with the patients than the R.N., and their informed observations are vital to good patient care.

Does the Hospital Provide Follow-up Services?

Intermediate and home care programs are sometimes needed by patients when they are released from the hospital. These programs must be approved by the state in order for your insurance company to reimburse you.

What Is the Autopsy Rate?

This question may unsettle some prospective patients who do not wish to be reminded of their mortality. However it has been shown that hospitals with the highest autopsy rates have the professional staff with the highest inquisitiveness. This means that doctors at these hospitals are concerned about the quality of care and how it may be improved. An autopsy enables a physician (and review committees) to check his diagnosis against the actual cause of death.

Other Questions

A vice-president of the Blue Cross Department of Health Care Services adds some other criteria: What kinds of specialists have privileges to practice at the hospital? Are they Board-Certified? Does the hospital have the facilities and personnel to qualify as a Primary Emergency Facility?* Is there an intensive care unit? Does the hospital have a large number of foreign medical graduates among the interns and residents? This may indicate communication problems for patients and may also mean that the hospital is having trouble attracting American students. Does the hospital follow the American Hospital Association's "Patient's Bill of Rights"? (See Appendix D.) What is the average length of stay? How does the per diem rate compare with other hospitals of comparable size? (Maternity charges are often good indicators of comparative costs.)

If you do not have an accredited hospital in your community and you are seriously ill, ask your doctor if he can care for you in the nearest accredited hospital or recommend someone who can. Consider the cost of getting there an investment in good quality care.

THE RIGHT TO KNOW

You are not always in a position to shop around for a hospital because your doctor may not have privileges at some hospitals or may need certain sophisticated equipment that is available only at one or two hospitals. Although you do have the right to know certain facts about your hospitals, meaningful information is not always available or has not been published. Comparisons are usually very interesting and if you are aware of large differences in costs at various

---

* A Primary Emergency Facility is an institution that has certain emergency facilities and personnel available twenty-four hours a day.

hospitals, hospital administrators may keep a closer eye on expenses.

Herbert S. Denenberg, former Pennsylvania Insurance Commissioner, was a pioneer in providing the public with information about health care. To inform consumers in his state, he published data on more than 100 hospitals and medical centers in Pennsylvania. He provided a chart that encouraged the public to compare the average daily charges (per diem rates), bed capacity, occupancy rate, and average length of stay. In addition, information was provided about medical school affiliation and whether psychiatric care, chronic care, and rehabilitative care were available. His chart also identified hospital beds that did not meet safety standards. With this kind of information, a consumer can make a more intelligent decision about choosing a hospital and perhaps discuss alternatives with his doctor before agreeing to enter a hospital.[18]

If your state does not offer similar information on hospitals, you can still get hospital facts if you are willing to invest some of your time in a little research. The annual *Guide to the Health Care Field* by the American Hospital Association contains comprehensive statistics on all hospitals in the United States that are members of the American Hospital Association. For example, you can find out if a hospital is accredited, has a residency and/or internship program, a professional nursing school, and if it is certified to participate in Medicare. You can also find out if the hospital has various facilities and services, such as an organ bank, renal dialysis equipment, inhalation therapy, or intensive care units. It will also give you information on the type of ownership, the number of beds, percent occupancy, number of births each year, number of personnel, and the payroll of the hospital, as well as a host of other pertinent items.

To obtain per diem rates, call the hospitals. Remember that there are three major money-making departments in a hospital: the pharmacy, radiology, and the clinical laboratory. It is quite possible and even probable that some hospitals will keep their per diem rates low (an item that the public feels they understand because it is a fixed amount and visible) and make up their deficit on the money-making areas (which are not quoted and are variable according to patient needs). A useful approach would be to ask what the laboratory charge is for a routine type of procedure such as a hemoglobin or a urinalysis. A similar approach could be used with the x-ray and the pharmacy.

BEING HOSPITALIZED

After experiencing long delays in treatment and much psychic trauma during his hospitalization, one author[19] has suggested some rules to be followed in "that most challenging of human experiences—going to the hospital."

1. Don't get sick on Friday. If you are hospitalized on Friday (or Saturday) not much will be done for you until Monday unless your condition is very serious. Most hospitals function on the five-day week with only skeletal staffs for laboratory, x-ray, and surgical care. Patient care is provided over the weekend, but it is usually just custodial.

2. Don't go to the hospital alone. If you are sick enough to be hospitalized you won't have the patience or the strength to answer all the questions and complete the forms that most hospitals require before admission. Take a friend or relative with you for moral support and assistance during admission.

3. Bring money. Even though you have insurance coverage, you may still be asked for a large cash deposit. This deposit varies with hospitals but is currently around $500.00.

4. Don't take a private room. Most doctors agree that you are better off with at least one roommate. Then in the event of a medical emergency, your roommate can summon help. If you have a private room, the call bell

may not be answered promptly or you may be in such a state (unconscious) that you cannot use it.

5. Take nothing for granted; ask questions; and, if necessary, complain. Notice the color of your pills; if they vary, ask why! It could be an error. If you get flustered when your doctor comes to see you and tend to forget to ask about things that have been bothering you, make a list and make certain you get answers you can understand.

6. Make certain that surgery is necessary. Much surgery is not necessary, so get another doctor's opinion before you agree to have an operation.

7. Make certain that you are not being confused with another patient. Some patients have the same last names. All patients wear similar gowns. Most rooms have a similar appearance and most doors (except for the room numbers) look alike. It is no wonder that mistakes are made.

8. Carefully check your bill for a record of everything that is done for you—each box of tissues, each pill, and each x-ray. Then check this against your final bill. This procedure will reduce the chances of error.

9. Ask if there is a patient representative in the hospital. The patient representative is supposed to assist you in adjusting to the hospital routine. Her duties will be discussed in a later section. If your hospital does not have one, ask "Why not?"

ENCOURAGING TRENDS

Due to the various pressures on them by consumers, by government agencies, and by third-party payers, hospitals are changing. These modifications mean that the consumer is receiving more humane treatment, better and faster treatment, and, in some cases, less expensive treatment. Some examples of these changes follow.

Patient Representatives

During the past decade, hospitals have grown in size and complexity. This growth has often been a mixed blessing. On the one hand, large size means that more services and facilities are available to patients; on the other hand, size has resulted in a depersonalization of health care. Patients have complained about this lack of personal care and hospitals around the country are responding to these charges. Several hundred patient representatives, sometimes called ombudsmen or consumer advocates, are now functioning in the nation's hospitals. This relatively new occupational category is designed to assist the patient through the institutional maze of the hospital and reduce the anxieties and problems that most patients experience. Too often patients suffer in silence, believing that a good patient is a quiet one. This belief may be fostered by nurses and doctors, but it is wrong! As a patient you should let others know when you are suffering. It doesn't matter if it is physical or mental anguish, something can usually be done. Patient representatives explain hospital procedures, check complaints about poor nursing care, interpret a consent form for surgery, and in general function on behalf of the patient. These representatives also attempt to sensitize the staff to the needs of the patient.[20,21]

Public Relations

Other evidence of the hospital's concern for the consumer is reflected by the increasing interest in public relations. One example of this trend is the fact that hospitals in several states have signed up for customer relations courses offered by a major airline. These brief (one day, six hours) classes emphasize a "positive self-image" for hospital employees. It is well-known that a patient often makes judgments about hospitals from the moment he arrives at the admitting area. Personnel coming into contact with the patient have an important effect on his attitudes about the quality of care he receives while in the hospital. For this reason, admitting area personnel, clerks, messengers, and elevator operators are often the first to receive the public relations training.

What does a stewardess have to offer hospital personnel? Hospitals and airlines have at least two common concerns—"just as courteous and reassuring service can distinguish one airline from another, the manner in which patients are received and cared for can distinguish one hospital from another." Also, "stewardesses and hospital personnel must deal with people whose personalities may be altered by the stress and anxiety they feel over their surroundings."[22] Airline personnel have learned to calm nervous passengers and can offer useful suggestions to hospital workers who have to deal with frightened patients.

Seven-Day Week

Since sickness befalls people without much regard to the time of day or the day of the week, people who become ill on the weekend often have to wait until Monday to have comprehensive care in a hospital setting. They may be admitted to the hospital on a Friday or a Saturday but, as mentioned earlier, they will receive basically custodial care until Monday. In 1964, the Albany Medical Center Hospital in Albany, New York, changed to a seven-day week because (1) there was a long list of patients waiting to be admitted to the hospital, (2) many elective patients did not want to be admitted to the hospital on a Friday or Saturday because they knew that little would be done until Monday, and (3) this over-the-weekend delay was unnecessarily prolonging hospital stays. Also, it was felt that prompt provision of treatment would result in better patient care. The advantages of the seven-day week have been:[23]

- More rapid diagnosis.
- Earlier treatment.
- Increased use of beds and equipment.
- Shorter patient stay.
- More patients cared for per year.
- Fewer new buildings required.
- Costs spread over larger numbers of patients.
- Lower cost to the patients.

In the late 1940s, nurses around the nation were delighted to forsake the ten-hour day for an eight-hour one; now in some hospitals nurses are back to the ten-hour day and they like it! There is a difference. In the early 1940s, nurses worked a forty-eight-hour week; now they are working a seventy-hour week (in seven days) but they get paid for eighty hours and get the next seven days off. This approach allows the hospital to change "the patient's hospital day to conform as much as possible with his normal life pattern." The benefits of this program are improved patient care, better continuity and flexibility of care, increased communication, better staff rapport, and more patient-centered care. Because nurses endorse the seven-day program, there is less turnover; sick leave is only one-third of that for nurses in the traditional forty-hour week. Also, the program provides greater opportunities for in-service education while nurses are on duty.[24]

Consortiums

Eight hospitals in Hartford, Connecticut, have formed a consortium that involves shared facilities, shared services, and a combined medical staff. The hospitals, which vary in size from 128 to 925 beds, have agreed to "coordinate and further the health delivery, medical, educational, research, administrative, and other activities of its members . . . ." Their objectives include: (1) the best quality of care at the lowest possible prices; (2) coordinated programs in preventive care and research; (3) the elimination of unnecessary duplication of services and the provision of incomplete coverage; (4) the integration of educational programs in medicine, dentistry, nursing, and allied health; and (5) the education of the public regarding the health care needs of the community. The consortium has bylaws and a governing board made up of three representatives (an administrator, a board member, and a physician) from each hospital.

Several major factors led to the establishment of the consortium. State and federal planning agencies had been urging hospitals in the Hartford area to share facilities and personnel. Also, several studies had shown needless duplication of facilities such as open-heart surgery and high-energy radio therapy. Quality of care tends to decline when specially trained teams needed for these facilities are not kept busy. Finally, some important health care needs, such as trauma and burn units, were not provided at any of Hartford's hospitals.[25]

A more loosely structured organization is found in Washington State, where five rural community hospitals situated 80 to 160 miles from Seattle have formed a Health Services Consortium with a teaching hospital in Seattle to share knowledge and technology. The five hospitals, ranging in size from twenty-six to eighty-nine beds, felt that there was a need for better communication between urban and rural physicians which hopefully would result in better patient care. The W. K. Kellogg Foundation provided a three-year grant to foster this cooperation. Results have been encouraging. The consortium has spawned regular meetings between personnel of the six hospitals including "nursing directors, business managers, x-ray and laboratory technicians, in-service education directors, medical records personnel, and pharmacy directors." This type of cooperation provides obvious benefits for the community hospital, but the urban medical center also gains. Better rapport with rural physicians may mean better patient referrals into the urban center with its waiting pool of specialty physicians which depends on a substantial volume of patients as well as appropriately referred ones. The medical center also receives funds from the community hospitals for providing consultants in various areas of expertise at the community hospitals. Another advantage for the medical center is the chance to strengthen its educational base; "some physicians like to teach, and the opportunities to develop the strong continuing medical education program can be an attraction."[26] Hopefully, this type of sharing will proliferate in the future.

Guarantees

Some hospitals are even guaranteeing patient satisfaction in such services as nursing care, food, and housekeeping. Dissatisfied patients do not have to pay their bills. These guarantees do not cover physician services or the results of medical care. See the box on pp. 188–190.[27]

BLANCHARD VALLEY HOSPITAL'S GUARANTEE TO OUR PATIENTS

Although we can't guarantee the results of your medical care, we do guarantee:

1. That the services you receive will be performed to your satisfaction. This includes your nursing care, your food, the cleanliness of your room, services of all our ancillary departments and our Emergency Department. In fact, any and all services you receive at Blanchard Valley Hospital.

2. If you are not satisfied, the service(s) which do not meet your expectations will not be charged to you,

---

subject to the simple requirements listed in 3A through E below.

3. If you are not satisfied with the service(s) you are receiving at Blanchard Valley Hospital, charges for such service(s) will not be billed to you or your insurance company IF:

A. You advise us within 24 hours of the time service(s) is not rendered to your satisfaction and if, upon investigation, your complaint is found to be justified, you allow us an additional 24 hours to make necessary changes which, hopefully, will be acceptable to you. Should the service(s) still be unsatisfactory, the "no charge" guarantee will be in effect and your account will be credited with an appropriate amount which represents the cost of such service(s).

B. The guarantee stated above does not cover waiting for services in those departments where the more seriously ill patient is treated first.

C. To be eligible for the "Guaranteed Services" program, all of your past accounts with the Blanchard Valley Hospital Association and any past accounts for a person for whom you or your guarantor has financial responsibility must be paid in full.

D. Because of the nature of human illness, we cannot guarantee the results of your medical or paramedical care nor can we guarantee the services provided by your physician(s) or dentist(s).

E. Patients wishing to discuss and/or take advantage of the "Guaranteed Services" program should call Ext. 251. If your phone is not activated, ask your nurse to make the call for you. A member of the Administrative Staff is on call 24 hours per day and will contact you immediately upon receiving your call.

4. The concept of the "Guaranteed Services" program is to credit your account for those services as outlined

above, which you find unacceptable. Cost liability incurred in this program will be funded from the hospital's investment income so that the program's cost will not be charged to any other patient.

Crediting a patient's account under the "Guaranteed Services" program is not an admission of liability, either expressed or implied, in relation to hospital services rendered.

Source: Courtesy of Blanchard Valley Hospital, Findlay, Ohio.

Lower Costs

Everyone is aware that hospital costs have soared in recent years, so it is encouraging to learn about some innovative approaches that have resulted in lowering the cost of certain procedures.[28] For example, a dilatation and curettage (D & C) which normally involves a two-day hospital stay is now being done in ten hours. The patient comes to the hospital at 7:00 a.m., has the necessary tests and pre-operative medication; by 8:30 her operation is completed; after two hours in the recovery room, she is taken to a small comfortable day-care room where she later has lunch and rests until her physician sees her at 4:30. When he determines that her condition is satisfactory, he releases her and she can be taken home by a friend or relative. Her visit did not utilize an expensive hospital in-patient room. This approach to shortening hospital stays is being utilized for other appropriate procedures, such as removing cysts, hernia repair, and oral surgery. There are at least two other advantages of this same-day surgery: it reduces the chance of acquiring a hospital-born infection, and for children it means that they do not have to spend those terrifying nights in the hospital.

Another innovation is the self- or minimal-care unit for ambulatory patients. In this unit, patients who are not acutely ill administer their own medications and go on their own to receive necessary treatments. They eat all their meals in the public dining room of the hospital and in general look after themselves at a considerable saving of money.

Cardiac patients with pacemakers can have their devices checked by telephone, avoiding an expensive personal visit. An inexpensive transistorized unit placed against the chest will send impulses from the pacemaker over the phone to hospital personnel where it is evaluated.

More hospitals are sharing the cost of expensive equipment, such as computers, and facilities such as laundries and laboratories.

Hospitals, which are the most highly organized part of our delivery system, have an opportunity and an obligation to initiate solutions to our current problems. They have the professional expertise and the prestige to undertake the task. They can not, however, do it alone; they will need the support of all segments of the system, including the medical profession, other health professionals, fiscal intermediaries (third-party payers), and the consumer.[29]

ENDNOTES

1. *Guide to the Health Care Field* (Chicago: American Hospital Association, 1974), pp. 17–19.
2. Robert N. Wilson, "The Physician's Changing Hospital Role," in W. Richard Scott and E. H. Volkart (Eds.), *Medical Care* (New York: John Wiley & Sons, Inc., 1966), pp. 406–408.
3. U.S. Department of Health, Education, and Welfare, *Public Health Service-Labor Seminar on Consumer Health Services* (Washington, D.C.: U.S. Government Printing Office 1968), p. 26.
4. Peter Rogatz, "Excessive Hospitalization Can be Cut Back," *Hospitals, Journal of the American Hospital Association* 48; August 1, 1974, 51–56.

5. U.S. Department of Health, Education, and Welfare, *Health Planning and Resources Development Act of 1974* (Washington, D.C.: U.S. Government Printing Office, 1974).

6. Malcolm T. MacEachern, *Hospital Organization and Management* (Berwyn, Ill.: Physicians' Record Company, 1962), pp. 84–112.

7. John H. Knowles, "The Hospital," *Scientific American* 229; September, 1973, 135.

8. Kenneth E. Raske, "The Components of Inflation," *Hospitals,* Journal of the American Hospital Association 48; July 1, 1974, 68.

9. Ibid., p. 69.

10. *Scientific American* 229, p. 135.

11. "What JCAH Surveyers Look For," *American Medical News* 16; March 5, 1973, 7.

12. S. D. Klotz, *Guide to Modern Medical Care* (New York: Charles Scribner's Sons, 1967), pp. 92–93.

13. "Accreditation," *Modern Health Care* 1, No. 3, June, 1974, p. 108.

14. *American Medical News* 16; March 5, 1973, 8–10.

15. "Respect is First Demand," *Hospitals,* Journal of American Hospital Association 48; August 16, 1974, 57.

16. James C. G. Conniff, "How to Tell a Good Hospital From a Bad One," *Today's Health* 52, No. 11, November, 1973, pp. 42–45.

17. Consumers Union, *The Medicine Show* (Mount Vernon, N. Y., 1974), p. 344.

18. Herbert S. Denenberg, *Shopper's Guide to Hospitals* (Pennsylvania Insurance Department, n.d.).

19. Thomas Thompson, "How to Survive the Hospital," *Good Housekeeping* 178; June, 1974, 69, 131–134.

20. Ruth Ravich and Helen Rehr, "Ombudsman Program Provides Feedback," *Hospitals, Journal of American Hospital Association* 48, No. 18, September 16, 1974, pp. 63–67.

21. Donald Robinson, "At Last, Hospitals Are Lowering Your Costs," *Family Health* 6; August, 1974, 22–25+.

22. "TWA Offers Hospitals Coffee, Tea—or a Positive Image," *Modern Healthcare* 1; April, 1974, 102–104.

23. Ferdinand Haase, Jr., "Experiences with a 7-day Week," *Resident and Staff Physician* 18, No. 3, March, 1972, pp. 27–32.

24. Regina T. Cleveland and Carol L. Hutchins, "Seven Days' Vacation Every Other Week," *Hospitals,* Journal of the American Hospital Association 48; August 1, 1974, 81–85.
25. Howard L. Lewis, "A Togetherness Spirit in Connecticut," *Modern Health Care* 2; July, 1974, 25–29.
26. *Modern Health Care* 1, pp. 120–121.
27. William E. Ruse, Administrator, Blanchard Valley Hospital, Findlay, Ohio, personal communication, November 5, 1974 and December 9, 1975.
28. *Family Health* 6; August, 1974, pp. 22–25.
29. *Hospitals* 48; August 1, 1974, 56.

Chapter Nine

Prescription Drugs

A patient buying prescription drugs has much less say in what he's getting than he does with most other products. Prescriptions are written by doctors and filled by pharmacists, but paid for and taken by patients. Because of their importance in health care and because they are so potent and complex, prescription drugs are among the most carefully regulated of products. In this chapter we will follow the development of a prescription drug from its discovery through the many tests that it must undergo before it reaches the consumer. We will examine the role of the Food and Drug Administration in approving new drugs as well as the problems faced by physicians who must choose the proper medication for their patients.

THE FOOD AND DRUG ADMINISTRATION

The Food and Drug Administration (FDA) is one of six major divisions* of the Department of Health, Education, and Wel-

* The other five divisions are: the National Institutes of Health, Health Services and Mental Health Administration, Social and Rehabilitation Service, Social Security Administration, and the Office of Education.

fare. The FDA has several bureaus, one of which is the Bureau of Drugs, which is responsible for regulating the American supply of prescription and over-the-counter drugs. Over-the-counter drugs are those that can be sold in pharmacies and supermarkets without a prescription. The Bureau of Drugs derives its authority over prescription drugs from the Food, Drug, and Cosmetic Act. It has several major responsibilities:[1]

1. To see that all prescription drugs are safe and effective and that they are properly labeled.

2. To make certain that prescription drug advertising is accurate and balanced and honestly presents the benefits as well as adverse effects of drugs. This advertising is rarely seen by the general public. It is directed at doctors and other health professionals.

3. To see that good manufacturing practices are observed and that high quality is maintained in the nation's drug supply.

4. To disseminate important drug information to consumers and providers.

A NEW DRUG ON THE MARKET

When a pharmaceutical company develops a new drug, it quickly applies for a patent to protect its product. It then submits to the Food and Drug Administration (FDA) an Investigational New Drug (IND) application which must be approved before any human (clinical) studies can be done. The IND application must include the following detailed information:[2]

1. The physical and chemical properties of the drug
2. The manufacturing process

3. Results of preclinical studies (this includes animal trials)
4. Proposed plan for human trials
5. Training and experience of the investigators
6. Other related information which may be requested

After the acceptance of the IND, human trials may begin, with the FDA closely watching the various phases of testing. The subjects being tested in the trials must give their informed consent in all but exceptional cases—where it might affect the outcome of the experiment.

Once the IND experimentation is completed, a New Drug Application (NDA) may be submitted to the FDA. This must be acted upon within 180 days. "The NDA involves additional data relating to manufacturing, marketing, and promotional plans. Methodology for process controls must be outlined, and the manufacturer must assure that each batch of the drug will be equivalent to that upon which the NDA is based. In most cases, the manufacturing facility must be inspected. The proposed labeling (including the required package insert) must be approved by FDA. After NDA clearance, the manufacturer must submit periodic reports of ongoing clinical studies and prompt reports of any unexpected adverse reactions."[3] Acceptance of a NDA is by no means automatic. The FDA rejects many NDAs because of inadequate animal test data, insufficient proof of safety in human trials, lack of clinical efficacy, or other important deficiencies in the application. The new drug is not put on the market until the stringent testing and inspection required for IND and NDA have been completed, a process that may take several years. In fact, five years is not considered unusual.

The need for such careful controls in the United States developed over a period of many years. In 1938, more than 100 people (most of them children) died after taking an "elixir of sulfanilamide." As a result of this tragedy, the Food, Drug, and Cosmetic Act was passed that same year, requiring the manufacturers to prove that a new drug was safe before putting it on the market. In 1962, the sedative thalidomide was being tested in the United States under an IND. Dr. Frances O. Kelsey of the Food and Drug Administration was not satisfied that the drug was safe. In spite of great pressure by the pharmaceutical industry and by certain members of Congress, she withheld her approval of thalidomide in this country. Then the storm broke in Europe and thalidomide was linked with *phocomelia* (birth defects characterized by mere buds developing instead of arms and legs); Dr. Kelsey then became a heroine for withholding her approval. The FDA ordered the recall of thalidomide but, to its dismay, found that precise records had not been kept by all the physicians participating in the experimental phases. Only 80 percent of the drug was recovered. More stringent requirements are now in effect to make certain that 100 percent of an IND can be recalled.

At least eleven cases of phocomelia have occurred in the United States as a result of the testing of thalidomide. An additional seven cases were found to be related to the use of thalidomide obtained from abroad.

The thalidomide tragedy in Europe was responsible for a major change in the 1938 Food, Drug, and Cosmetic Act, and in 1962 the Kefauver–Harris Amendment was passed. This required that a new drug be proven not only safe, but also effective. Prior to this, a pharmaceutical company had only to show that a new drug did no harm; it did not have to show that the drug did any good. The 1962 amendment also enabled the FDA to supervise closely the results of clinical trials, and the manufacturers had to report promptly to the FDA any adverse effects concerning the safety and effectiveness of a drug already on the market.[4]

Until the passage of the Kefauver–Harris amendment, the FDA had been unable to prevent ineffective drugs from being foisted on the American public. These included a number of worthless cancer drugs that often had delayed accepted treatment by reputable physicians. The amendment also gave the FDA authority to determine the effectiveness of thousands of drugs already on the market. The FDA decided to accept generally as effective those drugs produced before 1938. This included well-known and useful drugs such as quinine, insulin, thyroid, morphine, and codeine as well as a few lesser known drugs whose effectiveness had not been proven. This latter group was prescribed so rarely that it was not considered to be a threat to the public health.

Because it did not have sufficient personnel to take on the huge task of determining effectiveness of products developed between 1938 and 1962, the FDA turned to the most respected scientific groups in the United States—the National Academy of Sciences (NAS) and its research division, the National Research Council (NRC). It was hoped that decisions by such prestigious groups would be accepted by the pharmaceutical industry and the medical profession. "Eventually, some 200 experts—both research authorities and practicing physicians—were assembled in thirty panels to consider roughly sixteen thousand therapeutic claims involving more than four thousand products marketed by nearly three hundred different companies. About 15 percent of these were such over-the-counter products as mouth washes, dentifrices, and cold remedies."[5] The panel had a variety of data to examine: FDA files, published medical articles, and information from the drug manufacturers. It was decided to classify each product into one of six different categories:[6]

Effective—those with "substantial evidence" of effectiveness.

Probably effective—those for which some additional evidence was required to rate the drug as effective.

Possibly effective—those which might eventually be shown to be effective but for which little evidence of efficacy could be found.

"Effective but . . ."—those rated as effective for some recommended uses, but not for all and which, therefore, would call for labeling changes.

Ineffective as a fixed combination—those fixed-ratio combination products for which it was felt that one or more components might be effective if used alone, but which were not acceptable in combination for reasons of safety or because of the lack of the evidence of the contribution of each component to the claimed effect.

Ineffective—those with "no substantial evidence" of effectiveness.

The study lasted several years and resulted in about 2,000 of the over 4,000 1938–1962 products being classified as "effective" and 760 judged "ineffective" or ineffective as a fixed ratio combination. About 600 have been taken off the market and others approved only after significant changes were made in their labeling.

PATENT RIGHTS ON
A NEW DRUG

The patent system rewards a pharmaceutical company for investing money in the research and development of new drugs. The patent gives the developer exclusive rights to produce and sell the drug for a period of seventeen years. The company may also license production and sales of the drug to other firms. There are many who contend that most companies recoup their research and development costs within three years after a drug reaches the market. Therefore, a period of seven to ten years has been proposed as more realistic. The pharmaceutical industry states that because of stringent FDA regulations it takes up to six years to get some new drugs on the market, which means that a company has only eleven years in which to recover research and development costs.

The pharmaceutical industry also states that competition is a healthy situation and that the patent is the basis of competition in the industry. It contends that without it drug companies would not be willing to invest such large sums of money in research. The other view is that such extensive patents give the pharmaceutical companies control of the drug market at the manufacturing level and the prescribing level. The point is made that: "exclusive patents, combined with multi-million-dollar drug advertising campaigns, can keep new or small companies out of the high-profit circle and effectively stifle price competition in the market place."[7]

What happens when the patent runs out and a drug can be prescribed under its generic name? Not surprisingly, the company that held the patent tends to maintain the lion's share of the market. Physicians who have been prescribing one company's product for many years tend to continue to do so and pharmacists, when filling generically written prescriptions, tend to use the company which held the patent.[8] So the advantages of the patent system actually extend beyond the seventeen years and provide continuing high profits.

The Department of Health, Education, and Welfare has asked the drug industry to consider life-cycle pricing. This means that the price for a new product introduced into the market would be relatively high during the first few years until the research and development costs were recovered. Then the price would begin a slow decline until it reached a competitive price at the end of the patent life. The Pharmaceutical Manufacturers Association (PMA), an organization of approximately 100 pharmaceutical companies which market 95 percent of the prescription drugs in this country is violently opposed to such an idea. The PMA states that any dilution of patent rights or other tampering by the government would "destroy initiative, raise costs, lower productivity, and build bureaucracy to expensive and cumbersome levels."[9]

QUALITY OF DRUGS

The FDA concerns itself with the composition, safety, and efficacy of prescription drugs. It has established regulations on good manufacturing practices, which all manufacturers are required to follow. Included are requirements for such categories as buildings, equipment, personnel, procedures, distribution, records, and packaging and labeling. The FDA regulations fulfill two objectives. One is to supplement the quality control of the individual firms; the other is to prevent the marketing of dangerous or ineffective drugs.

An FDA inspector may spend several weeks or months at a pharmaceutical marketing plant, checking the quality of the incoming raw materials, observing the various steps in the manufacturing process, and sampling the finished product to see that it contains exactly what the label says it contains.

The FDA now has an Intensified Drug Inspection Program (IDIP), which includes an in-depth review of the manufacturing and quality control practices in a plant. The IDIP procedure is as follows:[10]

1. The FDA District Director meets with top management of a firm selected for IDIP, explains the program, and solicits management cooperation.

2. An inspector—or team, in the case of a large manufacturer—conducts the inspection operation, remaining in the factory for sufficient time to determine that the firm is operating in full compliance with the law, or—if it is not—what corrective actions are indicated. This may take from several days to several weeks.

3. The inspector outlines in detail to management what is required to produce a satisfactory product.

4. The inspector leaves, then returns to the plant after sufficient time for corrective action. Steps 2, 3, and 4 are repeated until the FDA is satisfied that the manufacturer is operating in a completely satisfactory manner, or it is concluded that the manufacturer is incapable of operating satisfactorily, in which case necessary court action may be taken.

5. During the above procedures, there may be additional conferences between the FDA District Director and top management of a firm. Also, there may be—and frequently are—recalls and seizure action to remove

from the market any unfit drugs detected during inspection.

Because of improved FDA regulations in recent years, there has been a dramatic decrease in the number of recalls.

In addition to the above activities, the FDA has eighteen regional laboratories throughout the United States, where it tests drugs that have been purchased in the retail marketplace. The FDA would like to be able to test between 150,000 and 300,000 samples of drugs annually. To reach this goal, it is moving toward the establishment of a "National Center for Drug Analysis," where automated test equipment and mass production techniques can be utilized. Such a center will take over much of the testing, but regional outlets will be maintained for emergency testing and routine surveillance.

DRUG SAFETY

A common misconception is the belief that it is possible to have a completely safe drug. *This is not so!* Any drug, under certain conditions, can cause impairment, tissue damage, or even death. The goal is to develop drugs with a high degree of safety. This is not an easy task. Even with the most demanding criteria and careful testing, a few undesirable drugs still reach the public. Some of the unfortunate side effects of a drug may not show up until it has been used by thousands of patients.

ADVERSE DRUG
REACTIONS

Drugs are one of mankind's most widely used and effective means of preventing and treating diseases and other illness. However, drugs may produce undesirable reactions which may be as serious as the sickness. There is always the risk that the use of a drug will cause the individual to have an adverse reaction which could be as minor as a mild headache, rash, nausea, or as severe as convulsions, heart arrest, or death.[11]

Estimates of the extent of adverse drug reactions vary widely. In terms of death, estimates range from 29,000[12] to 130,000[13] per year. In terms of suffering, adverse drug reactions "may spare a patient's life but leave him blind or deaf, afflicted with kidney, liver, or brain damage, bone necrosis, ulceration of the bowel, intestinal hemorrhage, skin scars, extreme sensitivity to sunlight, or other disabilities that may last for months or years."[14] In terms of cost, according to the FDA, six million people in the United States suffer from drug reactions each year at a cost of $627 million in hospitalization costs, doctor's services, and loss of productive work.[15] Another source[16] states that "one-seventh of all hospital days is devoted to the care of drug toxicity," at an estimated cost of $3 billion in extra room and board charges. A drug reaction patient is usually hospitalized about twice as long as a similar patient with the same disease who does not have a reaction. The above figure was arrived at when daily hospital rates were $60. At today's prices, the cost would be over $6 billion! This figure does not include doctor's services or the loss of productive work nor does it take into account out-of-hospital problems. If a patient has a drug reaction while taking medication at home, but does not go to the hospital or report it to his doctor, researchers will be unaware of the incident and it will not be recorded. Even if the patient does inform his physician, the doctor may not report it and the case will not be recorded as an adverse reaction. Why would a doctor not report something as serious as a drug reaction? A study by the General Accounting Office (GAO)* of the effectiveness of the FDA's system of handling reports of adverse reactions revealed the following reasons for physicians not reporting:[17]

* The GAO independently reviews and evaluates the planning, implementation, and results of various federal government programs. It provides needed feedback on program effectiveness and efficiency to the Congress and the President.

1. The FDA is looked upon as a regulatory agency and physicians are concerned about government involvement in medicine.

2. Many hospitals lack the manpower and the doctors lack the time required for reporting adverse reactions to the FDA.

3. Some doctors didn't know how or what to report to the FDA.

4. Some doctors believed reporting adverse drug reactions could result in malpractice suits.

5. The FDA failed to acknowledge the reports they had submitted.

The FDA has two methods of obtaining information about adverse drug reactions, spontaneous reporting and intensive monitoring. Sources providing spontaneous reports include private and federal hospitals, doctors, patients, drug manufacturers, or any one experiencing or observing an adverse reaction. Under intensive monitoring, specific groups of patients are closely observed for any adverse reactions. Monitoring, because it is so expensive, is not widely used and accounts for about 2 percent of the adverse reaction reports.[18]

Despite the statistics on adverse drug reactions, some feel that most drugs in use today are remarkably safe when their risks are weighed against their benefits. After a study of drug reactions in Boston hospitals[19] one researcher stated that most drug reactions, although associated with discomfort, are minor. The five most common reactions reported in the Boston study were nausea, drowsiness, diarrhea, vomiting, and rash. Of the Boston patients who died because of drug toxicity during the study, one third had advanced cancer and another third had advanced alcoholic liver disease; "thus, less than one third of the drug attributed deaths occurred in patients with a reasonably good short-term prognosis."

However you view the information on adverse drug effects, it is evident that some risk is involved in taking a prescription drug (or any drug). These side effects are merely your body's way of telling you that the medicine is acting adversely. When your doctor writes out a prescription for you he may mention possible side effects. Listen carefully and, if you have other side effects, call your physician promptly. He will know whether the reaction is expected or not and whether you should continue taking the medicine.

PRESCRIPTIONS FOR
CONTROLLED SUBSTANCES

Drugs that have the potential for addiction or abuse have been designated as "controlled substances" and classified into one of five groups or "schedules." Although there are many drugs in each group, we have listed only a few of the better-known examples:

Schedule I:	Marijuana
	Mescaline
	Peyote
Schedule II:	Amphetamines
	Methadone
	Opiates
Schedule III:	Barbiturates
	Lysergic Acid
Schedule IV:	Phenobarbital
	Meprobamate
	Chloral Hydrate
Schedule V:	Compounds with less than 200 mg. of codeine per 100 g.

Schedule II drugs, which include narcotics, are the most carefully controlled. In one state, for example, prescription blanks for Schedule II drugs are issued to pharmacists by the state in serially numbered groups of 100 forms each in triplicate. (It is a misdemeanor for an unauthorized person even to possess these prescription blanks.) A physician prescribing a Schedule II drug must fill out the triplicate form and sign all three copies. He keeps one copy; the patient takes the original and the other copy to the pharmacist, who files the original and endorses the copy when he fills the prescription. He sends the copy to the State Bureau of Narcotics Enforcement. These copies are reviewed carefully so that abuses of the system by patients or physicians are kept at a minimum.

When prescribing a Schedule II drug, a physician must make a record of: (a) the name and address of the patient, (b) the date, (c) the character and quantity of drug involved, and (d) the pathology and purpose for which the prescription is issued. This record must be preserved for two years and is, of course, open to inspection by appropriate state officials. The pharmacist must record the above items a, b, and c, as well as the name, address, and federal registry number of the physician who prescribed the Schedule II drug. A Schedule II prescription cannot be refilled; a new prescription form must be made out if the physician wishes his patient to have more of the drug.[20]

However, all dangerous drugs do not fall under the strict controls regulating the legal dispensing of Schedule II drugs. Prescribed sleeping pills and tranquilizers, for example, are less carefully controlled and such prescriptions are refillable by phone. You might assume that a physician could write himself a prescription for any controlled substance. Not so! It is illegal for anyone to prescribe, administer, or furnish such a drug for his own use.

"THE NAME GAME"

The *chemical name* of a drug is based on its chemical structure. For example, the chemical name *2-methyl-2-propyl-1,*

3-propanediol dicarbamate is a precise identification of a compound and is meaningful to a chemist. The chemical formula of this compound is

$$\text{H}_2\text{NCOO}-\text{CH}_2-\underset{\underset{\text{CH}_2\text{CH}_2\text{CH}_3}{|}}{\overset{\overset{\text{CH}_3}{|}}{\text{C}}}-\text{CH}_2-\text{OOCNH}_2$$

The *generic name* is a shorter one that is usually found in the scientific literature. It may or may not be a shortened form of the chemical name. The generic name is the one that physicians and pharmacists generally learn in their professional training. The compound above is known generically as *meprobamate*.[21]

Who decides on the generic name? Those most closely involved in the creation of the drug and its eventual use usually submit a name to the U.S. Adopted Names Council. The Council is composed of representatives from the American Medical Association, U.S. *Pharmacopeia,* the American Pharmaceutical Association, and the FDA. When agreement is reached on a name, it is submitted to the World Health Organization (WHO), which works with the official pharmaceutical organizations of many nations. The *brand* or *trademark name* is used by a company to distinguish its product from that of a competitor which may contain identical active ingredients. A company can choose any brand name it wishes, but generally it attempts to derive one that is easily remembered. For example, the tranquilizer referred to above carries different brand names. One company has named it Miltown; another, Equanil.

Obviously, the chemical name of a compound is too long and cumbersome for your physician to write out on his prescription pad. The question then arises, should he prescribe by generic or by brand name? This is another hotly contested issue, with the pharmaceutical companies claiming that brand name products are better known and are superior in reliability and predictability. The other side contends that there is no proof that generic drugs are inferior in any way to brand name drugs, and in fact, generic drugs are much more desirable if one considers the price factor.

According to Dr. John Adriani, past Chairman of the AMA's Council on Drugs, the problems of drug utilization and prescription methods are complex and becoming more complex as the number of drugs increases. He described the situation as "nearly chaotic." In his testimony before a Senate subcommittee, Dr. Adriani stated:

> Proprietary or brand names are, in essence, aliases. An alias, no matter how used, tends to confuse or be deceptive. An alias is intended to conceal the identity of whatever or whomever is being designated by an alias. The use of brand names for drugs serves no constructive purpose; on the contrary, the practice hampers rational drug utilization, rational prescribing and dissemination of drug information. Brand names should be abolished. The public's best interests shall not be served until this is done.[22]

Dr. Adriani suggested that the generic name should appear in large, boldfaced type on every label which identifies drugs, and the brand name should appear beneath in parentheses— but in type only one-eighth the size. The chemical name could appear between the generic and brand names.

Under Dr. Adriani's system, a pharmacist dispensing a prescription would be required to label the contents with the generic name. If the physician wanted his patient to have a particular brand name, it could be put in parentheses below the generic name, so that the physician and the patient would know whether or not the specified drug had been supplied. This system will not restrict physicians in their prescribing, since they can still order a drug by brand or generic name. But, by using such a system, brand names will be deemphasized. If this happens, pharmacists will need fewer items on their shelves, since "for every prescription drug, there is an average of 30 names—aliases that can obscure the identity of the medication not only from patients but from prescribing physicians."[23] The disappearance of brand name drugs would also do away with the duplicative "me-too" proliferation that now occurs.

Ordering by generic name enables the pharmacist to use the least expensive product. Since he must fill the prescription exactly as ordered, he does not have this choice when the brand name is used.

DRUG PRICES

Pharmaceutical companies are in business to make money. They have done this with considerable success. In the past ten years, the price of drugs has been the subject of much controversy. Basically, in arriving at the price of a drug, the company considers direct manufacturing costs, overhead, clinical factors, marketing and distribution costs, and profit potential. This may sound simple, but a business administration professor, after an in-depth study of the pharmaceutical marketplace, concluded that it was very confusing.

A drug company that has a patent on a drug that is considered a major breakthrough will be the only seller in the marketplace. This is an enviable position, and one which encourages the practice of charging "what the traffic will bear." This practice adds support to the contention that patents should not be allowed to continue for such long periods of time.

Profit may be measured in a number of ways, including total dollar profits, or profits as a percent of sales. The most useful measurement, however, is the rate of profit based on invested capital. Table 9.1 shows the return on stockholders' equity (in percent).

No matter how it is measured, the business of making and selling prescription drugs is highly and consistently

TABLE 9.1 1974 Financial Data on Ten Prescription
Drug Producers

Company	Return on Stockholder's Equity (in percent)
Bristol Myers	21.3
Eli Lilly	24.3
Merck	28.7
Pfizer	18.8
Smith Kline Corporation	21.6
Squibb	17.1
Schering–Plough	29.1
Sterling Drug	19.5
Upjohn	21.9
Warner–Lambert	16.8

Source: Forbes, January 1, 1975, p. 170.

profitable. Does the drug industry charge too much for its product? The industry points to the various risks involved, and pinpoints five in particular:[24]

1. The possible development of a competing product superior to one of the company's major products, causing its virtually complete replacement in a short time.

2. The possible discovery of unanticipated side-effects for a drug, leading to immediate limitations on the clinical indications for which it may be prescribed.

3. The possible discovery that a drug can be mis-used in ways that create a significant social problem, leading to limitations to its marketability, or even removal from the market.

4. Possible withdrawal or restriction of a drug by the Food and Drug Administration until additional required evidence of safety or efficacy is produced.

5. The possible development of a quality control program which necessitates withdrawal of a product from the market until the problem is identified and eliminated.

Others point out that much risk has been reduced in recent years because of certain trends. For example:

1. There has been a decline in the number of new drugs introduced annually since 1957. The quality of these new drugs, however, has improved, and thus drug longevity in the marketplace has increased. This means that drug companies are investing more in research, but are also earning more money over a longer period of time because their products have been well tested before being marketed.

2. In the past, the introduction of "me-too" drugs and duplicative drug products resulted in substantial losses to the pharmaceutical industry. The more stringent requirements of a New Drug Application has relieved the industry of the pressure to invest research money on these preparations.

3. Because of the above points, operations have become fairly stable and the pharmaceutical companies are now better able to do long-term planning.

Those involved in the argument cannot seem to agree on what constitutes "high risk" or "fair profit." A satisfactory definition of these terms apparently depends upon whether you are within the industry or outside it.

Surveys of drug prices over the years have resulted in remarkably similar results: prescription drug prices vary considerably from city to city and also within any given city. A recent survey of 147 pharmacies in seventeen states showed that consumers in some cities were paying from twice to ten times as much for identical drugs![25] If all states were included in the survey, even greater discrepancies may have appeared. Other studies have revealed that the same drug is usually more costly in a low income area than in a high-income area. Price differences between generic and brand-named drugs also show wide variations. Table 9.2 illustrates the tremendous differences in wholesale prices that pharmacists pay for generic and brand-name drugs. When a pharmacist pays a wholesale price that is forty-one times more for a brand-named drug than a generic one, he passes the price ratio on to the consumer. Thus, if your physician prescribes serpasil, you are likely to pay a much higher price than you would if he prescribed reserpine, the generic equivalent.

Today, we are still fighting the same battle to reduce

TABLE 9.2 Comparative Wholesale Prices of Selected Brand-Name and Generic-Name Drug Products, 1975

Product	Price	Price Ratio
Reserpine: 1,000 0.25-mg		
Serpasil (CIBA)	$39.50	
Reserpine (H. L. Moore)	.95	41.6:1
Pentaerythrotetranitrate: 1,000 10-mg		
Peritrate (Warner-Chilcott)	29.30	
Pentaerythrotetranitrate (Vita-Fore)	1.50	19.5:1
Chlorpheniramine: 1,000 4-mg		
Chlortrimeton (Schering)	22.74	
Chlorpheniramine (Winsale)	1.45	15.7:1
Meprobamate: 1,000 400-mg		
Equanil (Wyeth)	68.21	
Meprobamate (Interstate)	4.90	13.9:1
Oxytetracycline: 100 250-mg		
Terramycin (Pfizer)	20.57	
Oxytetracycline (H. L. Moore)	1.95	10.6:1
Tripelennamine: 1,000 50-mg		
Pyribenzamine (CIBA)	28.15	
Tripelennamine hydrochloride (Lannett)	4.00	7.0:1
Tetracycline: 1,000 250-mg		
Achromycin (Lederle)	45.06	
Tetracycline (H. L. Moore)	8.40	5.4:1

Source: Drug Topics Red Book 1975 (Oradell, N.J.: Medical Economics, Co., 1975)

the price differential between trade and generic-named drugs as we did in 1967, when William F. Haddad, then executive vice-president of the U.S. Research and Development Corporation, in his testimony before the U.S. Senate, said ". . . drug manufacturers deliberately keep prices high and use tactics, techniques, and strategies to perpetuate the false and malicious arguments that drugs sold under their generic names are unsafe."[26] He pointed out that by law trade and generic name drugs are identical. All drugs must meet rigid federal standards. He contended that the drug industry has for years been successful in frightening patients, politicians, and doctors with arguments that generic name drugs are unsafe. The result? Huge and consistent profits! Mr. Haddad referred to the drug industry as "the last of the robber barons, operating with near-feudal authority in one of the most vital segments of American life."

HEW now has a policy of basing reimbursement of prescriptions on the lowest cost at which a drug is generally available. This policy currently affects Medicaid prescriptions; when Medicare coverage is extended to cover outpatient prescriptions, the policy will apply to those too. If a physician prescribes a brand-named drug which is above the reimbursement level, and he insists that no other brand be dispensed, HEW will not pay the excess. In such a case, it is likely that the patient will have to make up the difference.[27]

ADVERTISING

A company can produce the best drug in the world, but unless physicians prescribe it for their patients, it will not be sold. Therefore, pharmaceutical companies must reach and convince physicians of the superiority of a given product. To this end, they spend enormous amounts of money, primarily on personal promotion and media advertising aimed at the approximately 375,000 practicing physicians in the United States.

Although the effect of drug advertising has not been carefully studied, one cannot help but be awed by its content and volume. The FDA became concerned over content and has proposed regulations which require "fair balance" in the presentation of a drug's merits and limitations. For example, the FDA states that "fair balance" is lacking if:[28]

1. Information is included in an advertisement that is not approved for inclusion in the package insert.
2. Advantages are claimed for a drug without simultaneous disclosures of disadvantages.
3. Obsolete information is used.
4. Claims are exaggerated.
5. Animal or laboratory data are cited as clinical evidence.
6. A statement by a recognized authority is used without also citing any unfavorable data from that authority.
7. Statements are used out of context.
8. Statistics are used in a misleading way.
9. Headline or pictorial matter is misleading.

These requirements have helped to reduce the number of complaints about the reliability and objectivity of direct mail and journal advertisements.

The claim is made that "the volume of drug advertising bombards and overwhelms the physician, capturing his prescribing practices by mass and weight alone." Apparently, the average medical practitioner receives about 4,000 direct mail promotional pieces a year. Assuming a five-day work week, the average M.D. receives about fifteen such pieces per day! It has been stated that the pressure of advertising by pharmaceutical companies results in a "trip hammer effect of weekly mails, the regular visits of the detail man, the two-page spreads, and the ads which appear six times in the same journal, not to mention the added inducement of the free cocktail party and the golf outing complete with three golf balls stamped with the name of the doctor and the company in contrasting colors."[29]

Reaching physicians and convincing them of the superiority of a given product is a very expensive procedure. It is estimated that drug companies spend about $4,500 per physician per year to accomplish this goal. It is so expensive, in fact, that smaller drug firms often cannot compete in the brand name push. Consequently, they promote generic name drugs, dealing mainly with pharmacists, and thus are not able to bring their low-cost wares to the attention of the physician.

The "detail man," euphemistically designated as a "medical services representative," visits physicians and promotes his company's drugs. He has been given intensive training in the effects that specific drugs have on various diseases. He informs the physician of the advantages of his company's drugs and, if asked, can discuss the disadvantages. He actually has a variety of functions:[30] "To carry information from his company to doctors; to report information from doctors back to his company; to transmit knowledge and experience from doctor to doctor; to provide companionship and support for some doctors; and, finally, to spread non-drug but professionally important information within the community of doctors."

The detail man at one time was quite liberal with free drug samples. The idea was ostensibly to enable the physician to try a product on his own patients to discover its advantages. In reality, so few patients would be involved that the test would not provide any useful information. The physician who received such samples, however, often became familiar with the drug and prescribed it for his patients after the free "samples" were gone. Free drug samples are still available, but now are dispensed by the detail man only on request from the doctor.

The large amount of money spent on physicians is considered a good investment. One study of the assimilation of a new drug by 141 doctors showed that 57 percent of them had received their initial information about the drug from the detail man. Another survey, this time in Canada, revealed that 46 percent of the physicians queried considered the detail man as "the most informative and/or most acceptable type of drug promotion."[31]

Not everyone, however, agrees on the desirability of the detail man. One physician, who feels rather strongly, has described him as follows:

> He masquerades as an educator, or, at least his parent firm stresses his role as a medical educator. He hopes to ingratiate himself to the physician by providing him with scientific information, albeit somewhat biased, regarding the product of his employer, by leaving samples of his product to help the patients or the physician use the product in question. He will graciously offer to fill the physician's family needs with his employer's product before taking his leave. If the physician is busy, as most are, and gets a thumbnail resume of the new product reportedly better than any other similar product he has used, he may well try it. He has the starter samples available so that he can somewhat reduce the cost of the drug to the patient, not to mention the fact that by handing out these samples he gains further good will from the patient, and the prescription for the drug is a natural by-product.[32]

YOUR DOCTOR
AND DRUGS

How is a physician prepared to make decisions about drugs for his patients? To understand this, we must go back to his medical school training. The medical student's main course in pharmacology (and often his only one) is taken in the second preclinical year. Also, pharmacology is taught only as a basic science, when it should also be presented as a clinical science. The course generally includes "principles of drug action, such as absorption, distribution, metabolism, mechanism of action, tissue storage, toxicity, and excretion; review of specific drug groups; laboratory demonstrations; and prescription writing."[33]

Some schools now offer advanced courses in pharmacology during the clinical years of medical school. Unfortunately, not many physicians have had the advantage of such advanced courses.

How does a physician keep up to date when there are some 1,200 drugs and literally thousands of drug combinations at his disposal? Add to this the fact that "seventy percent of currently marketed drugs were either unknown or unavailable fifteen years ago, when more than half of the Nation's physician's were receiving their pharmacology training in medical school."[34] There are multitudinous sources of drug information available to the practicing physician, but these sources are not necessarily objective, well organized, or concise. They include: over 1,500 medical journals; drug compendia (volumes of condensed drug information); formularies (list of drugs); textbooks of pharmacology; professional meetings; post-graduate seminars; visits of detail men; as well as mailings of drug advertisements and drug samples.

The average physician does not have time to sift through this fantastic mass of information. In fact, pharmacologists (drug specialists) admit to having a problem "keeping up." As one asserted, ". . . my professional role is to keep up with drugs and I am unable to do so. I classify myself as a neuro-pharmacologist, which means I only have to keep up with drugs which act on the brain. In terms of original literature, I wonder if I even accomplish keeping up with this narrow field."

Rational prescribing has been described as using the right drug for the right patient at the right time and in the right amount. Because many physicians have trouble keeping up to date in drug developments, they are unable to meet the requirements of rational prescribing. It has been estimated that 25 percent of all drug therapy provides little or nothing in terms of patient benefits. Consumers should be aware of the fact that the misuse of prescription and over-the-counter drugs is a serious public health problem.[35] To deal with this problem, a nationwide program of public education has been suggested to:[36]

1. Alert consumers to the existence and magnitude of the problem created by the misuse of prescription drugs.
2. Discourage self-medication.
3. Point out the dangers of both over- and underutilization of prescription medication.

4. Find ways to counteract the impact of advertising which tends to create a psychological dependence upon drugs as a solution to the stresses of daily living.

THE PHARMACY

Drug products usually move in large quantities from the manufacturer to the drug wholesaler, who distributes them in smaller quantities to the retail outlets, such as independent pharmacies, chain drugstores, and prescription pharmacies. *Independent pharmacies* are the traditional drugstores owned and operated by one person, or by a partnership, or as closed corporations in which the capital stock is held by a few individuals. The owners need not be pharmacists, but most states require that only pharmacists may dispense prescriptions. Since 1964, the number of independent pharmacies has been steadily declining.[37] *Chain drugstores* usually involve four or more outlets, which are owned and managed by a central office to provide continuity and homogeneity to their operations. Chain drugstores are currently enjoying a steady increase in growth. *Prescription pharmacies* are usually community pharmacies, which derive more than 70 percent of their income from prescriptions. They do not emphasize general merchandising functions, and so usually occupy less space than other drugstores. Other retail outlets include pharmacies in department, food, variety, and discount stores.

Hospital pharmacies have traditionally provided prescription drugs for in-patients (those occupying a bed in the hospital), and about two-thirds of hospitals with 200 beds or more provide prescription drugs for out-patients. It is interesting to note that while all community pharmacies must be under the immediate supervision of a pharmacist, this protection to the consumer is not always given to large numbers of hospital in-patients. For example, pharmacy permits are required of hospital pharmacies in only ten states. The reasons for this lack of control over hospital pharmacies are not clear. Hospital pharmacies generally serve as profit-making departments, with the profits used to subsidize other hospital services. Prices for out-patient prescription drugs are about the same as prices at community pharmacies, even though drug costs and operating expenses may be considerably lower and no income taxes may be involved.[38]

The pharmacist's duties have changed considerably in the past fifty years. Prior to World War I, approximately 90 percent of all prescriptions dispensed were compounded from bulk drugs. The pharmacist constantly weighed, measured, and mixed up the prescriptions, and really made use of his mortar and pestle. Today, almost 98 percent of all prescriptions are prefabricated by the manufacturer.[39] Another change that is evident when you walk into most drugstores today is the vast array of merchandise available. Most pharmacists find that they cannot succeed financially if they depend solely on prescription drug sales, so they branch out.

There are state and federal laws that require that all prescription drugs be dispensed by or under the direct supervision of a licensed practitioner of pharmacy (or medicine), who must be licensed by the state in which he is practicing.[40] The pharmacy itself must also be licensed by the state. An interesting exception to this licensing arrangement is that, if a physician wishes to dispense drugs, his license to practice medicine also licenses him to do this; neither he nor his office requires any additional approval by the state! Why this condition is allowed to continue is a question yet to be answered. Neither his training nor his experience places him in a position where he should be above complying with the licensing laws that regulate those who are specialists in the field of drugs.

IS THE FOOD AND DRUG ADMINISTRATION HOLDING UP PROGRESS?

The following charges are sometimes heard: "The Food and Drug Administration (FDA) is over-regulating the pharmaceutical industry," " The United States is experiencing a serious slowdown in the development of new drugs," "The American public is being denied certain drugs which are available in other countries."

The charge about over-regulation usually comes from the pharmaceutical industry and its supporters who feel that FDA regulations curtail their profit potential. However, historically, the profits of the industry are remarkably good, and during the past twenty-five years, no major pharmaceutical house has been forced out of business. "The high profitability reflects the absence of competition; the stability of profits demonstrates the absence of risk to investors."[41] The Bureau of Drugs of the FDA is merely acting as a consumer advocate in carrying out its responsibilities of assuring safe and effective drugs, fair advertising, and good manufacturing procedures.

Regarding the alleged slowdown in the development of drugs in the United States, several factors must be considered. The commissioner of the FDA feels that laboratory breakthroughs are needed before new drugs can be developed. Apparently, "truly dramatic new progress in medicine now waits on some basic innovation in molecular science, some breakthrough in our understanding of disease mechanisms, some new therapeutic concept, or some new tool."[42] When talking about the development of new drugs, we first have to define what is significant in terms of results from the patients' point of view. Many new drugs that appear on the market here and in other countries are only new in a narrow sense. They may be very similar to established drugs or they may be combinations of established drugs so that the only new thing about them is the way in which they have been combined. Really new drugs have always been rare. Over a recent twenty-year period, no matter how many new drug applications were received, the number of important new drugs has remained constant—about a half dozen a year.[43]

Other factors are also involved in the low number of new drugs approved. There are still deficiencies in our knowledge of the relevance of animal toxicity findings to man, especially children. There is an understandable hesitation to test new drug products on our young. Consequently, when a drug does reach the market the label often states: "This drug not approved for use in children." Another factor that has slowed some drug development has been the poor quality of drug investigation. Apparently, the pharmeceutical industry often confuses quantity with quality and has inundated the FDA with mountains of data that often fail to answer important questions required in clinical investigations.

Is the American public being denied certain drugs which are available in other countries? The answer is yes, and we should be thankful for it! The FDA feels that because prescription drugs are so vital, they must do what they're supposed to do. The FDA considers the elimination—or refusal to allow sale—of ineffective drugs as important as the development of new effective ones. Treatment with ineffective drugs not only does the patient no good, but may do harm through loss of valuable time in proper treatment. In addition, all drugs involve some risk; if there is no counterbalancing benefit, an ineffective drug is worse than useless. Other countries, with less stringent regulations, have licensed drugs that had serious consequences. The thalidomide disaster was mentioned earlier in this chapter. Another example was a drug used in England and Wales for bronchial asthma that resulted in 3,500 deaths. The drug was implicated in 7 percent of all deaths of children ten to fourteen years of age in a seven-year period. A third example occurred in Switzerland, Austria, and Germany, when the use of an appetite-suppressing drug caused an epidemic of primary pulmonary hypertension, a serious and often fatal condition.[44]

The FDA feels that relaxing the requirements for safety and effectiveness will only increase the risks, not the benefits, of drugs. In recent Senate hearings, it was joined by two rather unlikely allies, the American Medical Association and the Pharmaceutical Manufacturers Association. "Spokesmen for these groups, along with a number of prominent heart and cancer specialists, made it quite clear that even though the U.S. has the most demanding requirements of any nation in the world, all safe and effective drugs, or their equivalents, are available here."[45]

PHYSICIAN-OWNED
PHARMACIES

The issue of physician dispensing has been the subject of considerable controversy between pharmacists and medical groups. The case for physicians selling drugs is strongest in isolated areas in which no pharmacy is available. The M.D. is then providing a needed service for his patients. Such situations, however, are very rare today. Pharmacists, viewing physician dispensing as an encroachment, oppose it except under the isolated conditions described above. The AMA, on the other hand, "has decided it is not unethical for a physician to dispense so long as the patient is not exploited."* The AMA is thus in the position of insisting that the patient must have free choice of physician, but need not have free choice of pharmacist.[46]

Should physicians own pharmacies? The proponents of this idea point to the following advantages:

1. *Convenience to patients.* Often such pharmacies are located in the same medical buildings as the doctor's office.
2. *Reduced prices.* Physician-owned pharmacies can sometimes purchase drugs at prices that are not available to many community pharmacists.
3. *Small inventories.* These pharmacies need to stock only those drugs prescribed by a small number of physicians.

Although low inventories and relatively low acquisition costs could mean lower prices for patients, there is no evidence that the average prescription prices set by physician-owned pharmacies are any lower than those set by other pharmacies in the community.

The opponents of such pharmacies object because of the obvious disadvantages:

* The AMA does not specify what "exploited" means.

1. *Captive audience.* When a physician both prescribes drugs and has a financial interest in the pharmacy which dispenses the drugs, his patient loses his freedom of choice in having his prescription filled. Some doctors steer patients to their pharmacies by telephoning prescriptions directly to the pharmacy, writing the prescription in code, and using prescription blanks with the name of the pharmacy on it.

2. *Conflict of interest.* A physician who stands to make a profit on the sale of prescription drugs may be tempted to overprescribe. One study described by *Consumer Reports* showed that physician-owners of pharmacies prescribed antibiotics or sulfas 25 percent more often than did physicians without a financial interest in the pharmacies. Not only that, but "physician-owners of companies which market penicillin preparations prescribe penicillin at a rate approximately eight time higher than do control physicians."[47]

WHAT CAN YOU DO?

As a consumer, you are not entirely helpless. If, for example, you favor generic prescribing and are against physician ownership of drugstores or drug packaging plants, you can make your feelings known. The pen is still a powerful instrument. Write to your legislators and to local and state medical societies.

Drug advertising and promotion have encouraged patients to expect a prescription every time they visit their doctor. If he doesn't prescribe a medication, many patients feel they have not received proper treatment and may go to another physician.

To keep things in perspective, you should consider several important points about drugs.

1. We do not have—and probably never will have—a drug answer to all health problems.

2. Many conditions are resolved spontaneously and need no drug therapy.

3. For many conditions, such as the common cold and other viral infections, antibiotics are not helpful.

4. All drugs have a potential for harm as well as benefit and should be taken only when necessary. The millions of drug reactions that occur each year in the United States are eloquent testimony to this fact.

5. Many patients misinterpret usage directions on prescription labels. In one study,[48] patients were asked to interpret instructions on each of ten prescription labels. Not once was a label uniformly interpreted by all patients! For example, in interpreting the prescription that read "tetracycline, 250 mg. every six hours" only 36 percent of the patients correctly indicated that they would take the drug every six hours for a total of four doses in a twenty-four-hour period. If your doctor writes a prescription for you, be sure that you understand exactly how to take it. Also, ask about any possible side effects.

If your physician prescribes a medication, be sure that he gives you a copy of the prescription. If he has a direct telephone line or a pneumatic tube connecting him with the pharmacy, you would be well advised to look elsewhere for an M.D. Other practices to watch for include: the writing of the prescription in code so that only a certain pharmacy can fill it; the use of a prescription blank with a pharmacy name on it; or the encouragement for you to go to a particular pharmacy. If you observe any of these practices, inform your local medical society. Your physician may ask the name of your pharmacy and call in a prescription for you. This is an ethical practice and may save time. You may, however, wish to compare prices at various drugstores. This can often be done over the phone, but make certain before you leave your doctor's office that you are able to read the prescription. Prices do vary considerably for the same drug, even within a given city.

Recently, the U.S. District Courts in several states have ruled that pharmacists may advertise prescription drugs at discount prices. These rulings invalidated state statutes which had outlawed such advertising. As a result of this court action, consumers in affected states are expected to save up to 40 percent on the cost of their prescription drugs.[49]

In many states, it is now mandatory for pharmacies to post the prices of the top-selling prescription drugs; some states, however, still restrict this practice. If your state does not require price posting, or does not allow discount advertising, request an explanation from your elected representatives. If you are going to be taking a certain drug for an extended period, ask your physician to prescribe it in large quantities, which are generally more economical. This practice will also save many trips to the pharmacy.

You should ask your physician to prescribe, whenever possible, by generic name rather than brand name. This often results in a saving to you. But this is not so if a drug is protected by a patent or if the pharmacy does not stock the generic name (pharmaceutical companies have convinced many pharmacists of the alleged superiority of brand-named products, a position not agreed on by FDA officials). Your physician's opinion should be respected, however, and if he feels the brand name is the best for you, follow his advice. Many state and federal programs, which include all of the armed services, Medicare, and Medicaid, prescribe generically whenever possible and realize great savings for the taxpayer.

If your physician is unwilling to follow the above suggestions, ask him for an explanation. If you are still not satisfied, another doctor may better serve your needs.

ENDNOTES

1. "Prescription Drugs and America's Patients," *FDA Consumer,* November, 1972, p. 5.
2. Task Force on Prescription Drugs, *The Drug Prescribers* (Washington, D.C.: U.S. Government Printing Office, 1968), p. 35.
3. Ibid., p. 32.

4.   Ibid.
5.   Milton Silverman and Philip Lee, *Pills, Profits, and Politics* (Berkeley: University of California Press, 1974), p. 122.
6.   Ibid., pp. 122–123.
7.   Task Force on Prescription Drugs, *The Drug Makers and the Drug Distributors* (Washington, D.C.: U.S. Government Printing Office, 1968), pp. 38.
8.   "When a Patent Runs Out . . . ," *American Druggist* 169; May 15, 1974, 32.
9.   "Generic Reimbursement Policy Will Soon Be Instituted by HEW," *American Druggist* 169; January 15, 1974, 13.
10. Task Force on Prescription Drugs, *The Drug Prescribers,* p. 33.
11. Comptroller General of the United States, *Assessment of the Food and Drug Administration's Handling of Reports on Adverse Reactions from the Use of Drugs* (Washington, D.C.: United States General Accounting Office, 1974), p. 5.
12. Hershel Jick, "Drugs—Remarkably Nontoxic," *The New England Journal of Medicine* 291; October 17, 1974, 825.
13. Silverman and Lee, *Pills, Profits, and Politics,* p. 264.
14. Ibid., p. 259.
15. Comptroller General of the U.S., *Assessment of the Food and Drug Administration's Handling . . . ,"* p. 5.
16. Kenneth L. Melmon, "Preventable Drug Reactions—Causes and Cures," *New England Journal of Medicine* 284; June 17, 1971, 1361.
17. Comptroller General of the U.S., *Assessment of the Food and Drug Administration's Handling . . . ,"* p. 5.
18. Ibid., p. 3.
19. Jick, "Drugs—Remarkably Nontoxic," pp. 824–828.
20. State of California, *California Pharmacy Law* (Sacramento: Department of Consumer Affairs, 1974), pp. 58–76.
21. Task Force on Prescription Drugs, *The Drug Makers and the Drug Distributors,* p. 8.
22. S 5416, *Congressional Record,* May 20, 1969.
23. "How to Pay Less for Prescription Drugs," *Consumer Reports* 40; January, 1975, 52.
24. Task Force on Prescription Drugs, *The Drug Makers and the Drug Distributors,* pp. 47–48.
25. Silverman and Lee, *Pills, Profits, and Politics,* p. 355.
26. U.S. Congress, *Hearings* on Competitive Problems in the Drug Industry, 90th Cong., 1st sess., 1967, p. 12.

27. *American Druggist* 169, p. 13.
28. Task Force on Prescription Drugs, *The Drug Prescribers,* p. 14.
29. Task Force on Prescription Drugs, *The Drug Makers and the Drug Distributors,* p. 28.
30. Ibid., p. 29.
31. Task Force on Prescription Drugs, *The Drug Prescribers,* p. 14.
32. Ibid., p. 15.
33. Ibid., pp. 6–7.
34. Ibid., p. 9.
35. Donald C. Brodie, *Drug Utilization and Drug Utilization Review and Control* (Washington, D.C.: U.S. Government Printing Office, 1971), p. 2.
36. Ibid.
37. Task Force on Prescription Drugs, *The Drug Makers and the Drug Distributors,* pp. 61–62.
38. Ibid., p. 73.
39. "What's the Future of the Detailman?" *American Druggist* 169; June 1, 1974, 50.
40. Task Force on Prescription Drugs, *The Drug Makers and the Drug Distributors,* p. 61.
41. Martin S. Feldstein, "The Medical Economy," *Scientific American* 229; September, 1973, 163.
42. *Evening Tribune* (San Diego), April 24, 1974, A-21.
43. John P. Wiley, Jr., "What's Holding up New Drug Development?" *FDA Consumer* 7; September, 1973, 21–24.
44. Ibid., p. 24.
45. Feldstein, *Scientific American,* p. 165.
46. Task Force on Prescription Drugs, *The Drug Makers and the Drug Distributors,* p. 75.
47. "Doctors Who Profit from Prescriptions," *Consumer Reports* 31, No. 5, May, 1966, p. 236.
48. "Many Patients Misinterpret Usage Directions on Rx Labels," *American Druggist* 169; March 15, 1974, 26.
49. *Evening Tribune* (San Diego), May 13, 1975, A-2.

Chapter Ten

Emergency
Medical
Services

Although Bellevue Hospital in New York City claims to have used the "world's first ambulance" in 1869, records indicate that Cincinnati General Hospital used a vehicle to transport patients prior to 1865.

By the nineteenth century, ambulance vehicles gradually became motorized and until World War II were mainly hospital-based. During the war, hospitals suffered from a lack of staff so ambulance services were taken over by volunteer groups. No specific level of training was required for ambulance personnel and people gradually accepted the ambulance simply as a transport vehicle for the ill and injured. After the war, lessons learned in battle about the positive results of immediate emergency treatment of the injured were not transposed to civilian life. Back home, federal monies were being poured into medical research following the successes of penicillin and new surgical procedures. Hospitals were receiving grants for research but not in the area of emergency medical services. Since ambulance service had generally operated in the red, hospitals were not eager to revive this service. Those hospitals that still operated ambulances did not upgrade their service to keep pace with other developments in the medical field, nor did they even achieve the standards present before the war. During these years, it was possible for any individual or organization to set themselves up as an ambulance service.

Medical schools also neglected emergency problems and the area of first aid and emergency care outside the hospital disappeared from the curricula of these schools.[1]

The problems of the delivery of emergency medical care mounted. Sporadic corrective measures were stimulated by reports such as the National Research Council's 1966 report on "Accidental Death and Disability: The Neglected Disease of Modern Society."

HOSPITAL EMERGENCY DEPARTMENTS

Concern has been directed not only to the problems of emergency care before arrival at the hospital emergency department, but also to the problems of emergency care available within the hospital. The functions and responsibilities of the hospital emergency service have changed dramatically in the last fifteen years. Increasingly, it has become for many people their source of entry into the medical system. For others, it is a place to obtain medical care when their personal physician is unavailable. Gradually, hospitals themselves have allowed the emergency department to become responsible for elective surgery and non-emergent diagnostic procedures. The use of the emergency facility for non-emergent purposes decreases its efficiency in the care of actual emergencies.[2]

Traditionally, the emergency department has been the most neglected department in the hospital. It is frequently crowded, underfinanced, underequipped and poorly designed. There is also a staffing problem. In many instances, the emergency department's personnel, including the physicians, are not specifically trained in emergency medical care. However, this deficiency has been recognized and efforts are being made to provide special courses to certify emergency room nurses. At the physician level, emergency medicine has been established as a Board-Certified specialty.

"Ironically, some hospitals reduce the staff in the emergency department on weekends—the period of highest accident frequency—and either close ancillary facilities or drastically reduce their staff."[3]

Hospital emergency departments are only one of the many components of emergency medical care that need drastic revision.

THE EMERGENCY MEDICAL SERVICES SYSTEMS ACT

Until recently, organization and coordination of emergency services at local, state, and national levels were almost nonexistent. In 1973, the Emergency Medical Services Systems (EMSS) Act was passed by Congress in response to a growing concern about this pressing problem. The purpose of the act was to provide federal financial support, technical assistance, and encouragement for the development of better emergency medical services in communities throughout the nation. Under the act, three types of federal grants were established:[4]

1. Feasibility Studies and Planning Grants
2. Establishment and Initial Operation Grants
3. Expansion and Improvement Grants

The EMSS Act required the recipients to direct their efforts to the development of certain major components in an emergency care system which will be dealt with in detail later in this chapter.

This act has had a tremendous impetus on improving the delivery of emergency medical care. Many areas are presently developing plans and establishing systems using the guidelines provided. Of course, these funds are not intended to subsidize operations indefinitely; communities must be prepared to finance the system when the federal support ceases. There are other federal sources of income which may also be used. The Office of Civil Defense funds emergency communication centers, and the Department of Transportation's Division of Emergency Medical Programs supports highway safety projects.[5]

Up to this point, planning, delivery, and management of emergency medical systems has often been fragmented, inadequate, and maldistributed. Manpower roles have been poorly defined and financing has been insufficient and sporadic. Generally, the public has been uninformed about the potential of emergency medical systems and unacquainted with their technical aspects. Consumers do, however, recognize haphazard or inept care when they receive it.

In order to organize a responsive, efficient service, knowledgeable personnel must be prepared. Local, state, and federal authorities are beginning to view an effective EMS system as a necessary public service, just as important as fire and police protection.[6]

AN EFFECTIVE EMERGENCY MEDICAL SERVICES SYSTEM

The purpose of the 1973 EMSS Act was to encourage the improvement of emergency medical services. The act designated an "emergency medical service system" as a system which:[7]

a. provides for the arrangement of personnel, facilities, and equipment for the effective and coordinated delivery of health care services in an appropriate geographical area under emergency conditions, and

b. is administered by a public or nonprofit entity which has the authority and the resources to provide effective administration of the system.

The EMSS Act states that an emergency medical services system shall have the following components:[8]

1. Personnel:
    Include an adequate number of health professions, allied health professions, and other health personnel, including ambulance personnel, with appropriate training and experience. This means sufficient numbers of such personnel to provide emergency medical services on a 24-hour basis within the service area of the system.

2. Training:
    Provide for its personnel appropriate training (including clinical training) and continuing education programs which are coordinated with other programs in the system's service area; emphasize recruitment and necessary training of veterans of the Armed Forces with military training and experience in health care fields; and recruit and train appropriate public safety personnel in such areas.

    "Appropriate public safety personnel" includes police, firemen, and other public employees charged with maintaining public safety.

3. Communications:
    Join the personnel, facilities, and equipment of the system by a central communications system so that requests for emergency health care services will be handled by a communications facility that utilizes emergency medical telephonic screening; utilizes the universal emergency telephone number 911; and will have direct communication connections and interconnections with the personnel, facilities, and equipment of the system and with other emergency medical services systems.

    A "central communications system" includes a system command and control center which is responsible for establishing those communication channels and providing those public resources essential to the most effective and efficient emergency medical services management of the immediate problem, and which has the necessary equipment and facilities to permit immediate interchange of information essential for the system's resource management and control. The essentials of such a communications center are that (a) all requests for system response are directed to the center; (b) all system resource response is directed from the center; and (c) all system liaison with other public safety and emergency response systems is coordinated from the center.

4. Transportation:

Include an adequate number of necessary ground, air, and water vehicles and other transportation facilities to meet the individual characteristics of the system's service area. Such vehicles and facilities must meet appropriate standards relating to location, design, performance, and equipment; and the operators and other personnel for such vehicles and facilities must meet appropriate training and experience requirements.

5. Facilities:

Include an adequate number of easily accessible emergency medical services facilities which are collectively capable of providing services on a continuous basis, which have appropriate standards relating to capacity, location, personnel, and equipment, and which are coordinated with other health care facilities of the system.

6. Access:

Provide access (including appropriate transportation) to specialized critical medical care units in the system's service area.

"Appropriate transportation" means a vehicle equipped to enable the emergency medical technician or more highly trained personnel to administer to the patient's in-transit needs.

"Specialized critical medical care units" include intensive care units, burn centers, spinal cord centers, and detoxification centers.

7. Effective Utilization:

Provide for the effective utilization of the personnel, facilities, and equipment of each public safety agency providing emergency services in the system's service area. "Effective utilization" of personnel, facilities, and equipment of public safety agencies means the integration of public safety agencies into standard and disaster operating procedures of the areawide system, including the shared use of personnel and equipment suited to use in medical emergencies, such as helicopters and rescue boats.

8. Policy Making:

Be organized in a manner that provides persons who reside in the system's service area and who have no professional training or financial interest in the provision of health care with an adequate opportunity to participate in the making of policy for the system.

9. Payment for Service:

Provide, without prior inquiry as to ability to pay, necessary emergency medical services to all patients requiring such services.

10. Transfer:

Provide for transfer of patients to facilities and programs that offer such follow-up care and rehabilitation as is necessary to effect the maximum recovery of the patient.

"Follow-up care and rehabilitation" includes physical and psychiatric care and vocational rehabilitation.

11. Record Keeping:

Provide for a standardized patient record-keeping system to record the treatment of the patient from initial entry into the system through his discharge from it. This system should be consistent with ensuing patient records used in follow-up care and rehabilitation of the patient. A "standardized patient record-keeping system" means uniform records and forms throughout the emergency medical services system's service area, such as standard forms of ambulance and emergency department use which are integrated into the patient care record, discharge summary, and follow-up records.

12. Public Education:

Provide programs of public education and information in the system's service area stressing the general dissemination of information regarding appropriate methods of medical self-help and first-aid.

13. Review:

Provide for periodic, comprehensive, and independent review and evaluation of the extent and quality of the emergency health care services provided in the system's service area.

"Independent review" means review by persons not associated with the emergency medical services system and not residing or working within the service area of such system or within the State or States in which the service area of such system is located.

14. Disaster Capacity:

Have a plan to assure that the system will be capable of providing emergency medical services in the system's service area during mass casualties, natural disasters, or national emergencies.

15. Reciprocal Services:

Provide for the establishment of appropriate arrangements with emergency medical services systems or similar entities serving neighboring areas for the provision of emergency medical services on a reciprocal basis where access to such services would be more appropriate and effective in terms of the services available, time, and distance. Arrangements among emergency medical services systems or similar entities serving neighboring areas shall be written agreements, signed by individuals authorized to act for the respective parties with respect to such agreements, and reviewed and reevaluated at least once a year.

To meet the above federal criteria for an EMS system, and qualify for funds, is a difficult undertaking. It involves cooperation between health agencies at the local, regional, and state level as well as incorporation of existing emergency care facilities.

Although the EMSS Act covered the major components of an EMS system, the following areas are discussed in more depth: rating systems, ambulance service, total systems, personnel, and communications.

RATING EMERGENCY
DEPARTMENTS

Any effective EMS system must include a rating of hospital emergency services. The rating should include the entire service capabilities of a hospital, not just its emergency department. For example, how quickly can a hospital deal with an emergency? How many seconds does it take to assemble a team to deal with a cardiac arrest?

There is no reason for every hospital to have a complete emergency service. But it must be a matter of public knowledge which hospitals are equipped to handle particular emergencies. Not having every hospital duplicate emergency services will conserve both manpower and money. When a hospital's emergency service capabilities are assessed, everyone, including the hospital itself, knows how the services rate. Deficiencies, once identified, can usually be corrected.[9] Each hospital can contribute, according to its capacity, to the total EMS system. And it should be understood that a low rating as an emergency facility does not necessarily indicate the quality of medical care available in other parts of the hospital. Once emergency services are rated, signs on highways and streets can indicate the closest facilities appropriate to handle a particular emergency.

AMBULANCE SERVICE

Jacksonville, Florida, has developed one of the finest ambulance services in the nation. It utilized the sophisticated communications systems already established for the fire department, replacing the pull-lever fireboxes with telephones. When a call is made, the problem area is indicated on a master map and the ambulance is dispatched. The telephone enables the person reporting the emergency to give specific details concerning the type of emergency and the number of people involved. Jacksonville purchased modern specially designed and equipped ambulances which contain wrecking kits to help remove crash victims from vehicles. Each fireman volunteering for rescue work is given additional training and salary. Each ambulance is in communication with a hospital and can transmit information to a physician for advice on further emergency treatment. These may seem like ordinary procedures and qualifications but the U.S. Public Health Service estimates that not one in 100 U.S. ambulances can communicate with a hospital and no more than one in twenty ambulance attendants get better than minimal training. In many parts of the country, undertakers still provide much of the ambulance service.

There are many options open to a community that is considering the best way to handle emergency vehicle services. The provision of good ambulance service is no mystery; a community can have any level of service that they are willing to pay for.

TOTAL SYSTEMS

Various groups must get together to create a functional system. In many instances, the resources are already present, but they must be organized into an efficient cohesive unit. Florida has developed a total system which involves all professional services with no county lines that act as barriers to health care. Each area's needs will be different. For this reason, emergency medical services grant applications must have the approval of state and regional planning agencies.[10]

Illinois has developed the Illinois Trauma Care Center,[11] which establishes emergency procedures for early recognition of critical injury and subsequent mobilization of medical services to ensure the best possible care. These are based on the techniques of evacuation, early resuscitation, diagnosis, and comprehensive treatment developed during the Vietnam War. As in all emergency medical care systems, communication plays a key role. A radio network connects local, areawide, and regional trauma centers. A patient can be taken without delay to the hospital best able to care for his needs. The communications systems also alert the hospital so that it can be ready to deliver the services needed. This Trauma Care System is comprised of three types of facilities: 1) local trauma centers, 2) areawide centers, and 3) regional centers. Each *Local Trauma Center* is located in a community hospital. A physician must be available at all times and the hospital must be connected to the emergency radio network. The hospital must also have an intensive care unit, capabilities for basic patient resuscitation and a helicopter ambulance landing site. *Areawide Trauma Centers* provide standard specialized care for the critically injured patient. A physician must be on duty at all times and specialists available within minutes. The *Regional Trauma Centers* are the most specialized hospitals in the system and have the most sophisticated equipment and comprehensive medical staff.

To illustrate the importance and sophistication of the communications system in the delivery of emergency medical care, let us look at three unique features of the Illinois system.[12]

1. Trauma Coordinators:

These people are responsible for the integration of all the components of the system. They arrange for transportation to the proper treatment facility; determine, through radio contact, the severity of the injuries; and, if necessary, establish radio contact between physicians and on-the-scene personnel. They alert the staff at the receiving center about the condition of the incoming patient and summon specialists if necessary.

2. Trauma Data Registry:

The registry is a collection and storage of data on computers of every patient admitted to a Trauma Center. It can provide patient histories and clinical summaries for given injuries as well as death and disability rates for injuries. Each physician at a Trauma Center can instantly retrieve information from a central computer on the type of problem confronting him. The information is visually displayed on a television screen.

3. Hospital Emergency Area Radio:
   This radio links the trauma centers to other hospitals, police vehicles, ambulances, and occasionally helicopters.

PERSONNEL

Of course, any system is only as good as the personnel available to run it. One of the most important developments in emergency care in the last decade is the basic 81-hour course for Emergency Medical Technicians (EMTs) developed by the National Academy of Sciences, the American Academy of Orthopedic Surgeons, and others. Most states now have EMT training programs which are partially funded by the Department of Transportation under the National Highway Safety Act of 1966.

With the assistance of the federal government's Department of Transportation, the National Registry of Emergency Medical Technicians has attempted to set four uniform standards of training.[13]

1. EMT – Ambulance
   This is the basic 81-hour course, composed of 71 hours in classroom practice and demonstration lessons and ten hours in in-hospital instruction. It should enable the attendant to deliver life-saving care. The registry suggests that a hospital assume responsibility for the clinical training.

2. EMT – Advanced (Paramedic)
   Involves an additional 480 hours of training. Paramedics are mobile intensive care personnel who deliver emergency medical care at the scene of an emergency and during transportation to a hospital. Depending on the laws of the state, paramedics may perform procedures such as defibrillation and endotracheal intubation, pro-

vide medications, and administer intravenous fluid therapy when in voice and telemetry contact with a physician or qualified registered nurse.

3. EMT – Hospital
    In many areas this program is still in the planning stage. It is thought that the program will be offered as a two-year course in junior colleges. The training will be varied, allowing the student employment possibilities in many in-hospital jobs such as inhalation therapy, cardiac care, and intensive care.

4. EMT – Nonambulance
    This classification is designed for R.N.'s, licensed practical nurses, x-ray technicians, orderlies, law enforcement personnel, industrial safety specialists, military corpsmen without field experience, and others. It requires three months of patient or health care experience and satisfactory completion of 81 hours of training.

As registered ambulance attendants become more prevalent, and their expertise apparent, state laws will be changed to allow them to perform up to their level of training.

With the recent focus on emergency care, many areas are including EMT courses in their master plans for comprehensive health care. In San Diego, California, a two-semester community college course of 108 hours is offered to allow for presentations by representatives of major EMS providers such as hospitals, the ambulance industry, Poison Information Center, Burn Unit, and others with whom the EMT is in contact almost daily.

COMMUNICATIONS

Without an effective communications system, the various components of an EMS system will not have a means of coordination and control. Figure 10.1 illustrates the steps that a good communications system should provide to properly coordinate an EMS system.

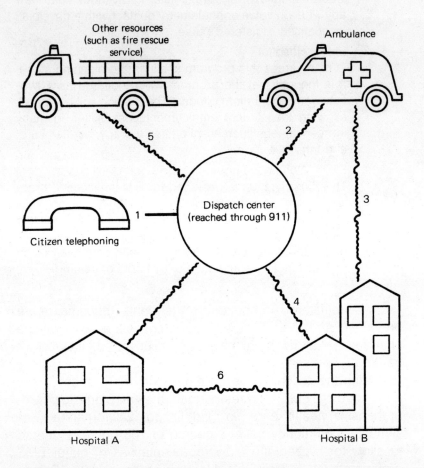

Other resources
(such as fire rescue
service)

Ambulance

5

2

3

Dispatch center
(reached through 911)

1

Citizen telephoning

4

6

Hospital A

Hospital B

FIGURE 10.1 Links in An Effective Emergency Communications System (Reproduced with permission from *A Guide for Hospital Participation in an Emergency Medical Communications System*, published by the American Hospital Association.)

Six steps are included in this system:[14]

1. Telephone link between citizen and dispatch center
2. Two-way radio communications between ambulance and dispatch center

3. Two-way voice and telemetry communications between ambulance and hospital

4. Two-way radio communications between hospital and dispatch center

5. Two-way radio communications between dispatch center and other resources

6. Interhospital radio communications that bypass dispatch center.

Most areas are planning to implement a "911" universal emergency telephone number. The variety of telephone numbers now used to call for emergency help has resulted in considerable delay. In some metropolitan areas, as many as fifty different telephone numbers are used due to poor planning, geographic and political boundaries. The 911 number is expected to be the universal entry mechanism for citizens needing emergency help.

WHAT CAN YOU DO?

Reduce the need for emergency care by becoming better informed about potential hazards. Of the leading causes of death, trauma (accidental injury) ranks first for Americans between the ages of one and 45. An effective, aggressive health education program is necessary to eliminate as many emergency medical situations as possible.

Take a first-aid course so that you will be of assistance to yourself and others in the event of an emergency. At the present time, only 5 percent of trauma victims receive competent lay help at the scene of an accident.

Learn which hospitals in your area have adequate EMS facilities so that you do not waste time when an emergency arises.

Write the EMS number(s) for your area in your telephone directory or on your telephone. Will you need a different number if you are in another part of the city? (If your city had the 911 system, that's the only number you would need.)

Compare your EMS system to those that we have discussed. If you are not satisfied with the comparison, contact your local and state officials and let them know that you want an efficient EMS system in your area.

ENDNOTES

1. Merlin K. DuVal, "The Hidden Crisis in Health Care," in John H. Noble, et al., (eds.) *Emergency Medical Services* (New York: Behavioral Publications, 1973), pp. 11–13.
2. Paul A. Skudder, et al., "Hospital Emergency Facilities and Services: A Survey," in John H. Noble, et al., (eds.) *Emergency Medical Services,* p. 28.
3. "Emergentology: A Key to Better Emergency Care," *Modern Medicine* 40; March 6, 1972, 133.
4. Division of Emergency Medical Services, Public Health Service, *The Emergency Medical Services Systems Act* (Washington, D.C.: U.S. Department of Health, Education, and Welfare, 1974).
5. Jay Nelson Tuck, "A Shot in the Arm for Emergency Services," *Modern Health Care* 1; June, 1974, 29.
6. Oscar P. Hampton, "A Rating System for Emergency Departments," *Prism* 2; July, 1974, 31.
7. Division of Emergency Medical Services, Public Health Services, *What is an Emergency Medical Services System?* (Washington, D.C.: U.S. Department of Health, Education, and Welfare, 1975).
8. Ibid.
9. Hampton, "A Rating System for Emergency Departments," p. 29.
10. Tuck, "A Shot in the Arm for Emergency Services," p. 29.
11. Illinois Division of Emergency Medical Services and Highway Safety, *Illinois Trauma Care System* (Northbrook, Ill.: Allstate Insurance Co., 1974).

12. Ibid.
13. American Hospital Association, *Emergency Medical Communications System* (Chicago, 1973), p. 30.
14. Ibid., p. 16.

Chapter Eleven

Medicare and Medicaid

Medicare and Medicaid programs are constantly being revised. In addition, Medicaid coverage varies considerably from state to state. Thus, if you wish precise information on Medicaid for your state, contact your local Social Services Department, or Public Health Department. If you want information on Medicare, contact any social security office.

MEDICARE

History

Prior to 1870, more than half of the nation's adult workers were farmers. They were virtually self-sufficient and did not become burdens to their neighbors. As time passed, there were fewer farmers and more hired workers, who tended to concentrate in the towns and cities. These hired workers and their families increasingly depended on a continuing flow of money income to provide for their needs. When this flow was interrupted, it meant destitution and poverty. Most local villages and towns recognized an obligation to help the needy when family efforts and assistance

249

by neighbors and friends was not enough to meet economic adversity. This help was provided through the poor relief system and almshouses, but like most charity systems, their demeaning and repressive features tended to discourage the needy from applying for this aid.

Around 1900, state governments started programs of assistance for the needy aged, the blind and deaf, homeless children, and the insane and feebleminded. In the early 1900s, other steps were taken to help provide for economic security. Workmen's compensation and retirement programs began. The federal government started providing benefits and services for persons who served in the military forces. Later, these benefits for the military included a full-scale system of hospital and medical care benefits.

Even with these provisions, the severe depression of the 1930s clearly showed that many Americans did not have economic security. To remedy this, the federal government, in 1935, passed the now famous Social Security Act. It established two social insurance programs: 1) a federal system of old-age benefits for certain retired workers, and 2) a federal-state system of unemployment insurance. The law also contains provisions to help states with three groups of needy persons: the aged, the blind, and dependent children. Since the inception of the Social Security Act, amendments have been made to broaden the scope and coverage of its provisions so that, now, virtually all gainfully employed workers are covered. To qualify for benefits under the program, workers contribute a small percentage of their salary during their working years.

The amendments that were of particular importance to health care were passed in 1965 and became effective July 1, 1966. These amendments to the Social Security Act were added to a new section, referred to as Title 18. It provided for two related health insurance plans for nearly all persons aged 65 and over: Part A, a basic *compulsory* program of hospital insurance, and Part B, a *voluntary* program of supplementary medical insurance (to help pay doctor bills). The hospital insurance (Part A) is financed by deductions from employees' wages, matching funds paid by employers, and by a tax paid by the self-employed. The medical insurance (Part B) is financed by monthly premiums paid by the individual and by a matching amount paid by the federal government. The whole program is administered by the Social Security Administration.

The Medicare Program, as Title 18 is now called, was particularly welcome. It is well-known that the elderly spend much more time in hospitals than any other segment of the population. Unfortunately, many persons over 65 are experiencing severe financial problems because they are entirely dependent upon their monthly Social Security checks. The spiraling costs of hospital and doctor care meant a crushing financial burden for those not covered by private insurance. Although Medicare has helped defray some expenses, it is by no means comprehensive; in a recent year, it paid only 40 percent of the personal health costs of people 65 and over. There are two parts to Medicare: hospital insurance and medical insurance.

Hospital Insurance
(Part A)

Medicare's hospital insurance helps pay for three types of care: 1) in-patient hospital care when medically necessary, 2) in-patient care in a skilled nursing home (after a hospital stay), and 3) home health care.

The term "benefit period" is often used to describe Medicare coverage. A benefit period is a period of time for measuring use of hospital insurance benefits. A benefit period begins when a Medicare recipient enters the hospital. It ends when the patient has not been a bed patient in a hospital or nursing home for 60 days in a row. A new benefit period begins the next time that a person enters the hospital and ends as soon as he has another 60 days in a row when he is not a bed patient in any hospital. There is no limit to the number of benefit periods a person may have.[1]

Hospital coverage

In each period, the hospital insurance portion of Medicare helps pay for up to 90 days of bed patient care in any participating general care, tuberculosis, or psychiatric hospital.* It pays all covered services for the first 60 days, except for a deductible of approximately $100. It also pays all covered services for the 61st through the 90th day, except for a deductible of approximately $25.

In addition to the above, each person has a "lifetime reserve" of 60 additional days. This is like the reserve fund in a bank account: a Medicare patient can use them if he needs more than the 90 days of hospital care in the same benefit period. Each "lifetime reserve" day used permanently reduces the total which remains.

Table 11.1 helps to visualize the benefits that hospital insurance can help pay for and those that it cannot pay for.

Medicare's hospital insurance also covers care in a Christian Science sanatorium and care in Canadian or Mexican hospitals under certain conditions.

Nursing home (extended care) coverage

In some cases, a hospital patient improves sufficiently so that he does not require intensive care at the hospital, but still needs full-time nursing care and certain other health services that cannot be provided in his home. Such a patient may be transferred to a nursing home for this type of care.

Medicare's hospital insurance pays for all covered services in an approved nursing home for the first twenty days in each benefit period; it also helps to pay for up to 80

* To participate in the Medicare Program, health facilities must meet standards which help assure that they will be able to provide high quality health care. In addition, they must not charge the Medicare beneficiary for services paid for by the program, and they must abide by Title 6 of the Civil Rights Act, which prohibits discrimination based on race, color, or national origin.

TABLE 11.1 Hospital Coverage

Medicare's hospital insurance can pay for these items.

1 A semiprivate room (2 to 4 beds in a room)
2 All meals, including special diets
3 Regular nursing services
4 Intensive care unit costs
5 Drugs furnished by the hospital during a stay
6 Lab tests included in the hospital bill
7 X-rays and other radiology services, including radiation therapy, billed by the hospital
8 Medical supplies such as casts, surgical dressings, and splints
9 Use of appliances such as a wheelchair
10 Operating and recovery room costs
11 Rehabilitation services, such as physical therapy, occupational therapy, and speech pathology services

*Medicare's hospital insurance **cannot** pay for these items.*

1 Personal convenience items that a patient requests such as a television, radio, or telephone in his room
2 Private duty nurses
3 Any extra charges for a private room, unless needed for medical reasons
4 The first 3 pints of blood received in a benefit period

Source: Social Security Administration, *Your Medicare Handbook* (Washington, D.C.: U.S. Government Printing Office, 1974), p. 13.

more days in that same benefit period. To qualify for extended care benefits, a patient must have been in a hospital for three days in a row prior to being transferred to the nursing home by his doctor. In addition, he must enter the nursing home within fourteen days of leaving the hospital. Table 11.2 clarifies nursing home coverage.

TABLE 11.2 Nursing Home Coverage

Medicare's hospital insurance can pay for these items.

1 A semiprivate room (2 to 4 beds in a room)
2 All meals including special diets
3 Regular nursing services
4 Rehabilitation services, such as physical, occupational, and speech therapy
5 Drugs furnished by the facility during a stay
6 Medical supplies such as splints and casts
7 Use of appliances such as a wheelchair

Medicare's hospital insurance **cannot** *pay for these items.*

1 Personal convenience items that a patient requests such as a television, radio, or telephone in his room
2 Private duty nurses
3 Any extra charges for a private room, unless for medical reasons
4 The first 3 pints of blood received in a benefit period
5 Doctor's services while in a nursing home (Medicare medical insurance, dealt with below, covers doctor's services)

Source: Social Security Administration, *Your Medicare Handbook* (Washington, D.C.: U.S. Government Printing Office, 1974), p. 19.

Home health benefits

If a patient has been in the hospital for at least three days and satisfies certain other criteria, his doctor may let him go home on the condition that he receive home health benefits. These benefits include such services as part-time nursing care, physical or speech therapy, and certain other services.

Medicare hospital insurance pays for as many as 100 home health visits for up to a year after the patient leaves the hospital or nursing home. To qualify, he must be receiving treatment for the same condition that required his admission in the first place.

Medicare medical insurance (Part B), which is explained in the next section, can also help pay for up to 100 home health visits in a calendar year. Under Part B, a person does not have to be hospitalized before receiving home health benefits. Table 11.3 clarifies home health services.

TABLE 11.3 Home Health Services

Medicare can pay for.

1 Part-time skilled nursing care
2 Physical therapy
3 Speech therapy
If part-time skilled nursing care, physical therapy, or speech therapy is needed, Medicare can also pay for:
> ▶ Occupational therapy
> ▶ Part-time services of home health aides
> ▶ Medical social services
> ▶ Medical supplies and equipment provided by the agency

Medicare **cannot** *pay for these items.*

1 Full-time nursing care at home
2 Drugs and biologicals
3 Meals delivered to a patient's home
4 Homemaker services

Source: Social Security Administration, *Your Medicare Handbook* (Washington, D.C.: U.S. Government Printing Office, 1974), p. 35.

Medical Insurance
(Part B)

Part B of Medicare is a voluntary program. Basically, it helps to pay for doctors' services, out-patient hospital care, home health care, out-patient physical therapy and speech pathology services, as well as other health services and supplies which are not covered by Medicare hospital insurance.

A person who elects this coverage pays approximately $7.50 a month, which is half of the cost of the insurance. The federal government pays the other half. This premium rate must be reviewed annually and may be increased to cover rising medical costs. (In 1966, this insurance cost $3.00.) Since it is a voluntary program, this protection may be cancelled by the person at the end of any calendar quarter. Approximately 96 percent of the elderly who are eligible have elected this coverage.

Under Part B, after a person's bills for covered services go over $60 in a year, medical insurance pays 80 percent of the reasonable charges for the rest of that year. "Reasonable charges" take into account the customary charges made by a doctor as well as the charges made by other doctors in the area for the same kind of service.

Doctors' services

Under this section, a person can select his own doctor and receive treatment in a hospital, his doctor's office, a nursing home, his own home, or at a group practice or other clinic. Table 11.4 outlines doctors' services under Part B.

In addition to the above coverage, medical insurance helps pay for surgical care by a dentist and for certain care by podiatrists and chiropractors.

Out-patient hospital services

Out-patient hospital services are services that people receive when they go to the hospital for diagnosis or treat-

TABLE 11.4 Doctors' Services

Medicare's medical insurance can help pay for.

1 Medical and surgical services
2 Diagnostic tests and procedures that are part of a patient's treatment
3 Other services which are ordinarily furnished in the doctor's office and included in his bill, such as:
   ▶ X-rays received as part of treatment
   ▶ Services of a doctor's office nurse
   ▶ Drugs and biologicals that cannot be self-administered
   ▶ Medical supplies
   ▶ Physical therapy and speech pathology services

Medicare's medical insurance **cannot** *pay for these services.*

1 Routine physical examinations
2 Routine foot care
3 Eye or hearing examinations for prescribing or fitting eyeglasses or hearing aids
4 Immunizations (unless required because of an injury or immediate risk of infection)
5 Cosmetic surgery unless it is needed because of accidental injury or to improve the functioning of a malformed part of the body

Source: Social Security Administration, *Your Medicare Handbook* (Washington, D.C.: U.S. Government Printing Office, 1974), p. 27.

ment but are not admitted as patients. Table 11.5 describes these services.

Other services and supplies

Part B helps pay for diagnostic tests, including x-rays, provided by independent laboratories (those not in a hospital

TABLE 11.5 Out-patient Hospital Services

Medicare's medical insurance helps pay for these items.

1 Services in an emergency room or out-patient clinic
2 Laboratory tests billed by the hospital
3 X-rays and other radiology services billed by the hospital
4 Medical supplies such as splints and casts
5 Drugs and biologicals which cannot be self-administered

Medicare's medical insurance **cannot** *pay for these items.*

1 Routine physical examinations and tests directly related to such examinations
2 Eye or ear examinations to prescribe or fit eyeglasses or hearing aids
3 Immunizations (unless required because of an injury or immediate risk of infection)
4 Routine foot care

Source: Social Security Administration, *Your Medicare Handbook* (Washington, D.C.: U.S. Government Printing Office, 1974), p. 29.

or doctor's office). It also helps pay for ambulance transportation, prosthetic devices, certain medical equipment such as wheelchairs and home dialysis systems, as well as medical supplies such as surgical dressings, splints, and casts.

Out-patient physical therapy and speech pathology

Part B helps pay for physical therapy or speech pathology by a physician, a Medicare certified physical therapist, or qualified speech pathologist. The treatment may be given at home or in the doctor's office, the hospital, a nursing home, clinic, or rehabilitation agency.

Medicare Exclusions

Medicare does not pay for the following:[2]

- Acupuncture
- Christian Science practitioners' services
- Custodial care
- Drugs and medicines purchased by a patient with or without a prescription
- Eyeglasses and eye examinations for prescribing, fitting, or changing eyeglasses
- Hearing aids and hearing examinations for prescribing, fitting, or changing hearing aids
- Homemaker services
- Injections which can be self-administered, such as insulin
- Meals delivered to the patient's home
- Naturopaths' services
- Nursing care on a full-time basis in the patient's home
- Personal convenience items that a patient requests such as a phone, radio, or television in his room at a hospital or nursing home
- Physical examinations that are routine and tests directly related to such examinations
- Private duty nurses
- Services performed by immediate relatives or members of a patient's household
- Services that are not reasonable and necessary
- Services payable by Workmen's Compensation or another government program
- Services for which neither the patient nor another party on his behalf has a legal obligation to pay

Limited Coverage

Medicare covers the following services and supplies in a very limited fashion:[3]

- *Chiropractic services.* Only manipulation of the spine to correct a subluxation that can be demonstrated by x-ray. Medicare does not pay for the x-ray or for any other diagnostic or therapeutic services furnished by a chiropractor.
- *Cosmetic surgery.* Only if it is needed because of an accidental injury or to improve the functioning of a malformed part of the body.
- *Dental care.* Only if it involves surgery of the jaw or related structures or setting fractures of the jaw or facial bones.
- *Foreign health care.* Only during an emergency where a Canadian or Mexican hospital is closer than the nearest U.S. hospital.
- *Immunizations,* unless required because of an injury or immediate risk of infection.
- *Private room* in a hospital or nursing home.

Medicare Problems

It is obvious that Medicare has many exclusions and limitations. This fact is painfully evident to those over 65 who have had medical expenses. They have found that Medicare pays only 40 percent of their bill. It is difficult for the elderly to understand that Medicare was never designed to pay all their medical costs; they do understand, however, that they are paying their highest medical bills at the time in their lives when they can least afford them. Statistics bear out the fact that the aged have frequent and costly illnesses. Persons over 65 have out-of-pocket expenditures for medical care that are three times as high as the out-of-pocket expenditures of those under 65.[4]

Apart from the exclusions listed earlier, Medicare is paying a smaller proportion of the medical costs of the elderly than it did in earlier years. Several factors are involved. The dollar amount of the hospital deductible has risen steadily; the hospital co-insurance has increased; the amount of the medical deductible under Part B has gone up;

and physicians' fees have increased. Also, an increasing proportion of physicians refuse to accept assignment for their bills. When a physician accepts "assignment," the patient is not billed for any amount over what the physician is reimbursed by Medicare. Without assignment, the patient is billed for the difference between the doctor's charges and the Medicare reimbursement amount. The percentage of physician refusal to accept assignment has risen from 39 percent in 1969 to over 50 percent today.[5,6]

PURCHASING PRIVATE INSURANCE

As Medicare has become less protective, the elderly have turned more to private health insurance policies for coverage of their health care costs. Since they do not usually work at jobs that qualify them for an employer's group coverage, they must choose from the myriad of private policies which have varying coverage and often are stated in confusing terminology. Combine this with the "hard-sell" and "scare" tactics of some insurance companies, and we find that the elderly are not getting their money's worth in the insurance marketplace. In fact, they have been characterized as the most duped of all the public in the accident and health insurance field.

Private health insurance companies and the policies they write are regulated by state departments of insurance. This regulation is a formidable task. For example, in a recent year, the Florida Department of Insurance recalled over 50,000 individual health insurance forms and policies for analysis. These figures refer to policies without regard to the age of the purchaser.[7]

In an attempt to guarantee certain minimum standards in health policies, the National Association of Insurance Commissioners has prepared a model bill. The subjects it covers are among the most important issues in health insurance regulation and are the greatest source of complaints brought to the attention of the state insurance departments. The list of items included in the model bill are:[8]

1) Terms of renewability
2) Initial and subsequent conditions of eligibility
3) Nonduplication of coverage provisions
4) Coverage of dependents
5) Preexisting conditions
6) Termination of insurance
7) Probationary periods
8) Limitations
9) Exceptions
10) Reductions
11) Elimination periods
12) Requirements for replacement
13) Recurrent conditions
14) The clear definition of terms such as "accidental means" and "nervous disorder."

Some states have already passed legislation covering many of these subjects.

The preexisting condition clause has been a major source of complaints reported to state insurance companies by the elderly. This clause enables the company to refuse to pay claims for current illnesses related to or developing from illnesses that began prior to the effective date of the policy. For example, "Mr. X suffers from arthritis in his knee and has been suffering from arthritis for some time. After the effective date of his insurance policy, an intense arthritic pain in his knee causes him to lose his balance. He falls and breaks his leg. With an ironclad preexisting condition clause, Mr. X's insurance policy would not pay for any hospital or medical costs incurred for his broken leg."[9] Many health insurance policies will not pay for any problems during the first two years of the policy if the claim is for a condition that the company believes existed before the coverage began. This would effectively exclude many of the health problems of the elderly. State insurance departments are working to reduce the period of preexisting condition or eliminate it completely.

Another serious problem reported by the elderly results from unscrupulous selling tactics used by some insurance agents. Overinsurance and unwise cancellation of a policy and simultaneous purchase of a new policy are two promotions that defraud the elderly. In regard to overinsurance, an agent will sell several policies to the same person to cover the same risks, implying that he will make money when he gets sick. However, insurance policies now have a "coordination of benefits" arrangement and, where duplication exists, only one will pay. With regard to the second abuse, a policy is sold and some months later, the insured elderly person is advised by the agent to cancel the policy and purchase a new one. The major advantage for the agent is the commission he receives on selling the policy. The disadvantage to the elderly person is that a new prior exclusion clause goes into effect and there is an additional wait for coverage of prior illness.

We have touched on a few of the abuses practiced by unscrupulous insurance agents. Fortunately, there are many reputable companies whose agents do not engage in such unethical methods. Since Medicare was not designed to cover all the medical costs of the elderly, private health insurance is needed to protect our aged from financial ruin when sickness strikes.* Unfortunately, many elderly persons do not understand the provisions of either Medicare or private policies. Also, every day, many more persons reach 65 years of age and need to be informed of their coverage and exclusions under Medicare. The education of over twenty-two million elderly regarding their benefits is a tremendous undertaking, and we seem to be losing ground.

---

* Some states use the Medicaid program to supplement Medicare for the eligible needy over 65.

There is one approach that would eliminate most of the problems this group has in purchasing health care: simply pay all of their medical expenses. Other countries such as Sweden, Denmark, and Great Britain, apparently less affluent than the United States, have done it. Why can't we?

MEDICAID

In 1965, at the same time that Medicare (Title 18) was passed, its companion measure, a medical assistance program commonly referred to as "Medicaid," was also passed. Relatively unnoticed at the time, Medicaid (Title 19)—the federal-state program of medical assistance for the needy —has since been very much in the spotlight. It has reached this prominent position partly because of the careful review it has received at all levels of government since its inception. Although Medicaid coverage varies from state to state, it usually includes services by physicians, dentists, pharmacists, optometrists, podiatrists, chiropractors, hospitals, extended care facilities (nursing homes), and home health services. It also usually includes comprehensive care; that is, preventive, diagnostic, treatment, and rehabilitative services. Another reason for Medicaid receiving so much attention is the publicity given to its abuses by some of the above vendors (providers of services). Some of these abuses included double billing, overutilization, and charges made for services that were not rendered.

The Program

Medicaid was established to consolidate the separate programs of medical assistance which were in effect, such as Old Age Assistance, Aid for Dependent Children, Aid to the Blind, and Aid to the Permanently and Totally Dependent. Medicaid provides for higher federal payments than was possible under the various individual programs. It also extends medical assistance to medically needy persons: those who have sufficient financial resources to take care of day-to-day expenses, but who cannot afford to pay for medical care.

To qualify its Medicaid program under Title 19, a state had to submit an acceptable plan to the Department of Health, Education, and Welfare. Each state, with federal approval, sets the amounts of income and resources an applicant may have and still be eligible for benefits; that is, be classified as medically needy (all persons on welfare and public assistance are automatically eligible).

There was no requirement that a state had to establish a Medicaid program. There was, however, pressure on the states to offer such a program because in January, 1970, the federal government stopped paying for medical care under public assistance programs other than Title 19. That is, in order to receive federal money for medical care for those on welfare and certain other programs, a state had to offer a Medicaid program. All but two states (Alaska and Arizona) met the deadline. Arizona was the last state to join, with its program going into effect in late 1975.[10]

Medicaid is administered at the federal level by HEW's Social and Rehabilitative Service, but primary responsibility is at the state level. The program is financed by federal and state funds, the exact proportion depending upon the "richness" of each state. Federal contributions vary from 50 to 81 percent, inversely in relation to a state's per capita income. This means that the highest federal funds go to the states with the lowest per capita income. A state with a per capita income which is equal to the national average receives about 55 percent federal money. To remain in the program, each state has to provide the following services:[11]

1) In-patient hospital care
2) Out-patient hospital services
3) Other laboratory and x-ray services
4) Skilled nursing services for individuals twenty years of age or older

5) Early periodic screening, diagnosis, and treatment for eligibles under twenty-one years of age
6) Family planning services
7) Physicians' services
8) Home health care services

Medicaid Problems

Medicaid's development has not been smooth. During the first few years, it was difficult to keep up with the changes in the programs that the various states enacted; coverage was cut back, taxes raised, and eligibility levels were reexamined in order to meet the financial reality of such a program. New Mexico was in such trouble that it temporarily withdrew from the program in 1969, and reentered offering only the bare minimum of services, and these only to persons on welfare, with nothing for the medically needy.

The federal government found that much of Medicaid expenditures were being eaten up by the inflation in medical care costs. Its estimates for the total federal, state, and local cost of Medicaid vendor payments were too low and Congress had trouble keeping up with the increased costs of the program.

One of the main problems with Medicaid seems to have been the lack of planning, at both the federal and state levels.[12,13] Many states optimistically rushed in to implement Title 19, only to find that they had to reevaluate seriously the whole structure of their programs. New York City, for example, had more than 2.5 million persons enrolled in its program in April, 1968, which at that time represented more than 25 percent of the nation's total Medicaid enrollment. By April, 1969, it had changed eligibility levels so that only 1.5 million qualified.[14]

Another major problem with Medicaid has been the definition of "medically needy" by the various states. Unfortunately, according to the Advisory Commission on Intergovernmental Relations, "many states set the levels of need far below any reasonable standards of adequacy, even when allowing for regional variations in the cost of living." This inequity creates a "migrational pull" to areas with more generous benefits. The federal government, although wishing to have fairly uniform standards, was understandably reticent about imposing such standards on the states.

When the various states participating in Medicaid were asked to outline their problems in implementing the program, they responded as follows:[15] The main problem was that providers' fees and charges (doctors, hospitals, and others) had risen sharply. Reasons for these increases included rising salaries, costs of buildings, and "profiteering," that is, raising of fees to take advantage of the maximum allowable under Medicaid. Another major stumbling block was the unwillingness of physicians or other suppliers of services to participate in the program. The reasons given for this included: fees were deemed inadequate, payment was too slow, and there was excessive "red tape." The third most frequently mentioned item was the shortage of personnel—doctors, nurses, auxiliary medical helpers, and others. The fourth problem area was the failure of the "medically indigent" to enroll and establish eligibility because they were unaware that they were eligible, or else wished to avoid the welfare "stigma" which they felt was associated with receiving aid.* Another complaint was the shortage of facilities and equipment such as hospital beds, clinics, and nursing homes.

SUMMARY

In spite of the problems that haunted the early development of both Medicare and Medicaid, both programs are providing needed benefits for two large segments of our population. The administration of both programs has been improved, and abuses, which were prevalent during the early

* In many states, Medicaid is administered by a Welfare Department.

years, have been greatly reduced. It is generally agreed, however, that an increasingly sophisticated and demanding portion of the public is overusing health services. Also, there is significant overservicing (providing unneeded treatments) by physicians. To deal with this problem, the Department of Health, Education, and Welfare introduced legislation in 1972 which set up Professional Standards Review Organizations (PSROs) around the nation.[16] Basically, the law mandated that review committees determine if services provided were medically necessary, that they were of acceptable quality, and that they were provided in the proper facility. (Many persons in acute hospitals could be cared for in less expensive facilities.) If these conditions are not met, then the government will not pay for those services provided for Medicare or Medicaid patients. PSRO regulations became effective in 1975, against the vigorous opposition of many physicians who felt that the government was interfering in the practice of medicine. Without PSROs, however, there was no way to prevent tax dollars from being spent on unnecessary hospitalization and unneeded treatments. Millions of dollars have been saved because of the utilization review provided by the PSRO law.

Much of the criticism that Medicare and Medicaid receive today is related to the fact that they do not provide enough benefits and, in the case of Medicaid, do not reach enough of our population. The solution to both of these problems awaits a change in our philosophy toward the elderly and the poor in our nation.

ENDNOTES

1. Social Security Administration, *Your Medicare Handbook* (Washington, D.C.: U.S. Government Printing Office, 1974), p. 10.
2. Ibid., pp. 42–43.
3. Ibid.

4. Barbara Cooper, et al., "National Health Expenditures, 1929–73," *Social Security Bulletin,* February, 1974, p. 3.

5. Special Committee on Aging, United States Senate, *Private Health Insurance Supplementary to Medicare* (Washington, D.C.: U.S. Government Printing Office, 1974), p. 6.

6. *American Medical News,* August 26, 1974, p. 2.

7. Special Committee on Aging, *Private Health Insurance Supplementary to Medicare,* p. 11.

8. Ibid., pp. 12–13.

9. Ibid., p. 14.

10. *American Medical News,* June 10, 1974, p. 1.

11. Albert J. Richter, Associate Commissioner, Medical Services Administration, Social and Rehabilitative Service, Department of Health, Education, and Welfare, personal communication, September 27, 1974.

12. Raymond S. Alexander, "Medicaid in New York: Utopianism and Bare Knuckles in Public Health"—II. "Administrative Dynamics in Megalopolitan Health Care," *American Journal of Public Health* 59, No. 5, May, 1969, p. 817.

13. Advisory Commission on Intergovernmental Relations, *Intergovernmental Problems in Medicaid* (Washington, D.C.: U.S. Government Printing Office, 1968), p. 56.

14. Edward O'Rourke, "Medicaid in New York: Utopianism and Bare Knuckles in Public Health"—I. "Introduction," *American Journal of Public Health* 59, No. 5, May, 1969, p. 814.

15. Advisory Commission, *Intergovernmental Problems in Medicaid,* p. 54.

16. Public Law 92-603, Title XI, Part B—1170.

Chapter Twelve

Nursing Homes

Nursing home patients have an average age of 82; about 10 percent of them are married; they take approximately six medications each day. They can expect to be in a nursing home more than two years and most will die in one of the nation's 24,000 nursing homes. The cost of nursing home care is approximately $4 billion per year, with about $2 of every $3 in nursing home revenues paid for by your tax dollar through Medicaid and Medicare.[1] How are these elderly persons being treated during their last years? Are your tax dollars being spent wisely on services for the more than 1.2 million aged who reside in nursing homes? In this chapter, we will attempt to answer these questions and others relating to nursing homes in the United States.

Citizens over 65 are the largest group of health care consumers in the country. In many cases, old age is accompanied by failing health and increasing financial dependence, if not outright poverty. Without exploring the sociological developments that led to the present situation, we can say that elderly people do not enjoy a prestigious position in our American culture. In their last years, many must depend on government assistance for their needs.

ALTERNATIVES TO NURSING HOME CARE

There are alternatives to placing all elderly people who are unable to care for themselves in nursing homes. The desire to be independent, to live in familiar surroundings, to feel in control of your life, to be with people, pets, and memories is no less strong at 70 than at twenty. Many elderly people can remain in their homes if assistance is available as it is needed, either sporadically or on a continuing basis. In most cases there is no question that a helping hand when needed is far superior to institutionalization. From a purely financial aspect, it is much less expensive to provide assistance to the elderly while they remain in their own residences than to provide 24-hour care in an institution. Furthermore, once you have institutionalized an individual, you nearly always lose whatever benefit that person may have been to society. Old age, even when accompanied by sporadic illness, does not destroy a person's ability to contribute substantially to that society.

Some concerned citizens are organizing services to assist the elderly. A program has been set up in Minneapolis that involves the over-65 person in deciding what services would be most helpful to senior citizens. The services decided upon and implemented were "daily meal deliveries; homemaker services (including bathing, housework, laundry, and maintenance); 24-hour transportation for medical care, shopping, and emergencies; legal assistance; once-a-day telephone reassurance to mitigate concern that one might become isolated and not found if sick; dial-a-friend to bring seniors who have common interests together; and assistance in obtaining health and counseling services."[2] Unfortunately, the Minneapolis type of program is rare and its success depends entirely on volunteer funding. Ideally, these kinds of services, plus others, should be available to the elderly.

Alternatives to nursing home care are used extensively

in other countries. For example, Great Britain, Denmark, and Sweden have earned a reputation for successfully developing ways to care for their aged through programs based on preventive medicine and home care. Americans have yet to achieve a comparable level of care for elderly citizens.

In Great Britain every effort is made to keep older people independent of institutional care as long as possible. Various community care programs are provided, such as hot meals served at centers throughout the country, home nursing and housekeeping services, night attendants and laundry services for the bedridden and infirm, "day hospitals" offering physical and occupational therapy for those who do not need institutional care but do require regular treatment. Transportation to and from day hospitals is provided. Psychogeriatric Assessment Units are in operation in many parts of England "where a patient can be examined by both a geriatric physician and a psychiatrist who then decide whether the patient need enter an institution (a mental hospital or nursing home) or whether, with help, he can manage in the community."[3] Nursing homes and hospitals are a last resort. Services to the elderly are predicated on the belief that an elderly person can, if given the opportunity, contribute greatly to the society in which he lives. The British philosophy seems to be: a society is enriched by interaction with all of its members, not solely its work force. In addition, the special housing needs of the elderly have been met. The units are small, easy to clean, close to shopping, medical centers, and public transportation. Considerations, such as handrails in the bathrooms, wider doorways to accommodate wheelchairs, and ramps rather than stairs have been included.

Denmark also makes every effort to keep the elderly living in their own homes. Services similar to those in Great Britain are provided as well as activities for healthy retired persons at the local level. When illness makes nursing home care absolutely necessary, the Danes are exploring a system of having the nursing home units adjacent to elderly housing units so that the transition from one phase of living to another is not traumatic. Friends, places, and familiar activities are still close by.[4]

Sweden also tries to avoid institutionalization of its elderly citizens through home care services. Its uniqueness is, however, in the model of nursing homes created. Sweden provides apartments for independent living, adjacent to a central service area and close to nursing home facilities. The transition from independent living to total bed care is not disruptive and the elderly move smoothly from one area to another. Optimum activity is encouraged through excellent opportunities for participation in community affairs, for working in the community, and for selling crafts. Physical fitness is encouraged by providing recreational facilities as well as the assistance of trained recreational personnel and physiotherapists. The elderly participate actively in the operation and decision-making policies of their homes.[5]

In the United States we do have all of the services just mentioned, but they are not generally available in one place or to a majority of our older citizens. Like the rest of our medical system, delivery is sporadic and maldistributed. It is ironic that unions strive primarily for earlier retirement for their members but do not use their power to save their retirees from the colossal neglect of the elderly so prevalent in this country.

Under our present system, it is usually very difficult to determine what services are available in a given area for the elderly who do not need a nursing home but do require some professional help. A call to the Public Health Department, the Accredited Nurses' Registry, or the Visiting Nurse Association will help you obtain assistance. Listed below are some questions you may consider:

1. Are nurses available for giving injections, changing dressings, and giving other needed medical attention to the elderly in their own home?
2. Are the services of therapists available either in the patient's own home or at a nearby facility?
3. Is a homemaker service available for them if they are temporarily or permanently incapacitated?

4. Are home health aides available to assist with the personal care?

5. Is a facility close by or close to public transportation that can provide treatment either for acute or chronic conditions on an out-patient basis?

6. Is free ambulance service available if needed?

7. Does their area have a "meals-on-wheels" service where, for a nominal sum, a warm, nutritious meal will be delivered to their residence in the event they are unable to prepare meals?

8. Are group housing plans available where they can live close to others with similar difficulties?

TYPES OF NURSING HOMES

Not all homes for the elderly are nursing homes and it is important to be aware of the different services available at each facility. It is best to choose a home offering the maximum independence that the person is capable of handling. If the older persons can cook their own meals and wish to, a retirement apartment or group residence may be what is needed. However, if nursing care, plus room and board, is necessary, a nursing home may have to be considered. The need for nursing home care may be only temporary while an elderly person is recuperating from hospital treatment or some acute condition. It is important to keep evaluating the condition of the person so that if enough improvement occurs, and he can manage without institutional care, he should be given the opportunity to do so.

Nursing homes are basically of two types, depending on the level of care they provide. Some homes do, however, provide both levels of care. *Residential,* or *intermediate care facilities,* provide a minimum amount of nursing care. They emphasize personal care and social services. The second type, referred to as *skilled nursing facilities,* usually provides 24-hour nursing service for convalescing or chronically ill patients who are unable to care for themselves.

Nursing homes are also categorized by their operating structure. Some are termed nonprofit institutions (which does not mean that they do not make a profit) while others are called profit or business enterprises. One might assume that a nonprofit organization sponsored by a religious or fraternal group would offer a more humane situation in which the elderly could live. Be careful! Each institution must be evaluated on its merits. Make no assumptions of quality where people are engaged in making a profit by providing a service to a weak and essentially powerless group.[6]

LICENSURE AND CERTIFICATION

If you are considering a nursing home, be sure to examine its license. If it is not on display, ask to see it; do not accept the word of the management. In all states, nursing homes must satisfy certain minimum requirements before they are granted a license to operate. Also, nursing homes wishing to qualify for reimbursement under the Medicare program must meet federal regulations. Inspections for this purpose are conducted by HEW. The inspection reports would be very helpful to anyone attempting to choose a nursing home. These reports were not available to the public until Congress passed a law in 1972 requiring HEW to make public both Medicare and Medicaid reports. Unfortunately, the Medicare extracts are available only at the local Social Security office; you may not order them by mail or phone. Most people don't know they are entitled to the information, and those who do must find their way to the Social Security office to obtain them. Consequently, the reports, which are paid for by your tax dollars and which would be very useful, are not readily accessible.[7] To overcome this problem, the National Consumers League developed a manual that offers suggestions for gathering and presenting information from official government inspection records on nursing homes. The League's address is: 1785 Massachusetts Avenue, NW, Washington, D.C., 20036.

In addition to the state and federal certifications, all nursing home administrators are required to be licensed. This license should be current. Do not consider a home in which the administrator does not have a current license.

If an administrator requests it, he can have an inspection by the Joint Commission on Accreditation of Hospitals (JCAH). The JCAH certificate, which was discussed in Chapter Eight, indicates that certain minimum criteria have been met. It is no indication, however, that high quality care is always available. Since it is a voluntary program, an administrator who requests JCAH inspection is usually attempting to provide good care. Unfortunately, less than 10 percent of nursing homes in America have requested and met JCAH standards.[8]

CHOOSING A NURSING HOME

To locate nursing homes available in your area, contact the following sources: local or state Health and Welfare Departments; the district office of the Social Security Administration or Veterans Administration, and the state branches of the American Nursing Home Association and the American Association of Homes for the Aging. Determine which homes provide the type of care needed, and how the elderly person can pay for it. Keep in mind that Medicaid and Medicare funds are often available. Much of this groundwork can be done by telephone. Then, using the checklist on pages 278–282, visit the home and see how it measures up to the suggested criteria. Now see if the home pleases the prospective resident. It is important that the elderly person participate as much as possible in decisions that affect his environment.

A CHECKLIST FOR RATING NURSING HOMES

Carry this checklist when you visit homes. It will help you compare one with another. As a rule of thumb, the best home is the one with the most checks. However, remember that different kinds of homes offer different types of services. You should compare skilled nursing homes with skilled nursing homes and residential homes with residential homes.

If the answer to any of the first four questions is "no," do not use the home.

1. Does the home have a current state license?
2. Does the administrator have a current state license?
3. Does the home meet Medicare and/or Medicaid standards?
4. Does it provide special services such as a specific diet or therapy that the patient needs?

PHYSICAL CONSIDERATIONS

5. Location
   a. Pleasing to the patient?
   b. Convenient for patient's personal doctor?
   c. Convenient for frequent visits?
   d. Near a hospital?
6. Accident Prevention
   a. Well-lighted inside?
   b. Free of hazards underfoot?
   c. Chairs sturdy and not easily tipped?
   d. Warning signs posted around freshly waxed floors?
   e. Handrails in hallways and grab bars in bathrooms?
7. Fire Safety
   a. Meets Federal and/or State codes?
   b. Exits clearly marked and unobstructed?

  c. Written emergency evacuation plan?

  d. Frequent fire drills?

  e. Exit doors not locked on the inside?

  f. Stairways enclosed and doors to stairways kept closed?

8. Bedrooms

  a. Open onto hall?

  b. Window?

  c. No more than four beds per room?

  d. Easy access to each bed?

  e. Drapery for each bed?

  f. Nurse call bell by each bed?

  g. Fresh drinking water at each bed?

  h. At least one comfortable chair per patient?

  i. Reading lights?

  j. Clothes closet and drawers?

  k. Room for a wheelchair to maneuver?

  l. Care used in selecting roommates?

9. Cleanliness

  a. Generally clean, even though it may have a lived-in look?

  b. Free of unpleasant odors?

  c. Incontinent patients given prompt attention?

10. Lobby

  a. Is the atmosphere welcoming?

  b. If also a lounge, is it being used by residents?

  c. Furniture attractive and comfortable?

  d. Plants and flowers?

  e. Certificates and licenses on display?

11. Hallways

  a. Large enough for two wheelchairs to pass with ease?

  b. Hand-grip railings on the sides?

12. Dining Room

  a. Attractive and inviting?

  b. Comfortable chairs and tables?

  c. Easy to move around in?

  d. Tables convenient for those in wheelchairs?

e. Food tasty and attractively served?
f. Meals match posted menu?
g. Those needing help receiving it?

13. Kitchen
   a. Food preparation, dishwashing and garbage areas separated?
   b. Food needing refrigeration not standing on counters?
   c. Kitchen help observe sanitation rules?

14. Activity Rooms
   a. Rooms available for patients' activities?
   b. Equipment (such as games, easels, yarn, kiln, etc.) available?
   c. Residents using equipment?

15. Special Purpose Rooms
   a. Rooms set aside for physical examinations or therapy?
   b. Rooms being used for stated purpose?

16. Isolation Room
   a. At least one bed and bathroom for patients with contagious illness?

17. Toilet Facilities
   a. Convenient to bedrooms?
   b. Easy for a wheelchair patient to use?
   c. Sink?
   d. Nurse call bell?
   e. Hand grips on or near toilets?
   f. Bathtubs and showers with nonslip surfaces?

18. Grounds
   a. Residents can get fresh air?
   b. Ramps to help handicapped?

SERVICES

19. Medical
   a. Physician available in emergency?
   b. Private physician allowed?
   c. Regular medical attention assured?

    d.   Thorough physical immediately before or upon admission?

    e.   Medical records and plan of care kept?

    f.   Patient involved in plans for treatment?

    g.   Other medical services (dentists, optometrists, etc.) available regularly?

    h.   Freedom to purchase medicines outside home?

20. Hospitalization

    a.   Arrangement with nearby hospital for transfer when necessary?

21. Nursing Services

    a.   RN responsible for nursing staff in a skilled nursing home?

    b.   LPN on duty day and night in a skilled nursing home?

    c.   Trained nurses' aides and orderlies on duty in homes providing some nursing care?

22. Physical Therapy

    a.   Specialists in various therapies available when needed?

23. Activities Program

    a.   Individual patient preferences observed?

    b.   Group and individual activities?

    c.   Residents encouraged but not forced to participate?

    d.   Outside trips for those who can go?

    e.   Volunteers from the community work with patients?

24. Religious Observances

    a.   Arrangements made for patient to worship as he pleases?

    b.   Religious observances a matter of choice?

25. Social Services

    a.   Social worker available to help residents and families?

26. Food

    a.   Dietitian plans menus for patients on special diets?

b. Variety from meal to meal?
c. Meals served at normal times?
d. Plenty of time for each meal?
e. Snacks?
f. Food delivered to patients' rooms?
g. Help with eating given when needed?

27. Grooming
a. Barbers and beauticians available for men and women?

ATTITUDES AND ATMOSPHERE

28. General atmosphere warm, pleasant and cheerful?

29. Staff members show interest in and affection for individual patients? Are courteous and respectful? Stop to chat with patients?

30. Administrator courteous and helpful?
a. Knows patients by name?
b. Available to answer questions, hear complaints or discuss problems?

31. Staff members respond quickly to patient calls for assistance?

32. Residents appear alert?
a. Residents are active and involved unless they are very sick?
b. Can decorate their own bedrooms?
c. Can wear their own clothes?
d. Have a chance for self-expression?
e. Can communicate freely without censorship?
f. Can work for themselves if they wish?

33. Visiting hours set for convenience of residents and visitors?

34. Civil rights regulations observed?

35. Visitors and volunteers pleased with home?

Source: Social and Rehabilitation Service, *Nursing Home Care* (Washington, D.C.: U.S. Government Printing Office, 1972).

Visit the home at different and unannounced times. Get a feeling for the general atmosphere. Talk to the residents. Do they appear talkative, alert, and clean? Is there interaction between the home and the community in which it is located?

It is unfortunate that so much research must be done at a time when the elderly themselves are often unable to cope with the task, either mentally or physically. Those left with the responsibility of making the decision may be unable or unwilling to take the time to examine the situation carefully. Therefore, disgraceful conditions are present and many helpless persons suffer.

If you have a complaint about a nursing home, for whatever reason, HEW[9] suggests you report it to:

1. The nursing home administrator.

2. Your local Social Security District office. It functions as a clearing house for complaints about all nursing homes, whether or not they receive government funds.

3. The patient's caseworker or the county welfare office if the patient is covered by Medicaid.

4. The State Medicaid Agency if the home is certified for that program.

5. The State Health Department and the State licensing authority.

6. The nursing home ombudsman if such an office has been established in your community.

7. The State board responsible for licensing nursing home administrators. (Get address information from the welfare department.)

8. Your Congressman and Senators. (Address Congressmen at House of Representatives, Washington, D.C. 20515; Senators at United States Senate, Washington, D.C. 20510.)

9. Your State and local elected representatives.

10. The Joint Commission on Accreditation of Hospitals (645 North Michigan Avenue, Chicago, Illinois 60611) if the home has a JCAH certificate.

11. The American Nursing Home Association (Suite 607, 1025 Connecticut Avenue, NW, Washington, D.C. 20036) if the home is a member.

12. The American Association of Homes for the Aging (529 Fourteenth Street, NW, Washington, D.C. 20004) if the home is a member.

13. The American College of Nursing Home Administrators (Suite 409, The Eig Building, 8641 Colesville Road, Silver Spring, Maryland 20910) if the administrator is a member.

14. Your local Better Business Bureau and Chamber of Commerce.

15. Your local hospital association and medical society.

16. A reputable lawyer or legal aid society.

PROBLEMS IN THE NURSING CARE FIELD

Evidence of our neglect of the elderly pervades our society. Although there are many good programs, excellent nursing homes, and dedicated people working in this field, our overall efforts to care for elderly citizens are grossly inadequate.

Nursing home care providers are in business and their biggest customer is the U.S. Government. Most patients' bills are paid either wholly or partially by either Medicaid or Medicare. Medicaid now pays about 60 percent of the nation's nearly $4 billion nursing home bill, and Medicare pays another 7 percent. Most nursing homes are reimbursed for patient care on a flat rate basis where the home receives so much a day for each patient; the other method of payment is the cost plus basis, where the home is reimbursed for its costs, plus a reasonable profit. The flat rate system is the most profitable for the nursing home operator because he receives the same amount of money regardless of the kind of care that he provides for the patient. The less care provided, the higher the profit. In such payment situations, healthy patients who require very little care, are very desirable patients. The charge has been made that many of the patients in nursing homes are so healthy that they should not be there at all. In fact, various studies have shown that from 30 to 80 percent of patients in nursing homes do not require skilled nursing care and could be cared for in other, less expensive ways.[10]

There are various ways to make increased profits and some operators use them. Unnecessary services are provided on a widespread basis. "Kickback" arrangements between suppliers such as pharmacies, physical therapists, and nursing home operators occur. Substantial evidence exists that many physicians are engaging in "gang visits" to nursing home and hospital patients. Under this practice, a physician may see as many as thirty, forty, and fifty patients in a day in the same facility—regardless of whether the visit is medically necessary or whether any service is actually rendered.[11] Of course, the government program (Medicaid or Medicare) is charged the same fee for each patient as for a regular individual visit. There is concern also that physicians investing in nursing homes may be more interested in admitting patients to the homes than in helping to secure the necessary services needed for them to remain independent.

Chain operators in the nursing home field are purchasing stock in hospital supply and pharmaceutical supply houses. This could involve the nursing home in the practice of purchasing goods at an inflated price, from companies in which they take a share of the profits.[12] There is apparently no limit to the number of schemes sharp operators can devise to increase their profits. Emphasis on profits can have two important effects: 1) the elderly may not receive the care they need, and 2) the public is defrauded because tax dollars are misappropriated. Nursing homes can be a very lucrative business. The growth of the industry has been impressive and the lure of profit from government-guaranteed payments brought a host of less dedicated operators into the field. Some nursing home operators are making a substantial profit at the expense of the taxpayer and the elderly.

The book *Tender Loving Greed* by Mary Mendelson, illustrates the seemingly endless ways by which nursing home operators are able to circumvent government regulations and take advantage of legal loopholes to increase their profits. There are government inspections and regulations but no legislation is effective unless it is enforced. According to the evidence collected by Mrs. Mendelson and the 93rd Congress, there is gross nonenforcement at all levels of government of regulations governing nursing homes.[13]

The abuses of the Medicare and Medicaid programs are partially the result of politics in health: the health care establishment fought vigorously against both programs. The result was a program whereby Washington poured our money into the health industry with a minimum of control on how it was to be used. The government took on the responsibility of paying for care of the sick and the poor, but not the responsibility to see that proper care was delivered. That was left in the hands of the providers. On paper, elaborate regulations governing Medicare and Medicaid reimbursement exist but, without enforcement, they are meaningless.

Since government has taken the responsibility of supposedly regulating nursing homes, it is accountable for the care administered in those homes. In many instances it has failed. Since we elect the government, we have failed. Only our concerned efforts will effect a change.[14]

When we mention the poor care administered in nursing homes, the usual solutions are "we need more money" and "we need more laws." More money will simply mean more abuses. As for more laws, there is overwhelming evidence that the laws we now have are not being enforced. The Senate Special Committee on Aging reports many examples of "cruelty, negligence, danger from fires, food poisoning, virulent infections, lack of human dignity, callousness and unnecessary regimentation."[15] After sixteen months of studying nursing homes, a Congressman stated "we have turned over the sickest, the most helpless and the most vulnerable patient group in the medical care system to the most loosely controlled and least responsible faction of that system."[16]

Who has assumed the responsibility for assuring the elderly of adequate institutional care when needed? We have seen that the government has not. Nursing home owners have not. Nor has the medical profession taken a leadership role in this area. Older people are dependent on others to make decisions for them when they are ill and unable to control their environment. Often, their families feel guilty because they cannot or do not care for the elderly themselves. In this country, many people fear the financial burden of providing appropriate care for their elderly. Many close their eyes to conditions in nursing homes, convincing themselves that it is the only alternative they have for providing care for an aging parent, relative, or friend. Not until a significant segment of our population shows concern for the neglected older persons in America will any substantial improvement occur. The informed and influential citizens of a society have a responsibility to protect the weak. In this country, we need to look critically at our attitudes toward the elderly. Only popular demand will initiate a course of action that will bring the level of care available in the United States up to the level currently available in many other nations.

ENDNOTES

1. "Nursing Home Care in the United States: Failure in Public Policy," *Congressional Record,* 93rd Congress, second session, Vol. 120, November 22, 1974.
2. *American Medical News* 17; September 9, 1974, 11.
3. Clair Townsend, *Old Age, The Last Segregation* (New York: Grossman Publishers, 1971), p. 149.
4. Ibid., pp. 151–153.
5. Ibid., pp. 153–155.
6. "How to Choose a Nursing Home," *Changing Times* 28; January, 1974, 35–36.

7. Mary A. Mendelson, *Tender Loving Greed* (New York: Alfred A. Knopf, 1974), pp. 223–224.
8. *Changing Times* 28, 37.
9. Social and Rehabilitation Service, *Nursing Home Care* (Washington, D.C.: U.S. Government Printing Office, 1972).
10. Mendelson, *Tender Loving Greed,* pp. 39–41.
11. U.S. Congress, *Hearings* on Medicare and Medicaid, 91st Congress, 2nd session, 1969, p. 34.
12. Mendelson, *Tender Loving Greed,* p. 26.
13. Mendelson, *Tender Loving Greed,* p. 29.
14. Ibid., p. 38.
15. Nursing Home Care in the U.S., *Congressional Record* 120, November 22, 1974.
16. Townsend, *Old Age, The Last Segregation,* p. 21.

Chapter Thirteen

Voluntary Health Agencies at Work

Most voluntary health agencies began when a small group of people who had been affected by a given problem or disease decided to try and help others with similar problems. The group usually calls in physicians for needed medical advice. As word of the group spreads, more join to help the cause. The needs of the community are more accurately assessed, money is solicited, and a program is soon under way. After a charter and constitution are established, an office is usually set up and persons from the community serve on various committees or on the Board of Directors. The Board has the legal responsibility for the actions of the agency; it makes policy decisions and may appoint a paid director who is responsible for the smooth functioning of the agency.

At the present time, there are about 70 national voluntary agencies in the health field. Hanlon[1] estimates that some 100,000 separate voluntary or disease-related agencies have been established in the United States, which are supported by millions of volunteers.

Voluntary health agencies are quite different from public health departments (which are dealt with in some detail in the next chapter). The most notable difference is that voluntary health agencies are not responsible to elected officials or civil service employees, nor does tax money constitute a major source of funding. Some voluntary groups do, however, obtain government grants to conduct specific programs.

Voluntary health agencies have several important functions.[2] To begin with, they provide assistance to persons who do not qualify for help through other programs. An example would be the loan of respiratory therapy equipment for a baby with multiple birth defects. Because they enjoy a freedom and flexibility not found in other structures, voluntary agencies can develop demonstration projects and experiment with new ideas. When these projects prove fruitful, they are usually taken over by tax-supported agencies and the voluntary agency is able to experiment with new programs. Another important function that voluntary agencies can assume is the role of speaking on behalf of the community on health-related issues such as air pollution controls, revenue sharing, or the diversion of gas tax money for the development of mass transit. Other functions include broad community health education campaigns and the support of medical research and professional education.

To illustrate the services being performed by the many voluntary agencies in this nation, we will examine the service programs of three local chapters in a metropolitan community of approximately one million people. The agencies: The American Lung Association, The American Cancer Society, and the American Heart Association. The programs described are typical of those in comparable urban areas throughout the United States. *No attempt has been made to include all the activities of these agencies.* The intent, rather, is to provide some insight into the many ways in which voluntary agencies assist people to solve their health problems.

THE AMERICAN LUNG ASSOCIATION (CHRISTMAS SEAL ORGANIZATION)

The American Lung Association is actually the granddaddy of voluntary health organizations in the United States. This group had its beginnings in Philadelphia in 1892, as the

Pennsylvania Society for the Prevention of Tuberculosis. It was a somewhat unique gathering, because doctors formed an alliance with the lay public, something unheard of prior to this time.[3] Lawrence F. Flick, who had recovered from tuberculosis himself, is credited with this unconventional approach to a health problem. Because of this, he has been referred to as the father of the voluntary health agency movement.

In 1904, the National Association for the Study and Prevention of Tuberculosis was formed. In 1918, the name was changed to the National Tuberculosis Association. As it became obvious that tuberculosis, although not beaten, was causing fewer deaths each year,* the organization widened its horizons to include other respiratory diseases (such as chronic bronchitis and emphysema) and air pollution. As a result of this change in emphasis, in 1968 the official name became the National Tuberculosis and Respiratory Disease Association.[4] As tuberculosis deaths continued to decline (currently 4,000 each year), the organization, in 1973, became the American Lung Association.

Moving up to the present, what happens daily at the over 1,300 chapters (affiliates) of the Lung Association around the United States? The phone is constantly ringing because someone needs help. About half the calls to the local Associations are from persons who have a health problem and don't know where to turn. Other calls relate directly to some respiratory problem. The following questions are common: "I have just moved into town; where can I get a free chest x-ray or skin test?" "I have emphysema. What section of town has the least air pollution?" "My doctor told me I had to use a breathing machine. I can't afford it. Can you help me?" The local Associations do not provide cash assistance or direct patient care; they provide education and referral services. The person making the last call would be referred to an appropriate clinic where help could be provided.

---

* Although there are fewer deaths, 30,000 persons are found to have new active cases of tuberculosis each year in the United States.[5]

A call may come in from a teacher who needs materials and audiovisual aids to help in presenting the health consequences of smoking to her class. The local Association can send out up-to-date pamphlets and information, as well as recent films and filmstrips. A social or professional group may call and ask for a speaker to address their meeting on a variety of topics related to respiratory diseases. If a general group wants an overview of the problem of tuberculosis today, one of the trained staff may make the presentation. If a professional group wishes to learn more about a technical aspect of treatment—chemotherapy, for example—a volunteer physician member will usually make the presentation.

The local Association also sponsors physical conditioning classes designed to improve the breathing of asthmatic children. These children, ages six to twelve, who are virtually incapacitated because of asthma, are referred to the program by their physicians. Classes of not more than twelve meet once a week for 90 minutes. For the first hour, the children are given special exercises to improve their breathing; during the last 30 minutes, they receive swimming pool therapy. Because of their severe breathing problems, these children have not been able to enjoy the water the way most children do. The parents are encouraged to see that the children continue the exercises at home. The local Association aranged for transportation for one child whose parents could not afford to send him to the clinic. One woman drives a round trip of about 240 miles once a week so that her son can participate in the eight-week program. When one class terminates, another begins. The results of this program with children are so encouraging that a similar program is planned for the ever-increasing number of adults suffering from emphysema.

The double-barred cross ‡ is the symbol of the American Lung Association. Most of its funds are raised through the well-known Christmas Seal Campaign.

The aim of the American Lung Association is the prevention and control of the various lung diseases in the United States, which affect some 47 million persons.[6] (See box.)

Emphysema sufferers in the U.S. (all figures estimated)	1,300,000
People with asthma	6,031,000
People with chronic bronchitis	6,526,000
People with tuberculosis on health department registers	215,000
People with any chronic respiratory condition	47,000,000

The American Lung Association hopes to carry out its purpose in three major ways: "improving the care of patients who have lung diseases; preventing damage to patients and non-patients alike through control of such things as polluted air and smoking; and advancing the knowledge and expertness of the professional people who give lung disease care."[7]

THE AMERICAN CANCER SOCIETY

The American Society for the Control of Cancer was formed in 1913 by a group of concerned doctors and laymen. In 1945, the organization was enlarged to include businessmen, physicians, and scientists, and it greatly expanded its programs and activities. At the same time, it changed its name to the American Cancer Society.

Cancer affects many Americans. In a recent year, about 365,000 Americans died of cancer. It will, over the years, strike two out of every three families. On the hopeful side, some kinds of cancer—such as skin cancer and most lung cancers—can be prevented. Of every six who develop cancer, two will be saved; another one out of six *could* be saved if proper treatment were received in time. This means that 111,000 cancer patients in the United States died needlessly in the past year; they could have been saved had they received earlier treatment.[8]

The phone also rings constantly at the local chapter of the Cancer Society, and people are requesting help. Common questions are "I want to have a cancer checkup; when can you do it?" "I'm sure I've got cancer because I coughed a lot early this morning. Can you tell me if I have cancer?" The Cancer Society does not provide this service, so the caller is usually referred to his own doctor or to other community resources for an examination. The Cancer Society is, however, able to provide considerable help for many people.

Dressings

Mrs. M., 47 years old, is suffering from breast cancer and has profuse draining from her lesion. Since Mrs. M. cannot afford the $60 to $80 a month for the dressings that she requires to care for her problem properly, the Cancer Society provides her with dressings free of charge. The dressings are made up by volunteers of the Order of the Eastern Star and given to the Cancer Society for distribution to needy patients. The Cancer Society has established "Cancer Cupboards" at local fire stations where Mrs. M. and others like her pick up their dressings. Also available at the "cupboards" are absorbent bed pads for incontinent patients (those who do not have bladder and/or bowel control).

Assistive devices

Mr. P. is a 67-year-old terminal lung cancer patient. Because of his condition, when he lies on an ordinary bed, breathing becomes very difficult, almost impossible. To help him with this problem, the Cancer Society pays for the rental of a hospital bed in his home. Mr. P. can adjust this bed so that he is able to breathe without difficulty. The Cancer Society also rents other devices when needed, such as wheel-chairs and over-the-bed tables for needy patients.

Reach to recovery

Mary L. noticed a lump on her breast one day when she was taking a shower. She thought about cancer but dismissed the idea as being silly. She thought: "I'm only 41, with two children in high school. I can't possibly have cancer." The lump didn't go away; in fact, it seemed to be getting larger. When Mary finally decided to ask her husband about it, he was quite alarmed. The Cancer Society had sponsored an education program at the telephone company, where he worked, and he recalled that a lump on the breast should be examined by a physician immediately. Mary called her doctor the next morning and was told to come into his office that same afternoon. A biopsy was done and her doctor decided that a *radical mastectomy* (breast removal) would have to be done.

This operation involves not only the breast but also the removal of lymphatic tissue in the inner portion of the upper arm on the infected side. This means that it takes considerable retraining to get the full use of that arm. After the operation, The Cancer Society sent a woman volunteer out to help Mary with her exercises and to encourage her to persevere until she had complete mobility in her arm. Mary was feeling sorry for herself and didn't think the volunteer was sympathetic enough. In the course of the conversation, Mary learned that the volunteer had had the same operation four years ago. Mary looked at her again and had to admit that she couldn't tell that the volunteer was wearing a breast *prosthesis* (artificial breast). Mary's spirits were lifted considerably and she began to think more positively.

Who can better understand the mental and physical trauma experienced by a mastectomy patient than one who has had a similar experience? The Cancer Society routinely assigns volunteers on this basis and finds that they work very effectively with all types of cancer surgery patients.

Freewheelers

Mr. K. is 69 years old and has lung cancer. He lives alone and is not able to drive himself, nor can he afford to take a taxi to the hospital for the cobalt treatment he needs. (A series of cobalt treatments may involve five visits a week for six weeks.) The Cancer Society has a group of volunteers who drive cancer patients to their doctor or to the hospital for their cobalt treatments. This group, called the "Freewheelers," has over 180 volunteers in one city, who provide the personalized service.

The volunteers

The volunteers who provide the above services are persons who feel a deep sense of responsibility toward others. They may be persons who have recovered from cancer themselves, or may have been affected because someone in their family had cancer. In any case, the thousands of volunteers across the country are an invaluable aid to cancer sufferers wherever they are.

Other programs

So far, we have been concentrating on patient and community services which, although very important, are only one part of the American Cancer Society's program. The largest portion of funds is allocated to research.[9]

Twenty-nine percent (over $26 million) provides for research to find better treatment measures and to discover more about the cause of many types of cancer. Other portions of the program include public education (17.2 percent of funds), professional education—for doctors and dentists (10.5 percent), and patient and community services which we have already discussed (22 percent). Fund raising and management requires 21.3 percent of the annual budget.

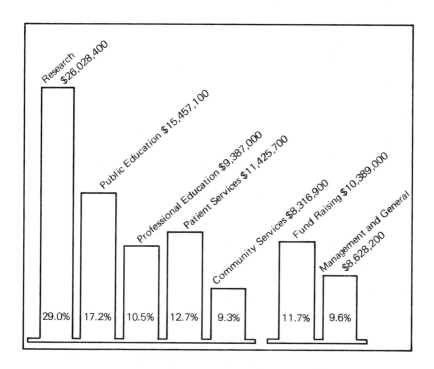

FIGURE 13.1 How ACS funds are allocated (based on total 1973–74 budget $89,633,000). Courtesy of the American Cancer Society.

The American Cancer Society raises its funds through an independent drive culminating in April, which the President of the United States has designated as "Cancer Control Month."

THE AMERICAN HEART ASSOCIATION

The American Heart Association was formed in 1924. Up until 1948, however, it was an organization of physicians spending most of their time with matters of professional concern such as more accurate blood pressure testing and the proper readings of electrocardiograms. Its main office was in the headquarters of the National Tuberculosis Association, which kindly donated the space and also contributed $10,000 to the Heart Association's budget. (This amount was sometimes as much as two-thirds of the Heart Association's budget.) In 1946, Doctor David D. Rutstein* persuaded the faltering organization to become a voluntary organization and admit the public into partnership. In 1948, Ralph Edwards put the weight of his radio program, *Truth or Consequences,* behind the professional efforts of the Heart Association. He developed "The Walking Man" Contest. Footsteps of the walking man were broadcast along with other clues each week. Fans could enter the contest to try to identify the footsteps by mailing in contributions to the Heart Association and including twenty-five words about the heart. The "walking man" turned out to be the late comedian, Jack Benny, and the Heart Association was the recipient of $1,570,000—a figure practically unheard of in those days![10] From that day, the Heart Association has been a healthy organization and has made vital contributions to research, public health education, professional education and training, and community service. A recent annual report[11] indicates a budget of over $54,000,000 spent on the fight against heart disease.

Work classification unit

Mr. M., age 55, six feet tall, and powerfully built, came into the Work Classification Unit of the Heart Association and said in a threatening manner, "You guys are going to write a good report about me!" After questioning, it was learned that he had suffered a heart attack a few months earlier and had been hospitalized. After returning home from

* Dr. Rutstein is now head of the Department of Preventive Medicine at Harvard and author of *The Coming Revolution in Medicine* and *Blueprint for Medical Care,* published by M.I.T. Press.

the hospital, he had another attack. Through perseverance and determination, he had gradually built himself up to the point where he could do one day's work. His company, however, would not let him come back to his job as a structural steelworker until he had a note from his doctor that he was healthy enough to do it. His doctor referred him to the Work Classification Unit. Probably realizing that he was not as healthy as he looked, he tried to bluff the staff at the Unit by saying, "I'm strong as a bull."

After doing a complete medical analysis on him which included, among other things, a chest x-ray, an electrocardiogram, and a Masters Two-Step Test, as well as a psychological examination, the Unit's personnel discussed his case. The Work Classification Unit calculates the calorie expenditure per minute required for hundreds of jobs. In his old job, Mr. M. needed to expend eight to ten calories per minute. Analysis of his condition indicated that he could not perform at that level, but could do a sitting job which expended about two calories per minute. He was referred to the Department of Rehabilitation for assistance. After training, he was able to set up a small appliance repair business, which did not require an energy expenditure of more than two calories per minute.

The goal of the Work Classification Unit is to help industry maintain cardiacs in gainful employment. Patients are usually referred to the Unit by their own physicians for evaluation and counseling. Through this program, hundreds have been helped to return to the work force and to continue to provide for their families.

Penicillin

Mrs. J. has a rheumatic heart condition which requires her to take a penicillin tablet every day. Depending on where she does her shopping, a month's supply normally costs from $5.00 to $8.00 which she can't really afford. Through the Heart Association and a pharmaceutical company, she is able to buy her penicillin at cost (90 cents for a month's supply). It is estimated that heart patients in this one metropolitan community alone have been saved over $1,000,000 on drug costs since the inception of this program.

"Dial-a-Dietitian"

Mary R. dialed a certain number and posed this question: "I am on a very low sodium diet; my doctor told me not to eat canned vegetables. Can I eat canned fruit?" *Answer:* Yes, as long as you don't have to lose weight. Canned fruit does not contain salt. Another call came in: "Can I eat ice milk on my low cholesterol diet?" *Answer:* Yes, ice milk may be used in moderation as long as you don't have to lose weight. Ice cream contains too much cholesterol and saturated fat. Another question: "How many calories are there in a piece of apple pie?" *Answer:* This depends on how the pie is made and how large a piece one has in mind. An average piece of apple pie contains 350 calories. Another question: "Can I use nondairy powdered creamer on a low saturated fat diet?" *Answer:* No, cocoanut oil, which is saturated, is used in most nondairy creamers. There are, however, a few polyunsaturated liquid creamers that are acceptable.

The service that answers these questions, and thousands like them each year, is "Dial-a-Dietitian." It is part of the Heart Association's service to those in the community who need nutritional information. The service is a cooperative venture involving the Heart Association and volunteer registered dietitians. When Mary phoned in her question, it was written down along with her name and phone number. She was told that she would receive the information from a registered dietitian. The question was then given to a dietitian of the Heart Association's Dial-a-Dietitian Committee who, if necessary, researched the question and then called Mary with a full explanation. Many heart patients are placed on a strict diet without adequate explanation. They may attempt to stay on the diet, but often get bored or confused, and really need some help and suggestions about what they can eat. Many of these patients "dial-a-dietitian" for assistance.

Calls sometimes come in which are medical questions: "I have a pain in my stomach. Do you think I need an ulcer diet?" or, "I think I have hypoglycemia. Please send me a diet." Persons asking such questions are referred to their personal physician.

Some questions are quite novel. For example, "Is it true that ginger under a horse's tail will make it run faster?" Answer: "Yes, but it is not recommended." At a time when you are being bombarded with information about food, and not all of it factual, it is very helpful to have a number to call where you are assured of competent nutritional advice. "Dial-a-Dietitian" is operating in many cities throughout the United States. Look in the telephone directory, or call your local Heart Association or Dietetic Association for the number in your area.

Heart patient project

Jim H. was 49 years old and happily married, with two children in high school. He worked as a car salesman and was quite successful in this competitive field. One afternoon, on a particularly busy day, as Jim was hurrying into a meeting, he had a pressing, burning sensation in his chest. He also experienced a feeling of impending doom. He stopped and sat down on a nearby chair. His right shoulder and arm felt strangely heavy and uncomfortable. Then he had the feeling that a steel band was being tightened around his chest; the pain was quite severe. It became very difficult—almost impossible—for him to get his breath, and then he lost consciousness. He woke up on his way to the hospital, but had no desire to move. Jim had just had a heart attack.

A heart attack victim needs special attention. Apart from medical care, he should have extensive counseling to help him adjust to a new way of life, necessitated by his weakened condition. If he cannot return to his old job, he also needs rehabilitative advice, and perhaps retraining, so that he may more easily return to the work force. Busy physicians do not have the time or the facilities to provide such comprehensive follow-up.

With Jim's consent, his physician referred him to the Heart Patient Project at a local hospital, where a team approach is being used to handle not only the medical aspects of treatment but also the nonmedical factors affecting the patient and his family.[12] After the fear of death had subsided, Jim was suffering from the following anxieties, which are typical of heart attack victims: Will I be able to go back to my old job? If not, how will I care for my family? How will my condition affect my sexual relationship with my wife? Will my family look on me as a burden?

Jim's family also had anxieties, such as: How should we react to him when he returns from the hospital? How can we keep him happy? Will he have another attack?

The director of the Heart Patient Project, who is a professional staff member of the local Heart Association, talked to Jim and his wife and explained the project and services offered. An evaluation was made regarding possible problems of convalescence and his return to work. The staff nurse later visited Jim's home to understand better the attitudes of the family and see if there were any physical limitations, such as stairs, which might slow Jim's progress when he returned home.

The project team consisted of the director of the project, the referring physician, the staff nurse, and a public health nurse who served as liaison between Jim and the project team. She listened to complaints and checked to see that his drug, diet, and exercise regime was being followed. The director coordinated the team, did a vocational survey, and discussed Jim's problem with his employer, explaining the implications of his heart condition. The project team reviewed Jim's case and agreed upon his outlook for recovery. Then the director and the public health nurse followed up on his progress. Jim's condition would not allow him to return to his old job because it involved too much stress. He was referred to the state Department of Rehabilitation, where he was assigned to a counselor who took his background and medical limitations into consideration in helping him to secure different work. Since Jim was familiar with accounting procedures and was interested in this type of work, he was able to undergo short-term training as a bookkeeper. After this training, his rehabilitation counselor helped him secure a position as a timekeeper and part-time bookkeeper with a small construction company.

The public health nurse maintained contact with Jim's family and was able to answer questions and provide reassurance on his recovery. The project team goes over Jim's case every week, reviewing the medical aspects, the home situation, and his vocational adjustment.

Thus, the Heart Patient Project coordinates a smooth transition for Jim from an acute heart attack through to rehabilitation. It keeps the family informed of his progress and offers suggestions for facilitating his return home from the hospital. Jim's personal physician is also kept up to date on Jim's condition and later Jim will return to him for periodic evaluation.

Information and referral service

The phone rings and someone says: "I had a heart attack two years ago. I think I'm all right now. What can I do?" Another question: "My doctor says that my wife needs surgery at the Mayo Clinic. Who will pay for it?" Another: A very obese young woman called to ask for help. Apparently, she would gorge herself with food, induce vomiting, and then gorge herself again. (She was referred for professional help.)

Most of the calls relate to heart disease, either that of the caller or a member of his family. The Heart Asociation attempts to provide help or to suggest where help may be found.

There are many frustrations at the Heart Association. As more people become more educated about the seriousness of heart disease* more are asking for assistance. The Heart Association cannot possibly help everyone, since it operates on a limited budget. Some callers, in their exasperation, say: "If you can't do that for me, what *can* you do?" One solution which would help many people would be a mass screening approach, where those interested could receive an accurate assessment of their state of health. At the present time, some health agencies provide limited free screening for such diseases as tuberculosis, glaucoma, and diabetes.

In addition to education and community service, the American Heart Association, in the year 1973 to 1974, spent 31 percent of its budget (over $16 million) on research (see Table 13.1). This makes it the largest nongovernment source of cardiovascular research in the world. Over the past twenty-five years, research expenditures by the American Heart Association have totaled over $212 million. Money for the work of the Association is raised through the Heart Fund Campaign. Fund raising costs run about 14 percent.

TABLE 13.1   How the Heart Dollar Was Spent 1973–1974

Research	$17,637,327	30.0%
Public Health Education	8,255,654	14.0
Professional Education and Training	7,964,737	13.6
Community Services	9,931,971	16.9
Fund Raising	8,190,416	13.9
Management and General	6,804,421	11.6
	58,784,526	100.0%

Source: American Heart Association, reprinted with permission.

---

* Heart disease is the number one killer in the United States today, accounting for about 53 percent of all deaths.

WHAT CAN VOLUNTARY HEALTH AGENCIES DO FOR YOU?

Voluntary agencies can provide free up-to-date information about a given disease and assistance with solving a problem. For example, if you are concerned about diet and heart disease, call your local Heart Association; they will be happy to send you suggestions for a diet which will help to minimize your chances of heart disease. They can also provide you with a list of the risk factors associated with heart disease so that you may, if you wish, change some of your own risk factors. Voluntary health agencies also provide excellent films, filmstrips, and speakers on request.

Voluntary agencies also give you a chance to help others. This may sound trite, but millions have experienced the personal satisfaction of helping their fellow man in time of need. The emphasis on material possessions and money and the growing isolation and indifference of people in the cities have taken away many opportunities to help others. Through one of your local voluntary agencies, you can share one of the most precious commodities you have to offer: your time.

FUNDS

Voluntary health agencies are not supported by your tax dollar. They raise money in a variety of ways: membership dues, public donations, and bequests from wealthy individuals. The oldest and the best-known approach is the Tuberculosis Christmas Seal Campaign. This program proved so successful for tuberculosis that, in 1934, it was adopted by the National Society for Crippled Children as the Easter Seal Campaign. The March of Dimes, associated with Franklin D. Roosevelt (himself a victim of polio), is another very successful approach. Money from the March of Dimes goes to support the National Foundation-March of Dimes.

With the increasing involvement of government in health care programs, voluntary health agencies face a serious dilemma. A taxpayer may well ask: "Why should I continue to contribute to the support of voluntary health agencies when an increasing portion of my tax dollar is already supporting health-related services and programs?" If many people feel this way, contributions to voluntary agencies will shrink and government involvement will have to increase. Some see this as a dangerous trend.[13]

ENDNOTES

1. John J. Hanlon, *Public Health Administration and Practice* (St. Louis: The C. V. Mosby Company, 1974), p. 310.
2. Jack E. Damson, *Charitable Organizations—Right On or Rip Off?* Unpublished material, June 25, 1974.
3. Richard Carter, *The Gentle Legions* (Garden City, N.Y.: Doubleday & Company, Inc., 1961), p. 63.
4. National Tuberculosis and Respiratory Disease Association, *NTRDA: The Facts* (New York, 1968), p. 2.
5. "Recommendation of the Public Health Service Advisory Committee on Immunization Practices, BCG Vaccines," *Morbidity and Mortality* 24; February 22, 1975, 69.
6. American Lung Association, *Annual Report, 1973–1974* (New York, 1974), p. 2.
7. Ibid.
8. American Cancer Society, *1975 Cancer Facts and Figures* (New York, 1974), pp. 3–4.
9. Ibid., p. 29.
10. Carter, *The Gentle Legions,* pp. 172–177.
11. American Heart Association, *Focus—The Future* (New York, 1974).
12. San Diego County Heart Association, *Heart Patient Project . . . A Pilot Demonstration* (San Diego, 1969).
13. Damson, *Charitable Organizations.*

Chapter Fourteen

The Public
Health
Department

Despite the fact that many of its activities go unnoticed, the public health department assumes a very important role in providing a better environment for citizens within its jurisdiction. In this chapter, we will examine the relationship of the State Health Department with local health departments, and look at examples of services provided at both levels.

THE STATE HEALTH
DEPARTMENT

Each state health department has the legal responsibility for the health of the people within its jurisdiction. The legal requirements are established by the state legislature and usually written (or codified) in the health and safety code of the state. Because of the immensity of carrying out this task, the State Health Department delegates many of its responsibilities to individual counties and cities throughout the state. This allows for more flexibility and ensures that local health problems can be taken care of quickly, without authorization from the state level. The State Health Department rarely provides direct personal services to the public. but does provide many services to the county and city health departments. These services include research and

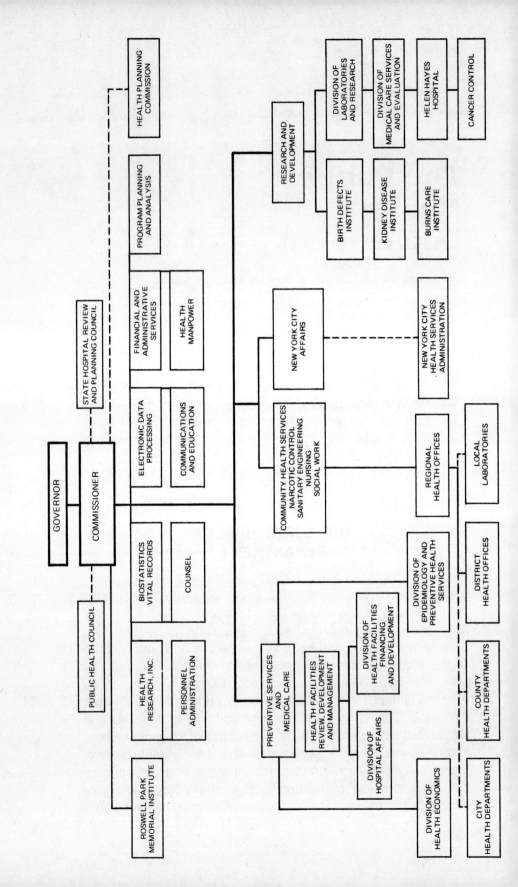

FIGURE 14.1 New York State Department of Health. Source: New York State Department of Health

special investigative studies, and provision of expensive equipment needed for sensitive assessment such as in monitoring air pollution, which is usually too expensive for the local health departments. It also provides consultation and advice. For example, in a recent year, certain mountain areas in one state had a particularly heavy snowfall. When this snow melted during the spring and early summer, many areas of the state had water pooling where it had never been before. This stagnant water provided a breeding ground for mosquitoes which can transmit encephalitis. On request from the local health departments, the State Health Department provided trained persons to make tests and provided advice and guidance on the best approach to the problem. As a result of this cooperation between state and local governments, very few cases of encephalitis developed.

Generally, the requirements of the State Health Department are written into law in such a way that local public health departments have considerable flexibility in implementing them. This does not, however, always occur. For example, a state law that requires that all children (except those whose parents have religious objections) be immunized for a given disease prior to their entry into school leaves little room for interpretation. It must be obeyed!

Figure 14.1 shows the organization and New York State's Health Department. Note the scope of its activities.

LOCAL PUBLIC HEALTH DEPARTMENTS

The first health departments in the United States were in the New England area in the 1860s. They were usually established in response to some sort of a crisis or epidemic. These early health departments concentrated on sanitation because at that time it was just about all they knew anything about. There were no antibiotics or immunization programs (Koch's now famous postulates were not established until 1881, and Pasteur's anti-rabies vaccine did not appear until four years later). Traditionally, most health departments have been primarily concerned with prevention, rather than treatment, of disease. This role is changing and some health departments are now providing treatment. In a few cities, "free clinics"* are a part of the health department function.

Structure

A primary health center is generally located in the downtown area of a city. Secondary health centers are located throughout the district to make services more accessible to the public.

Figure 14.2. depicts the organization of a local (county) public health department. In this local public health department, approximately 25 percent of the personnel are clerical; the rest are professional and technical staff, and include the following:[1]

Administrative Assistant
Air Pollution Chemists
Air Pollution Engineers
Clinical Psychologist
Communicable Disease Investigators
Dairy Inspectors
Epidemiologist
Executive Assistant
Health Educators
Health Information Specialist
Industrial Hygienist
Medical Social Workers
Microbiologists
Milk Technician
Nutritionist
Occupational Therapists
Physical Therapists
Physicians
Psychiatric Social Workers
Public Health Analyst
Public Health Engineer
Public Health Nurses
Registered Nurses
Sanitarians
Vector Controlment
Vector Ecologist
Veterinarian
Virologists
X-ray Technicians

* Free clinics are discussed briefly in Chapter Fifteen.

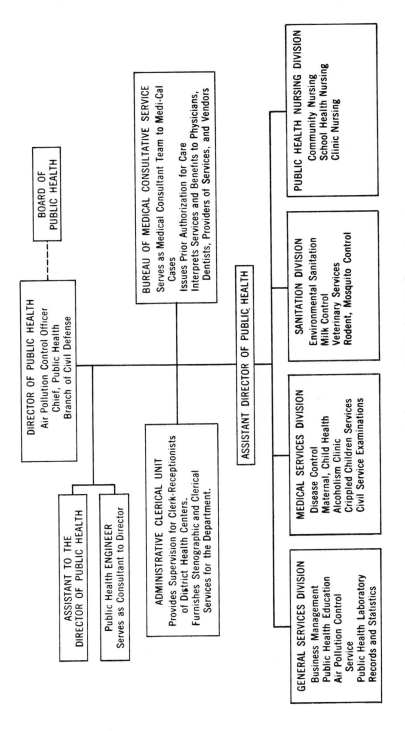

FIGURE 14.2 A County Public Health Department

Funds

Since the public health department is a tax-supported agency, fees are not charged for basic services. Fees are charged, however, for the following:

1. Permits to operate health-regulated businesses (restaurants, foodstores).
2. Certified copies of birth and death records.
3. Special public health services.
4. School nurses for some school districts.
5. Certain public health nursing visits.

The above, and certain other services, help to bring in approximately 50 percent of the annual budget for a local public health department. Approximately 40 percent comes from local property taxes and 10 percent from the State Health Department. To be eligible for the state contribution, the county health departments have to provide services covering specific areas. In California, these include environmental sanitation, maternal and child health, public health nursing, public health education, laboratory services, vital statistics, chronic disease, nutrition, occupational health, family planning, and social work. The local health department usually provides the State Health Department with an annual report providing information about these services.

We will examine the public health department of a metropolitan community of approximately one million people. Services offered by other public health departments may vary somewhat, but these examples will provide you with some insight into the scope of activities undertaken by local public health departments around the nation.

FAMILY PLANNING

Mrs. J. is 23 and the mother of four children. She has more than enough to do to look after them and certainly does not want any more. None of her children have been "planned." She had gone to the Health Department's prenatal clinic during her last two pregnancies. She asked the nurse at the clinic to give her some advice on birth control, and the nurse made an appointment for her with the Family Planning Clinic for the following week.

When Mrs. J. arrived at the clinic, she found herself in with a group of twelve other mothers who were there for the same purpose. A public health nurse talked to the group about the various types of contraceptives available. Mrs. J. had a chance to ask questions about the different methods of birth control, but she was most interested in the "pill," which she felt would be best for her. Next she saw the public health doctor, who took a careful health history, then gave her a complete pelvic examination, a pap smear, a gonorrhea culture, and a breast examination. Since Mrs. J. did not seem to have any health problems, the doctor concurred with her decision to have the pill. Mrs. J. has been on the pill for two years now and is very happy to find that she finally has some control over her childbearing.

The public health department at one time offered family planning services only to mothers. Now, however, these services are also available to unmarried women, and even sexually active minors.

CHILD HEALTH CONFERENCES

In the past, Child Health Conferences have been referred to as well baby clinics.

Mrs. L. brought her nine-month-old baby to the clinic, where she was met by a public health nurse and physician. On file was her baby's chart with a complete record of its growth, development, immunization data, and comments on formula, special foods, or vitamins that the baby had taken. The doctor reviewed the chart and then gave the baby a complete physicial examination.

Child Health Conferences are provided free of charge.

They are open to everyone. Babies are examined at two weeks, eight weeks, three months, six months, nine months, twelve months, and then once a year through age five. These conferences are for well babies only. If a sick baby is brought in, the public health department will not provide treatment, but will refer him to a private physician or clinic. If, in the course of a routine examination, the physician notes any medical problem, such as a heart murmur or an orthopedic problem, the baby is referred to an appropriate facility for treatment. Many such problems are referred to Crippled Children's Services.

Unfortunately, mothers do not always follow suggestions made by the public health department. If the child has a heart condition, cooperation is generally good, but if the child is anemic, most mothers do not seem to feel that the condition is important enough to change nutritional patterns in the home. Public health nurses follow up by visiting the home and encourage mothers to improve the diets of their children. In most cases, money is available to provide good nutrition. The problem is usually poor food selection and faulty preparation.

Medicaid* has reduced the number of mothers coming to Child Health Conferences because they can now take their babies to private physicians and the Medicaid program will pay for it. One drawback to the private physician approach is that there may be no follow-up.

One of the problems faced at the Public Health Center is missed appointments. These run as high as 50 percent for Child Health Conferences in some parts of the city. Health care is not always a high priority item, and the reasons given for not coming at the agreed-upon time range from "I forgot" to "Something came up." Some may miss an appointment just to annoy the doctor. Very few, however, miss their family planning appointments.

In an attempt to take health care to the people, Child Health Conferences are also held in school or church buildings in areas that do not have a nearby health center.

* Medicaid is dealt with in detail in Chapter Eleven.

HEALTH CARE PROJECT

The Director of Public Health administers a comprehensive health care facility which was established in a lower socio-economic section of the city. The project is supported by federal funds through the Model Cities Program. A Citizens Advisory Board assists the Director in planning and developing the program. Residents of the Model Neighborhood serve on the Advisory Board and comprise a majority of its membership. The facility offers general medical services for adults, general pediatric services for children, dental care, mental health services, an emergency medical care unit, public health services, social work services, and a medical para-professional training program.[2]

PUBLIC HEALTH
NUTRITION

Mary D. is eight years old. She has *cystic fibrosis,* a disease which affects the exocrine glands, especially those secreting mucus; it usually involves pulmonary disease, problems with the pancreas, and, in some cases, cirrhosis of the liver. Persons with the more serious manifestations of this disease do not usually live past young adulthood. A public health nurse has been working with her mother, explaining Mary's special nutritional needs. Because of cystic fibrosis, her body does not have an enzyme which normally breaks down food, so she does not absorb sufficient amounts of nutrients from her food, and she requires more vitamins and food than the normal child. She is always hungry. Her diet has to be high in proteins, vitamins, and calories, but low in fat because her body cannot properly metabolize fat.

 The nurse learned about the special nutritional needs of cystic fibrosis victims at in-service education sessions conducted by the public health nutritionist at one of the secondary public health centers. The nutritionist also briefs public health nurses on the nutritional problems faced by persons with diabetes or heart disease. On request, she discusses nutritional problems with various groups and organizations. She often speaks to groups such as TOPS ("Take Off Pounds Sensibly"), PTA's, Junior Chambers of Commerce, fraternal organizations, senior citizens, and health education and home economics classes at local colleges and universities. She may speak on problem areas such as food quackery, artificial sweeteners, or children's feeding problems. But underlying all her presentations is the emphasis on sound nutrition.

RECORDS AND STATISTICS

Mrs. K., age 62, came into the Bureau of Records and Statistics of the Department of Public Health. She asked for ten certified copies of her husband's death certificate. She needed these copies to "settle her affairs." They were necessary to provide evidence of her husband's death so that she could receive his life insurance, transfer money from his bank accounts to her own, transfer his stock certificates to her name, and apply for social security benefits.

Mrs. O., age 27, mother of three children, came into the Bureau and asked for a certified copy of her oldest son's birth certificate. She needed it to provide proof that he was of school age.

Another mother needed a certified birth certificate so that her son could provide proof of his age to the Little League team he wanted to join.

These are just a few examples of the daily requests that come into the Bureau. All births, deaths, and fetal deaths (*stillbirths*) which occur in the county are carefully recorded by the Bureau of Records and Statistics. Each death certificate, for example, has over 50 items of information on it; it includes personal data on the deceased, place of death, usual residence, physician's or coroner's certification, funeral director and local registrar information, and medical data such as cause of death and circumstances—accident, suicide, or homicide. The attending physician must sign the death certificate. If the physician has not seen the decedent professionally within ten days of death, he must report this fact to the coroner. If the coroner is uncertain about the circumstances of the death, he may order a complete investigation.

Under the "cause of death" portion of the death certificate, a physician must indicate not only the *immediate* cause of death, but also the *contributing* or *underlying* causes. For example, the immediate cause of death might have been ventricular fibrillation, while the contributing causes were "congestive heart failure" and "arteriosclerotic heart disease."

It is often very difficult to determine which is the immediate cause of death and which is the contributing cause. To provide guidance and uniformity in reporting causes of death, the World Health Organization has developed an *International Classification of Diseases, Injuries, and Causes of Death,* which provides immediate and contributing causal preferences for all combinations of diseases.[3] All this information becomes a matter of record and must be as accurate as possible.

In the early 1900s, most babies were born in the home and the attending physician filed the birth certificate with the Health Department at his convenience. Today, over 95 percent of babies are born in hospitals. The hospital now completes the birth certificate, the physician signs it, and it is sent to the public health department. A birth must be registered with the Bureau of Records and Statistics within four days of the event. Each week, the local public health department sends its birth (and death) certificates to the State Department of Health, where these vital statistics are compiled on a statewide basis.

Statistics from the Bureau are also used to plan public health programs and project population trends for city planning. Many businessmen study the information to determine the best locations for an office or service. Persons who are trying to trace genealogical information also depend on the Bureau's accurate statistics.

ENVIRONMENTAL SANITATION

In this metropolitan community, restaurants and cafes have a card approximately five inches square in their window with a large letter (usually an "A") on it. This is not a Duncan Hines rating; it indicates that the establishment has been inspected by the health department and meets their sanitary standards. More than thirty sanitarians* make unannounced visits to cafes and restaurants and check on the following kinds of things: *building and grounds:* general cleanliness, proper storage of food, absence of insects and rodents; *inside:* temperature of dishwater (must be 180° F. during the final rinse), proper procedures in handling food (cleanable cutting boards, a scoop for putting ice in glasses), hairnets worn by those wating on tables, and general cleanliness throughout—floors, walls, and ceilings. Points are deducted from 100 when deficiencies are found. Three ratings are possible: A: 90–100; B: 80–89; and C: below 80.

Any establishment with a "C" rating must clean up within thirty days or be closed by the health department. Approximately 95 percent of restaurants and cafes in this community have an "A" rating. Most establishments are happy to cooperate with the health department on this project.

College and university food service areas are also given these unannounced inspections. Even the candy bar and

---

* Sometimes called "environmental health specialists."

drink dispensers are carefully checked. On one occasion, a college student became very nauseated after drinking a beverage from a vending machine. He called the sanitation division of the public health department and reported the incident. The sanitarian investigated and found the valve in the machine was not working properly. It allowed the carbonated beverage to come into contact with the copper tubing and cuprous oxide was formed, which caused metal poisoning.

Public health sanitarians also inspect supermarkets and food stores and look for such things as mislabeling, spoiled canned goods (referred to as "springers" and "leakers" by the sanitarians), and the amount of fat in hamburger (no more than 30 percent). They also check for the presence of adulteration in foods (sulphites added to meat to make it look red). Prime cuts of meat are examined to make certain they bear an inspection stamp. The meat saws are also checked for cleanliness.

The public health department also assists the local zoo with "vector" control—prime concerns are mosquitoes, cockroaches, and rodents. Sanitation inspections also include such diverse areas as the public water supply, public swimming pools and beaches, tattoo parlors, kennels and stables, mobile home parks, and the galleys of sport fishing vessels.

From May through October, a tiny flagellate in the ocean goes through its prolific reproductive period. It increases in such numbers that it sometimes gives the water a pinkish hue and hence is often referred to as the "red tide." Shellfish eat these flagellates which secrete a toxin, causing the shellfish to be unfit for human consumption. The sanitation department posts warnings along the beaches, advising the public of the danger of eating shellfish during the "red tide." Not everyone, however, heeds these warning signs. Recently, several persons were poisoned from a mussel stew which they had made on a picnic. They used an old folk method to indicate the "safety" of eating the mussels by testing the stew with a silver coin.

They had time to ponder their mistake while they received treatment for food poisoning in a nearby hospital a few hours later.

PUBLIC HEALTH LABORATORY

When a physician sees a woman in his office for the first time and suspects that she is pregnant, state law requires that he take a sample of blood for analysis. A portion of the blood is sent to the Public Health Laboratory to determine whether or not the woman has syphilis. Physicians who suspect their patients have tuberculosis send sputum samples to the Public Health Laboratory for confirmation. In cases of suspected poisoning, the Public Health Laboratory analyzes the food to determine the source of the problem. Other services include testing for viruses, the testing of several hundred samples of milk each month to assure a high quality product, daily testing of samples of the public water supply from several locations throughout the city, and testing samples of the water in swimming pools and public beaches.

Occasionally the local Public Health Laboratory is unable to perform an analysis. In such a case, it sends the sample to the laboratory at the State Department of Health. If the state cannot perform the test, the sample is sent to the Communicable Disease Center in Atlanta, Georgia.

When a physician requests an analysis of a specimen, the Public Health Laboratory reports back to him that a given organism was, or was not, found in the specimen. It does not make a diagnosis; that is the prerogative of the physician.

The Public Health Laboratory has thirteen microbiologists, a milk technologist, and other personnel working on thousands of samples each month to assist other branches of the public health department and local physicians who have requested help.

PUBLIC HEALTH NURSING

Due to vision problems, twelve-year-old Susan R. was given a vision screening test at her junior high school. A note was sent home, indicating that she should have a complete eye examination by a professional. Several weeks passed and she did not have the examination. The public health nurse was informed of the situation and made a home call. She found that Mrs. R. was a thirty-six-year-old widow who was supporting four children on the salary which she earned as a housekeeper. Susan had a sister, 11, and two brothers, 7 and 5 years of age. The all lived in a two-bedroom trailer owned by Mrs. R.'s employer.

The public health nurse told Mrs. R. that she would qualify for Medicaid and that she could have Susan's eye examination and glasses, if needed, paid for under this program. The ophthalmologist who examined Susan recommended glasses for her and suggested that the rest of the children also have their vision checked.

The nurse, after seeing the other children, realized that they all needed dental care and probably should have complete medical examinations. She helped Mrs. R. set up appointments with a dentist and a physician. The medical examination revealed that Susan's eleven-year-old sister had a skin condition requiring treatment and that her youngest brother was anemic. The nurse also arranged for Mrs. R. to talk to officials of the Food Stamp Program. Mrs. R. was able to qualify for the federally-sponsored program, which is designed to help low-income families meet their basic nutritional needs.

The public health nurse then worked with Susan's mother and helped her plan her family's diet. The nurse also gave Mrs. R. some suggestions for handling the discipline problem which was arising with her two sons. Through the immunization clinics of the public health department, the children received all needed immunizations.

While working with this family, the public health nurse helped them establish contact and receive needed services from a variety of community agencies. Mrs. R.'s family is one example of many which the public health nurses see every month.

Much skill is needed in working with these troubled families. The nurse must be careful not to try to impose her value system on that of the family. She is there as a guest and the family is under no obligation to follow her suggestions. It is quite different from the hospital nursing situation, where the patient is in a more controlled environment and generally does exactly what the nurse asks. The nurse has no way of knowing whether or not a tuberculosis patient is taking his drugs. He may say that he is, but may, in fact, not be! Many seem to agree with the nurse and want to please her, but just don't bother to follow through on her recommendations. In nonmedical matters, the nurse generally tries to point out the various alternatives open to the family, but lets the family make the final decisions. The nurse is certainly qualified to make these decisions, but by so doing, she would be encouraging the family to develop too much dependency on her. Her goal, of course, is to help these families get through their present problems and become independent again.

In this community, a local medical school has arranged to have freshman medical students accompany the public health nurses on their home visits. This gives the fledgling M.D. an opportunity to see the patient in a family environment. He can see the various forces at play and is better able to understand the important effect of the family on the health of the patient.

Since the public health nurse often needs to talk to the head of the household, visits after 5 p.m. and on Saturday and Sunday are often required.

HEALTH PROBLEMS OF
SENIOR CITIZENS

There are thousands of retired persons in this community and over 100 different senior citizen groups, most of which are organized for recreation and sociability. These older persons need to be able to recognize the early signs of such chronic diseases as diabetes, heart disease, and glaucoma. They also need to be alerted to medical and nutritional quackery. Since falls in and around the home are one of the leading causes of disability in this age group, they also need information on home safety.

In spite of these obvious needs, prior to 1960, there was no organized program to provide information to these older citizens. The Bureau of Public Health Education decided to try to fill this void. The problem was to be able to provide the information in a way that would be acceptable to persons gathered together for recreation. It was obvious that the usual lecture-discussion approach would not be very successful. The public health educators developed many interest-arousing activities which could be adapted to the needs of the various groups. Since most senior citizens enjoy games, the health educators created games which included information about symptoms of various diseases. One such game is *Diabetes Bingo*. It is similar to regular bingo, except that in place of certain numbers, symptoms are listed that might indicate the presence of diabetes. Some of these symptoms include "diabetic relative," "blurring vision," "usually hungry," or "sudden weight loss." The game is usually followed by a question-and-answer session. Those persons with several of the symptoms are encouraged to see a physician. The symptoms may be indicative of some other medical problem, but only a doctor can determine this. Other popular games include *Password to Health* (dental health) and *Eyes Right* (glaucoma).

The Department of Public Health cooperated with the federal Public Health Service in the pre-testing of a game called *Medigame,* designed to stimulate better understanding of the Medicare program.

The public health educators have also developed exhibits and pamphlets which provide more information about health and safety for older citizens.

There are numerous mobile home parks in the area, housing thousands of persons. Seventy percent of these residents are over 50 years of age. To reach these persons, the public health educators have taken their programs to the mobile home parks and have received enthusiastic support from the senior citizens there.

Through these programs, the Public Health Department hopes to alert senior citizens to recognize developing symptoms of diseases, increase their understanding of these diseases, and to learn to utilize properly the community health resources which are available.

PUBLIC HEALTH EDUCATION

In addition to the preceding programs with senior citizens, the Bureau of Public Health Education is busy on many fronts. It conducts an orientation program for new public health personnel to acquaint them with the various departments and their functions. This orientation provides the new team members with an overall view of the Public Health Department, so that they can better appreciate how their efforts complement the total program.

The Bureau of Public Health Education also provides an orientation program for new welfare personnel. This orientation stresses health-related items with which welfare workers should be familiar, so that they can be of greater assistance to their clients. Some of the topics include basic information on nutrition, housing, and sanitation, as well as an introduction to medical assistance programs such as Medicaid.

The Bureau accepts, as trainees, graduate students who are working on a Master of Public Health degree (M.P.H.). For three months, these students work with public health educators and gain valuable on-the-job experience in the role of a public health educator.

Local college students majoring in Health Education often elect a course entitled "Supervised Field Experience." This course provides the students with an opportunity to gain practical experience with local health agencies. Many students choose the Public Health Department for their field experience and work under the supervision of full-time public health educators.

Other functions of the Bureau include: preparing news releases on items of public health concern for the mass media; assisting members of other departments in the preparation, organization, and presentation of information to the public; speaking to various community and college groups on health-related topics. In addition, to improve coordination between health organizations, public health educators attend many meetings of other health agencies in their capacity as representatives of the Public Health Department.

OTHER PROGRAMS

We have had a glimpse of some of the activities of a local Public Health Department. Many other programs are being carried on simultaneously, such as school health, industrial medicine, and tuberculosis control. Although the Public Health Department does not usually, provide treatment of diseases, there are a few notable exceptions. One is the Health Care Project mentioned earlier. Another is the Venereal Disease Control Program, which offers diagnosis and treatment of venereal disease cases and their contacts. The third is out-patient tuberculosis care for those unable to obtain it elsewhere.

ENDNOTES

1. Annual Report of the San Diego County Department of Public Health, 1974, p. 3.
2. Ibid., p. 5.
3. John J. Hanlon, *Public Health Administration and Practice* (St. Louis: The C. V. Mosby Company, 1974), p. 683.

Chapter Fifteen

Consumerism
in Health Care

The consumer movement has reached health care. For too long, the consumer has been tolerated in the system but not given the consideration due him. Some evidence of the change is reflected in hospitals where we now find a Patient's Bill of Rights and patient advocates circulating to help people adjust to the strange and often frightening environment of the hospital. Various groups are compiling physician and dentist directories to supply the consumer with information so that he can intelligently choose a provider of health services. The consumer is finally being recognized as an important part of the health care process.

HEALTH EDUCATION AND
HEALTH CARE

Health education bridges the gap between health information and health practices. It should also bring the health care consumer actively into the process of the health care delivery system by encouraging him to follow sound preventive practices, make appropriate use of available health services, and adhere more consistently to medical advice.

Because health education is prevention-oriented, money spent on it will ultimately save great sums now spent on crisis medicine.' A knowledgeable consumer has a much greater opportunity of getting what he is paying for. If he wants preventive medicine, and hopefully, he will, he can insist that it be made available. When a crisis is unavoidable, an informed consumer will have prepared the way for prompt, efficient care. He cannot assume that those in the medical and allied health professions will arrange to have competent services conveniently available for all consumers. More money and additional manpower will not in itself solve the problems of health care delivery. The consumer must be educated. He must be aware of good health practices; he must be interested in functioning optimally; he must be interested in heading off crisis situations regarding his health; he must insist that competent, convenient, preventive and crisis medical care be available; and he must use his influence to develop an efficient health care delivery system. But, until some reasonable organization is achieved, he must use knowledge and ingenuity to obtain optimum care under the present inefficient system.

PUBLIC HEALTH FACILITIES

The public health department, supported by tax dollars, offers many services which were discussed in some detail in Chapter Fourteen. If a particular service is not available, the department can inform you of an organization providing it. Since the public health department's main objective is to safeguard your health, its programs emphasize preventive medicine. The public health department's services are not widely advertised because of budget constraints, as well as concern by physicians and dentists (providers) that the public health department is encroaching on the private practice of medicine.

SOURCES OF HEALTH AND MEDICAL INFORMATION

There are many sources of health and medical information. The problem is one of arousing the interest of the consumer in assuming responsibility for his general well-being. Not only must he come in contact with the information, but he must be motivated to modify his behavior to be consistent with the new information.

Your Doctor

One excellent source of sound health information is your personal physician. However, physicians are primarily disease-oriented and are generally too busy to give patients advice about preventive measures. Patients may feel that since the doctor is so busy, they won't bother him with questions, and so the opportunity for patient education is lost. In fact, many patients leave their doctor's office with more questions than when they entered. It is possible to obtain information from your doctor, but it takes planning. Before you visit your doctor, make a list of the questions that have been on your mind. During or after your examination, ask the doctor each of the questions on your list, no matter how trifling they may seem. If your doctor tries to leave before you are finished, ask him to remain a few more minutes. Do not leave his office until you have answers that you can understand. Remember, since you are paying for his services, he is working for you and should at least take the time to answer your questions. If your doctor is not willing to do this, perhaps another doctor will better serve your needs.

Taped Telephone Messages

Many communities have health and medical information that is available by phone. In the privacy of your own home, you can dial, free of charge, and hear by phone a three- to five-minute taped health message. Some areas provide the information in more than one language. Usually, the recording has been approved for accuracy by the physicians in your area. Each tape also suggests other resources for those persons wishing more information. Some communities have as many as 200 different topics on tape, ranging from alcoholism, birth control and cancer, to poisoning, smoking and venereal disease. Call your local county medical society if you are interested in the taped health messages in your area. The taped messages are designed to help you:[2]

(1) remain healthy by giving preventive health information;
(2) recognize early signs of illness;
(3) adjust to a serious illness.

If your community does not have this system, call your local medical society and ask if they can initiate this service.

Voluntary Health Agencies

Voluntary health agencies are good sources of assistance and information on a particular organ (Heart Association) or disease (Cancer Society) in which they are involved. Often, they offer screening programs for early detection of problems, as well as preventive education programs. Voluntary health agencies were dealt with in some detail in Chapter Thirteen.

Patient Health Education Libraries

An innovative idea is being used by the Kaiser-Permanente Medical Care Program in Oakland, California. Kaiser has set up a health education library for members designed to emphasize the use of audiovisual material. There are twenty-four individual viewing booths available with technicians to assist the visitor in selecting and running the desired material. The health education materials are suitable for a lay audience. "The programs pertain to both health and disease in the human lifespan and include newborn and infant care, the child at each stage of growth and development, guidance for pre-adolescents, teenage problems, family life education, including family planning and prenatal care, immunizations, nutrition and weight control, disease prevention, and acute and chronic disease conditions."[3] The library is also becoming an important source of material for local health-oriented organizations.

Directories

Various directories and consumer guides are now being published to assist patients in making wiser choices in the health marketplace. Herbert Denenberg, past insurance commissioner for Pennsylvania, was one of the pioneers in this field. He developed a series of shopper's guides, which covered a variety of topics such as hospitals, hospital rights, surgery, dentists, and life insurance. His guides were written in a readable style and provided very useful information. For example, in his booklet "A Shopper's Guide to Surgery" he lists fourteen rules on how to avoid unnecessary surgery. These rules are essential reading for anyone faced with the possibility of surgery. The Pennsylvania Insurance Department at Harrisburg provides single copies of this "Guide" free of charge.

Many consumer organizations are publishing "doctor directories" fashioned after the first one produced by Ralph Nader's Health Research Group.* These directories con-

* If you would like to organize a group in your area to develop a Directory of Physicians, write to the Health Research Group at 2000 P Street, N.W., Washington, D.C., 20036, for assistance.

tain a wide variety of information that can assist consumers when they are choosing a physician. We have listed only a few examples of the kinds of questions answered.[4]

1. Education and Appointments:
   a) Where and when did the doctor obtain his medical training?
   b) If he is a specialist, is he Board-Certified?
   c) Does he teach at a medical school?
   d) Where does he admit his patients when they need hospitalization?
2. Fees and Billing:
   a) What is his standard fee for routine office visit (and routine hospital visit)?
   b) Does he accept Medicaid patients?
   c) Does he accept Medicare fee schedule as full payment?
3. Practice Information:
   a) Does he prescribe contraceptives on request?
   b) Does he prescribe drugs by generic name whenever possible?
   c) Does he allow patients to view their medical records on request?

Directories of dentists are also being compiled in various parts of the country. Contact the Public Interest Research Group in your area for more information.

Prescription drug surveys have been conducted in many cities to provide consumers with information concerning drug prices and services offered by various pharmacies. Often, consumers are not aware of the many services that are available from some pharmacists.[5] For example, does your pharmacist provide emergency prescription service after the regular store hours? Does he provide you with the total cost of all drugs purchased during the year for income tax purposes? Does he deliver? Does he accept major credit cards or personal charge accounts? Does he keep a patient profile (personal medication record)? This profile, which is required in some states, is a record of all the drugs that you have taken (or are taking). If you are going to more than one physician, it is possible that each doctor will prescribe drugs for you. One of these drugs may nullify the effect of the others, or worse yet, may set up an adverse reaction which could be very harmful. The patient profile enables your pharmacist to review your medications and alert your doctor to any such problems. Usually, before writing a prescription, a doctor will ask his patients if they are taking any other drugs, but many patients forget they are taking other medications.

Other Sources

Other good sources of health information include health classes available through adult education, community colleges, and the extension departments of many state colleges and universities. Your local library contains books and periodicals that deal with a variety of health topics. Also, government publications on many aspects of health are available free of charge. For a list of current health topics, write the U.S. Government Printing Office, Denver, Colorado 80202.

FREE CLINICS

The Haight-Ashbury Free Clinic in San Francisco, established by David Smith in 1967, is credited with starting the free clinic movement. The first free clinics were primarily drug treatment centers, but soon broadened their coverage so that they offered primary care and routine screening such as pregnancy and venereal disease testing, and treatment of minor infections.[6,7] Some, where personnel permit, offer follow-up care, medical and social referral, home health care, medically related counseling, preventive health education, plus some dental services. They also provide a system of access to the entire spectrum of existing health and social services. Since the free clinics attempt to help people in need, they often evolve into true community centers, offering legal aid, food programs, housing and message exchanges.[8] Some even provide out-reach programs, where volunteers go door-to-door in the community offering educational and screening programs for such problems as sickle cell anemia or tuberculosis.

Although no one model exists, free clinics have certain common characteristics. They are generally operated on a small budget and staffed with volunteer physicians, nurses, and others from the community, who donate their time. Professionals usually train others to do routine procedures. Everyone dresses in street clothes, not white gowns, and first names are used rather than titles. Free clinics are usually located in makeshift quarters which were not intended for health care delivery, hence the term "storefront medicine." Often, the clinics are located in areas of the city not provided for by mainstream medicine and, because they depend on volunteers, clinics are usually open only a few evenings a week.

The principles of free clinics may be summarized as follows: "1) Health care is a right and must be free at the point of delivery; 2) the community served must have the controlling interest in the planning, organization and administration of the clinics; 3) humanity, dignity and concern for the patient must be the mode in which health care is delivered; and 4) the present health care delivery system is a failure and the free clinics offer a model for a new health care delivery system."[9]

Obviously, free clinics are not without cost, but no charge is made at the time of service. "These are freedom clinics, developed to liberate the individual from his problems, physical or otherwise, to help him get on with his life, to actualize his potential, whatever it may be."[10] Free clinics raise funds in a variety of ways. Some depend on donations and augment their support by bazaars and street fairs; others, once they gain political understanding, obtain funding through city, county, state, and federal programs, and through third party billing. With adequate funds, clinics expand from several nights a week to more comprehensive, full-time care. Most expect patients to contribute "in kind," i.e., offer their skills—legal, social work, plumbing, painting, etc., in return for medical services. Free clinics do not further exploit the sick by charging them for care, but attempt to obtain support from other sources.

While free clinics have obvious advantages, there are some disadvantages. Since there are no appointments, waiting time is long, follow-up is casual, and continuity of care is very difficult. Free clinics must make certain trade-offs—if quality care is stressed, then fewer patients will be treated. Although they may de-mystify medicine by removing white coats and function on a first-name basis, they "often fall short of educating patients about their illness or about the politics of the health system."[11] In spite of these shortcomings, free clinics are serving a need for many who were not previously receiving health care.

PATIENT NONCOMPLIANCE

Most studies indicate that at least one-third of the patients in America do not follow their doctors' advice. Many studies have turned up a noncompliance rate of 50 percent or more. Research has been undertaken to determine why such a high percentage of patients do not follow the advice they have paid for. Several important reasons emerge:

1. Psychological factors (fear)
2. Environmental and social factors (can't afford it or may resent doctor's upper-class status)
3. Therapeutic regimen (how disruptive is the regimen to the patient's life style?)
4. Physician-patient interaction (personality conflict)

It has been suggested that the high incidence of noncompliance can be reduced by patient education, personality accommodation by both physicians and patients, involving the family in the treatment process, using methods such as group instruction for diabetics, and negotiating the treatment regime to adapt to the patient's schedule.[12]

Each consumer should be aware of any resistance on his part to follow the treatment prescribed and try to analyze why he is resisting the advice he has sought. There is very little use in going to a carefully chosen physician for care if one is not going to comply with his recommendations.

PROSPECTIVE MEDICINE

Prospective medicine is concerned with "improving the patient's survival odds."[13] That involves identifying the things in the patient's environment that may either make him ill or shorten his life. The idea is to solve problems before a crisis situation occurs. The prospective system is different from the more customary crisis-oriented medical care in that it is continuous, comprehensive, and occurs before disease is present. An analysis is made of the risk factors present in the patient's life. Once identified, an attempt is made to modify behavior so as to minimize these risk factors. Prescriptions that don't come out of bottles are used such as counseling, diet modification, and physical therapy. Identifying the risk factors to your health is in itself a valuable teaching device. Unfortunately, most physicians are trained to treat sickness, not promote health, so prospective medicine or preventive medicine is not widely practiced. If you are interested in having a physician who practices prospective medicine, call your local medical society for assistance.

THE HOSPITAL EXPERIENCE

As a patient in a hospital, you should be aware of your rights. Most general hospitals are community hospitals, financed by your tax dollars, supposedly run by and for the benefit of the community. As a consumer, it is your prerogative to insist that the hospital provide the best possible services efficiently. Without consumer control, we are not likely to get the cost and quality controls that are essential for any viable health delivery system.[14]

Hospitals are beginning to respond to consumer needs. Some hospitals are employing patient representatives to help patients maintain their dignity and to help eliminate many of the causes of fear and anger. Many hospitals now distribute booklets that tell patients what they can expect in the way of courteous, efficient treatment. The American Hospital Association circulates a "Patient's Bill of Rights" to its member institutions. (See Appendix D.)

Patient care conferences in hospitals are becoming more widespread in an attempt to help ensure more comprehensive personal care. The patient then becomes "a person" to those involved in his treatment, with needs other than his present medical requirements. Patients do have diverse needs and it is important that the hospital staff members keep these needs in mind in order to provide more effective care.[15]

THE PATIENT'S
RESPONSIBILITY

Successful health care requires the active cooperation of the patient "throughout the continuum of health care, from preventive services, through the range of diagnosis, treatment and rehabilitation."[16] Education is needed to obtain this kind of cooperation. In fact, education of the health care consumer is as important, if not more important, in assuring improved national health as increased money and manpower.[17]

With education comes responsibility. The consumer must begin to assume responsibility for his own health and become an active participant in the health care system. There is much evidence that the consumer's influence in the health care field is increasing. The power shift from the provider to the consumer is going to require significant attitudinal and behavioral changes on the part of both consumers and providers.[18]

Increasing public awareness and concern about the pollution of air and water, of radiation and pesticides, are pointing out the close relationship between man and his environment. As man becomes more conscious of environmental and public health problems, hopefully he will become more aware of his personal health problems and responsibilities. He may see more clearly the relationship between his actions and his health. Often, personal and cultural behavior patterns of nutrition, exercise, and the use of habit-forming substances have a harmful effect on our health which is as great as environmental pollutants.[19]

Informed citizens are our greatest source of untapped health manpower. People must be informed about how they can help themselves to optimal health. In the future, the major improvements in health will not be from physicians, nurses, and hospitals, but from life-style changes—elimination of alcohol, smoking, improper nutrition, as well as environmental and social changes. The idea of going to the physician so that he can make you well must change to one of going to the physician so that he can help you understand how you can keep yourself well.

Consumers are becoming aware of their rights (see box) and no longer unquestioningly accept decisions of others concerning their health and well-being.

CONSUMER RIGHTS IN HEALTH CARE

(A document of the Consumers Association of Canada)

I Right to be informed:
- About preventive health care including education on nutrition, birth control, drug use, appropriate exercise;
- About the health care system including the extent of government insurance coverage for

services, supplementary insurance plans, the referral system to auxiliary health and social facilities and services in the community;
- About the individual's own diagnosis and specific treatment programs including prescribed surgery and medication, options, effects and side effects;
- About the specific costs of procedures, services and professional fees undertaken on behalf of the individual consumer.

II Right to be respected as the individual with the major responsibility for his own health care:
- Right that confidentiality of his health records be maintained;
- Right to refuse experimentation, undue painful prolongation of his life or participation in teaching programs;
- Right of adult to refuse treatment, right to die with dignity.

III Right to participate in decision making affecting his health:
- Through consumer representation at each level of government in planning and evaluating the system of health services, the types and qualities of service and the conditions under which health services are delivered;
- With the health professionals and personnel involved in his direct health care.

IV Right to equal access to health care (health education, prevention, treatment and rehabilitation) regardless of the individual's economic status, sex, age, creed, ethnic origin and location:
- Right to access to adequately qualified health personnel;
- Right to a second medical opinion;
- Right to prompt response in emergencies.

Source: Canadian Medical Association Journal, Vol. 111, July 20, 1974, p. 175.

Naturally, getting good medical care is more than an individual matter, since only collectively can we assure the availability of doctors, hospitals, and a viable health delivery system. Health and medical care are matters of concern to the entire community. If we do not exercise our prerogatives as consumers, we will get only those services the providers of service wish to give us and, in the public health sector, only those services government wishes to finance. We must not only take charge of our personal health needs, but must exercise our lobbying power effectively for the health needs of the entire nation.

ENDNOTES

1. Clarence E. Pearson, "Cost Effectiveness and Reimbursement," in *Rx: Education for the Patient, Proceedings* (Carbondale, Ill.: Southern Illinois University, 1975), pp. 33–35.
2. San Diego County Medical Society, *TEL-MED Tape Library* (San Diego, Cal.).
3. F. Bobbie Collen and Krikor Soghikian, "A Health Education Library for Patients," *Health Service Reports* 89; May-June, 1974, 238.
4. "How to Develop a Local Directory of Doctors," *Consumer Reports* 39; September, 1974, 685–691.
5. Public Interest Research Group, *A Consumer's Guide to Humboldt Area Pharmacies* (Humboldt, CA: Action Community Pressworks, 1974).
6. "With a Little Help From Their Friends," *Health/Pac Bulletin,* No. 34, October, 1971, p. 6.
7. Alan D. Motzger and David E. Smith, "Free Clinics: An Alternative Approach to Health Care," in David E. Smith (ed.) *The Free Clinic: A Community Approach to Health Care and Drug Abuse* (Beloit, Wis.: Stash Press, 1971), p. 60.
8. Jeoffrey Gordon, "The Free Clinic Movement," *Modern Medicine* 39; August 23, 1971, 106.
9. Irene R. Turner, "Free Health Centers: A New Concept?" *American Journal of Public Health* 62; October, 1972, 1348.
10. *Modern Medicine* 39, pp. 106–107.

11. *Health/Pac Bulletin,* No. 34, p. 10.
12. Richard F. Gillum and Arthur J. Barsky, "Diagnosis and Management of Patient Noncompliance," *Journal of the American Medical Association* 228; June 17, 1974, 1563–1567.
13. *American Medical News* 17; September 2, 1972, 17–19.
14. Herbert S. Dunenberg, *Citizens Bill of Hospital Rights* (Harrisburg: Pennsylvania Insurance Department, 1973), pp. 1–2.
15. Liebe Kravitz, "Patient Care Conferences," *Hospitals, Journal of the American Hospital Association* 48; July 16, 1974, 55–57.
16. Joan M. Wolle, "Multidisciplinary Teams Develop Programing for Patient Education," *Health Services Reports* 89; January-February, 1974, 9.
17. "Opinion," *Modern Healthcare* 1; May, 1974, 7.
18. Marlene Kramer, "The Consumer's Influence on Health Care," *Nursing Outlook* 20; September, 1972, 574–578.
19. Edyth H. Schoenrich, "The Potential of Health Education in Health Services Delivery," *Health Services Reports* 89; January-February, 1974, 5–6.

Appendix A

Arranging the First Visit*

Arrange for the visit by calling the doctor's office and telling the receptionist that you are looking for a new doctor—that Dr. Such-and-Such has recommended him and that you want to meet him. Explain that you are not sick, but that you are looking for a doctor and that you would like an appointment for a physical checkup. Depending upon the nature of your call, whether for a physical examination or merely as a get-acquainted visit, ask the girl what the ordinary charge is. If that charge is acceptable to you, make the appointment.

Explain to the receptionist that you would like some information about the doctor. Don't be surprised if the receptionist is suspicious or curious. Very few people ask for such information and you may have to assure the girl that you are sincere. Don't become angry or upset if you find the girl reluctant to tell you about the doctor. Offer to let her send you the information by mail or to get it from her personally before you meet the doctor on the day of the appointment.

Here is what you should find out from the doctor's nurse or receptionist if you have not already learned it from the

* Reprinted with permission of the Macmillan Company from *The Commonsense Guide to Doctors, Hospitals, and Medical Care* by Richard H. Blum. © Richard H. Blum, 1964.

county medical society or from the *Directory of Medical Specialists*. The girl may not know, so give her time to find out, even if it means you have to call back or wait a while. Ask:

1. When did the doctor graduate from medical school? (This will give you an idea about his experience.)

2. Is he a general practitioner or a specialist? What specialty?
   a. If a specialist, does he have his Boards in his specialty? When did he get his specialty Board certificate?
   b. Is he a Fellow in the American College of Physicians? The College of Surgeons? The Academy of General Practice?
   c. If not Board-Certified, but still a specialist, how long was his residency training? Is he Board-Eligible?

3. To what hospital staffs does the doctor belong? Have the nurse or receptionist list the staff level which the doctor holds for each hospital (consulting, active, associate, courtesy). How long has he had the appointment to his present level in each hospital?

4. What category of surgical privileges does the doctor hold in each hospital for which he holds a staff appointment? This question is especially important for doctors from whom you expect the competence to do any kind of surgery.

5. How many patients does he see in an average day? (For general practitioners thirty is about average. Doctors who see more than thirty a day can be skilled, but at some point seeing too many patients leaves less time for each, including you. Sixty or more a day may be too many for your comfort.)

By the time you have asked these questions the girl may be exasperated or curious. Many receptionists are overworked; keep this in mind when you talk to the girl. Blame your questions on this book. Blame its authors if need be, but for the sake of your own good choice of a doctor don't be so embarrassed by the reluctance of the girl to answer that you don't try to get the information which you should have.

The next step is the get-acquainted visit itself. Be sure you are on time for the appointment. If the doctor does not run his office on an appointment system, that is a bad sign.

When you meet the doctor, observe him to see if he is polite. Does he make you feel at ease? When you have been seated, explain your purpose. It will be your job to put the doctor at ease, too, for very few people make a get-acquainted visit and the doctor may not know quite what to do or say. For him to be interviewed by a patient will be a new experience. So do not be surprised if the doctor seems nonplused or distressed. If he is, feel free to blame this book and its authors for giving you the idea of a get-acquainted visit.

Here are some of the questions you should ask the doctor during the visit and/or examination. The answers will help you to decide whether or not he is the doctor you want.

1. Do you make house calls? Tell him your address. Would you make a call to where I live?
   a. If you don't make house calls, how do you arrange for the care of your patients who get very sick at home?
   b. If you do make calls, what do you suggest as the basis for telling whether or not the patient's sickness requires a house call? What kinds of complaints are worthy of a house call? What do you suggest as a standard for judging a sickness over the telephone? You know that it is difficult to make a diagnosis over the telephone; how do you handle the telephone diagnosis problem?

2. Would you be willing to call in a consultant should I be worried about my illness, even if you feel I don't need one? (A consultant is a second doctor who is called in to give his opinion on a case.)

3. Would you be willing to tell me in advance what your fees would be?

4. If I need to go to some specialist, would you help me to keep you as my personal doctor—someone to help me find and use these specialists?

5. How would you suggest that we agree on the amount of time that we should take to talk over nonmedical problems should there be some occasion when I feel I need to talk about some personal trouble or other matter?

6. What do you charge for office visits and for house calls?

7. Would it be all right with you if I told you when I was worried about either my sickness or your treatment, even if we both knew my worries might be unnecessary ones?

8. If you were either sick or on vacation, what arrangements would you make for another doctor to take care of your patients?

9. What are your vacation plans, so that I will know when you will be gone?

10. Would you mind explaining things to me if there were things I wanted to know about my diagnosis or treatment?

11. Would you mind telling me what to expect on the cost of drugs you might prescribe so that we could figure the least expensive brand of medicine that would still do the job?

These questions will open a conversation between you and the doctor. His answers will lead you to new questions. The doctor may also want to ask you questions so that he can decide if you are the kind of person who he thinks would be a good patient for him.

Appendix B

Sources of Information on Health Careers

American Academy of Family Physicians
Volker Blvd. at Brookside, Kansas City, Missouri 64112

American Academy of Pediatrics
1801 Hinman Avenue, Evanston, Illinois 60201

American Academy of Physicians' Associates
2150 Pennsylvania Ave., Rm. 356, Washington, D.C. 20037

American Association for Health, Physical Education and
    Recreation
1201 16th Street, N.W., Washington, D.C. 20036

American Association of Blood Banks
1828 L Street, N.W., Suite 608, Washington, D.C. 20036

American Association of Colleges of Pharmacy
8121 Georgia Avenue, Suite 800, Silver Spring, Md. 20910

American Association of Dental Schools
211 East Chicago Avenue, Chicago, Illinois 60611

American Association of Medical Assistants
One East Wacker Drive, Chicago, Illinois 60601

American Association of Ophthalmology
1100 17th St., N.W., Room 304, Washington, D.C. 20036

American Association for Respiratory Therapy
7411 Hines Place, Suite 101, Dallas, Texas 75235

American Cancer Society
219 East 42nd Street, New York, New York 10017

American College Health Association
2807 Central Street, Evanston, Illinois 60201

American College of Hospital Administrators
840 North Lake Shore Drive, Chicago, Illinois 60611

American College of Nurse-Midwives
50 East 92nd Street, New York, New York 10028

American College of Obstetricians and Gynecologists
One East Wacker Drive, Chicago, Illinois 60601

American Corrective Therapy Association
Public Relations Officer
1781 Begen Avenue, Mountain View, California 94040

American Dental Assistants Association
211 East Chicago Avenue, Chicago, Illinois 60611

American Dental Association
211 East Chicago Avenue, Chicago, Illinois 60611

American Dental Hygienists' Association
211 East Chicago Avenue, Chicago, Illinois 60611

American Diabetes Association
18 East 48th Street, New York, New York 10017

American Dietetic Association
620 North Michigan Avenue, Chicago, Illinois 60611

American Foundation for the Blind
15 West 16th Street, New York, New York 10011

American Heart Association
44 East 23rd Street, New York, New York 10010

American Home Economics Association
2010 Massachusetts Ave., N.W., Washington, D.C. 20036

American Hospital Association
840 North Lake Shore Drive, Chicago, Illinois 60611

American Industrial Hygiene Association
210 Hadden Avenue, Westmont, New Jersey 08108

American Library Association
50 East Huron Street, Chicago, Illinois 60611

American Lung Association
1740 Broadway, New York, New York 10019

American Medical Association
535 North Dearborn Street, Chicago, Illinois 60610

American Medical Record Association
875 North Michigan Ave., Suite 1850, Chicago, Ill. 60611

American Medical Technologists
710 Higgins Road, Park Ridge, Illinois 60068

American Medical Women's Association
1740 Broadway, New York, New York 10019

American Medical Writers' Association
2900 Grove Road, Thorofare, New Jersey 08086

American National Red Cross
17th and E Streets, N.W., Washington, D.C. 20006

American Nurses' Association
Careers Program
2420 Pershing Rd., Kansas City, Missouri 64108

American Occupational Therapy Association
6000 Executive Blvd., Suite 200, Rockville, Md. 20852

American Optometric Association
7000 Chippewa Street, St. Louis, Missouri 63119

American Orthoptic Council
555 University Avenue, Toronto, Ontario, Canada

American Osteopathic Association
212 East Ohio Street, Chicago, Illinois 60611

American Pharmaceutical Association
2215 Constitution Avenue, N.W., Washington, D.C. 20037

American Physical Therapy Association
1156 15th Street, N.W., Washington, D.C. 20005

American Podiatry Association
20 Chevy Chase Circle, N.W., Washington, D.C. 20015

American Psychiatric Association
(Joint Information Service)
1700 18th Street, N.W., Washington, D.C. 20009

American Psychological Association
1200 17th Street, N.W., Washington, D.C. 20036

American Public Health Association
1015 18th Street, N.W., Washington, D.C. 20036

American Rehabilitation Counseling Association
1605 New Hampshire Avenue, Washington, D.C. 2003

American School Health Association
107 South Depeyster Street, Kent, Ohio 44240

American Social Health Association
1740 Broadway, New York, New York 10019

American Society for Medical Technology
5555 West Loop, Houston, Texas 77401

American Society of Clinical Pathologists
2100 West Harrison Street, Chicago, Illinois 60612

American Society of Electroencephalographic Technology
University of Iowa, Division of EEG & Neurophysiology
500 Newton Road, Iowa City, Iowa 52240

American Society of Radiologic Technologists
500 North Michigan Ave., Suite 8, Chicago, Illinois 60611

American Speech and Hearing Association
9030 Old Georgetown Road, Washington, D.C. 20014

American Veterinary Medical Association
600 South Michigan Avenue, Chicago, Illinois 60605

Arthritis Foundation
1212 Avenue of the Americas, New York, N.Y. 10036

Association of American Medical Colleges
One Dupont Circle, N.W., Washington, D.C. 20036

Association of Medical Illustrators
Medical College of Georgia, Augusta, Georgia 30902

**Association of Medical Rehabilitation Directors and
    Coordinators**
3830 Linklea Drive, Houston, Texas 77025

Association of Schools of Allied Health Professions
One Dupont Circle, Suite 300, Washington, D.C. 20036

Association of Schools of Public Health
1825 K Street, N.W., Suite 707, Washington, D.C. 20036

Association of University Programs in Hospital Administration
One Dupont Circle, Suite 420, Washington, D.C. 20036

Biological Photographic Association
P.O. Box 12866, Philadelphia, Pennsylvania 19108

Blue Cross Association
840 North Lake Shore Drive, Chicago, Illinois 60611

Council for the Advancement of Science Writing
201 Christie Street, Leonia, New Jersey 07605

Epilepsy Foundation of America
1828 L Street, N.W., Suite 406, Washington, D.C. 20036

Goodwill Industries of America
9200 Wisconsin Avenue, Washington, D.C. 20014

Hospital Financial Management Association
840 North Lake Shore Drive, Chicago, Illinois 60611

International Association of Milk, Food and Environmental Sanitarians
P.O. Box 437, Shelbyville, Indiana 46176

Maternity Center Association
48 East 92nd Street, New York ,New York 10028

Medical Library Association
919 North Michigan Ave., Suite 2023, Chicago, Ill. 60611

Muscular Dystrophy Associations of America
810 Seventh Avenue, New York, New York 10019

National Association for Mental Health
1800 North Kent St., Rosslyn Sta., Arlington, Va. 22209

National Association for Music Therapy
P.O. Box 610, Lawrence, Kansas 66044

National Association for Practical Nurse Education and Service
1465 Broadway, New York, New York 10036

National Association of Dental Laboratories
3801 Mount Vernon Avenue, Alexandria, Virginia 22305

National Association of Hearing & Speech Agencies
814 Thayer Avenue, Silver Spring, Maryland 20910

National Association of Social Workers
600 Southern Building, 15th & H Streets, N.W.,
Washington, D.C. 20005

National Council for Homemaker—Home Health Aide Services
67 Irving Place, New York, New York 10003

National Council on Alcoholism
Two Park Avenue, New York, New York 10016

National Council on the Aging
1828 L Street, N.W., Washington, D.C. 20036

National Cystic Fibrosis Research Foundation
3379 Peachtree Road, N.E., Suite 950, Atlanta, Ga. 30326

National Easter Seal Society for Crippled Children and Adults
2023 West Ogden Avenue, Chicago, Illinois 60612

National Environmental Health Association
Office of the Executive Director
1600 Pennsylvania, Denver, Colorado 80203

National Executive Housekeepers Association
Business & Professional Bldg., Gallipolis, Ohio 45631

National Federation of Licensed Practical Nurses
250 West 57th St., Suite 323-25, New York, N.Y. 10019

National Foundation
1275 Mamaroneck Avenue, P.O. Box 2000,
White Plains, New York 10602

National Hemophilia Foundation
25 West 39th Street, New York, New York 10018

National League for Nursing
Ten Columbus Circle, New York, New York 10019

National MEDIHC Program
Bureau of Health Resources Development
Federal Building, Room 514
7550 Wisconsin Ave., Bethesda, Maryland 20014

National Medical Association
2109 E Street, N.W., Washington, D.C. 20037

National Multiple Sclerosis Society
257 Park Avenue South, New York, New York 10010

National Rehabilitation Association
1522 K Street, N.W., Washington, D.C. 20005

National Safety Council
425 North Michigan Avenue, Chicago, Illinois 60611

National Society for the Prevention of Blindness
79 Madison Avenue, New York, New York 10016

National Urban League
55 East 52nd Street, New York, New York 10022

Registry of Medical Rehabilitation Therapists and Specialists
5308 Locust Street, North Little Rock, Arkansas 72116

Society for Public Health Education
655 Sutter Street, San Francisco, California 94102

Society of Nuclear Medical Technologists
1201 Waukegan Road, Glenview, Illinois 60025

Society of Nuclear Medicine
211 East 43rd Street, New York, New York 10017

Student American Medical Association
1400 Hicks Road, Rolling Meadows, Illinois 60008

Student National Medical Association
2109 E Street, N.W., Washington, D.C. 20037

United Cerebral Palsy Associations
66 East 34th Street, New York, New York 10016

ADDITIONAL SOURCES OF INFORMATION

Alcohol, Drug Abuse, Mental Health Administration
5600 Fishers Lane, Rockville, Maryland 20852

Bureau of Health Resources Development
Information Office
Bethesda, Maryland 20014

U.S. Office of Education
Division of Vocational & Technical Education
Dept. of Health, Education & Welfare, Washington, D.C. 20202

U.S. Training & Employment Services
Division of Occupational Analysis & Career Information
1741 Rhode Island Avenue, N.W., Washington, D.C. 20210

Appendix C

Priority Items of Public Law 93-641

1. Primary care services for medically underserviced populations, especially in rural or economically depressed areas.

2. Development of multi-institutional systems for co-ordinating or consolidating institutional health services.

3. Developing medical group practices, health maintenance organizations, and other organized systems for providing health care.

4. Training and increasing utilization of physician assistants, especially nurse clinicians.

5. Developing multi-institutional arrangements for sharing support services.

6. Promoting activities to achieve improved quality in health services.

7. The development by health service institutions of the capacity to provide various levels of care on a geographically integrated basis.

8. Promoting activities for preventing disease, including studies of nutritional and environmental factors affecting health and the provision of preventive health care services.

9. Adopting uniform cost accounting and other improved management procedures for health service institutions.

10. Developing effective methods of educating the general public concerning proper personal health care and effective use of available health services.

Source: U.S. Department of Health, Education, and Welfare, *Health Planning and Resources Development Act of 1974* (Washington, D.C.: U.S. Government Printing Office, 1975).

Appendix D

A Patient's Bill
of Rights

The American Hospital Association presents a Patient's Bill of Rights with the expectation that observance of these rights will contribute to more effective patient care and greater satisfaction for the patient, his physician, and the hospital organization. Further, the Association presents these rights in the expectation that they will be supported by the hospital on behalf of its patients, as an integral part of the healing process. It is recognized that a personal relationship between the physician and the patient is essential for the provision of proper medical care. The traditional physician-patient relationship takes on a new dimension when care is rendered within an organizational structure. Legal precedent has established that the institution itself also has a responsibility to the patient. It is in recognition of these factors that these rights are affirmed.

1. The patient has the right to considerate and respectful care.
2. The patient has the right to obtain from his physician complete current information concerning his diagnosis, treatment, and prognosis in terms the patient can be reasonably expected to understand. When it is not medically advisable to give such information to the patient, the information should be made available to an appropriate person in his behalf. He has the right

to know by name, the physician responsible for co-ordinating his care.

3. The patient has the right to receive from his physician information necessary to give informed consent prior to the start of any procedure and/or treatment. Except in emergencies, such information for informed consent, should include but not necessarily be limited to the specific procedure and/or treatment, the medically significant risks involved, and the probable duration of incapacitation. Where medically significant alternatives for care or treatment exist, or when the patient requests information concerning medical alternatives, the patient has the right to such information. The patient also has the right to know the name of the person responsible for the procedures and/or treatment.

4. The patient has the right to refuse treatment to the extent permitted by law, and to be informed of the medical consequences of his action.

5. The patient has the right to every consideration of his privacy concerning his own medical care program. Case discussion, consultation, examination, and treatment are confidential and should be conducted discreetly. Those not directly involved in his care must have the permission of the patient to be present.

6. The patient has the right to expect that all communications and records pertaining to his care should be treated as confidential.

7. The patient has the right to expect that within its capacity a hospital must make reasonable response to the request of a patient for services. The hospital must provide evaluation, service, and/or referral as indicated by the urgency of the case. When medically permissible a patient may be transferred to another facility only after he has received complete information and explanation concerning the needs for and alternatives to such a transfer. The institution to which the patient is to be transferred must first have accepted the patient for transfer.

8. The patient has the right to obtain information as to any relationship of his hospital to other health care

and educational institutions insofar as his care is concerned. The patient has the right to obtain information as to the existence of any professional relationships among individuals, by name, who are treating him.

9. The patient has the right to be advised if the hospital proposes to engage in or perform human experimentation affecting his care or treatment. The patient has the right to refuse to participate in such research projects.

10. The patient has the right to expect reasonable continuity of care. He has the right to know in advance what appointment times and physicians are available and where. The patient has the right to expect that the hospital will provide a mechanism whereby he is informed by his physician or a delegate of the physician of the patient's continuing health care requirements following discharge.

11. The patient has the right to examine and receive an explanation of his bill regardless of source of payment.

12. The patient has the right to know what hospital rules and regulations apply to his conduct as a patient.

No catalogue of rights can guarantee for the patient the kind of treatment he has a right to expect. A hospital has many functions to perform, including the prevention and treatment of disease, the education of both health professionals and patients, and the conduct of clinical research. All these activities must be conducted with an overriding concern for the patient, and, above all, the recognition of his *dignity* as a human being. Success in achieving this recognition assures success in the defense of the rights of the patient.

Source: Reprinted with the permission of the American Hospital Association.

INDEX

Accredited Nurses' Registry, 274
Active staff, 28
Advertising, dental, 58
Adriani, Dr. John, 209
Adverse reactions, 203–206
Allied Health, 105–133
    careers, 108–128
    physician acceptance of, 128–129
    trends, 106–108
American Association of Homes for the Aging, 277
American Cancer Society, 295–299
American Chiropractic Association, 88
American Dental Assistants Association, 49
American Dental Association (ADA), 61–62
American Dental Hygienists Association, 49
American Heart Association, 299–306
American Lung Association, 292–295
American Medical Association (AMA), 37–38, 139
American Nurses Association, 67, 70, 75
American Nursing Home Association, 277
American Osteopathic Association (AOA), 85
American Podiatric Association, 91
American Society of Allied Health Professions, 131–132
Associate Staff, 28
Association of American Medical Colleges, 13, 36
Attendants, 69

Baltimore College of Dental Surgery, 44
Better Business Bureau, 60

Blanchard Valley Hospital, 188–190
Board-Certified, 17, 338, 350
Board-Eligible, 17
Brand names (drugs), 208

Cancer, 295–299
Chemical names (drugs), 207–208
Cherkasky, Dr. Martin, 5, 23
Chiefs of service, 29
Chiropodist, 91
Chiropractic, 87–90
Choosing a hospital, 175–180
Choosing a physician, 24–30
Christian Science, 93–96
    practitioners, 93
Christian Science Journal, The, 93
Committee for Economic Development, 5
Consulting staff, 27
Consumer rights in health care, 344–345
Consumerism in Health Care, 333–347
Controlled substances, 206–207
Council on Chiropractic Education, 89
County Dental Society, 60
Courtesy staff, 28

Denenberg, Herbert S., 181, 337
Dennis, James L., 15
Dental Assistant, The, 50
Dental Auxiliaries, 48–51
    dental assistant, 49–50
    dental hygienist, 48–49
    dental laboratory technician, 50–51
Dental Care, 43–64
    emergency, 54–55
    historical view, 43–44
    preventive care, 55
Dental clinic, 59
Dental Education in the United States and Canada, 44

Dental fees, 54
Dentists
      choosing, 51–59
      diplomate, 47
      distribution of, 45–46
      education of, 44–45
"Detail man", 216–217
Dial-a-Dietitian, 302–303
Diplomate, 17, 47
Directory of Dental Specialists, 48
Directory of Medical Specialists,
      20, 27, 350
Doctor of Dental Surgery (D.D.S.),
      45
Doctor of Medical Dentistry
      (D.M.D.), 45
Doctor of Osteopathy (D.O.), 84
Doctor of Podiatric Medicine
      (D.P.M.), 91
Drug prices, 210–214
Drugs. See Prescription drugs

Eddy, Mary Baker, 93
Effective emergency medical ser-
      vices system, 234–238
Emergency departments, rating of,
      239–240
Emergency Medical Services, 231–
      247
Emergency Medical Services Sys-
      tems Act, 233–234
Emergency Medical Technicians
      (EMTs), 242–243
Emergency medicine, 17
Environmental Health Specialists,
      322

Fauchard, Pierre, 43–44
Fee-for-service, 136–137
Flexner report, 84
Flick, Lawrence F., 293
Food and Drug Administration
      (FDA), 195–205, 220–222
Food, Drug, and Cosmetic Act, 196
Foreign Medical Graduates, 36–37
Free choice of physician, 135–136
Free clinics, 339–341
      Haight-Ashbury, 339
Full privileges, 29

Generic names (drugs), 208

Georgetown University School of
      Nursing, 78
Governor's Committee on Hospital
      Costs, 159
Group Health Cooperative (GHC),
      141–143
Group practice, dental, 56–57
Guide to the Health Care Field, 181

Haddad, William F., 214
Hahnemann, Samuel, 96
Haight-Ashbury Free Clinics, 339
Health and Medical Information,
      335–339
Health Careers, 355–361
Health directories, 337–339
Health education and health care,
      333–334
Health education libraries, 336–337
Health Insurance Plan of Greater
      New York (HIP), 140–141
Health Maintenance Organizations
      (HMOs), 135–154
      consumer advantages, 147–
      148
      consumer disadvantages,
      148–149
      physician advantages, 149–
      150
      physician disadvantages, 150–
      151
      results, 151–153
Hill-Burton, 160–163
Homeopathy, 96–98
Hospitals, 157–193
      accreditation, 171–175
      accredited, 176
      as employer of nurses, 73–74
      choosing, 175
      classification of, 164
      consortiums, 186–188
      costs, 168–171
      development of, 157–160
      emergency departments, 232–
      233
      encouraging trends, 183–191
      federal support of, 160–164
      guarantees, 188
      hospitalization, 182–183
      organization of, 164, 166

Patient's Bill of Rights, 180, 333, 343, 367–369
size, 177

Infant mortality, 4
Intensified Drug Inspection Program, 202–203
Intermediate privileges, 29
International Chiropractic Association, 89
International Classification of Diseases, Injuries, and Causes of Death, 321
Internship, 12
Investigational New Drug (IND), 196–198

Joint Commission on Accreditation of Hospitals (JCAH), 171–175, 277
Journal of the American Dental Hygienists Association, 49

Kaiser Foundation Medical Care Plan, 143–146, 336–337
Kaiser, Henry, 144
Kefauver-Harris amendment, 198
Kelsey, Dr. Frances O., 198

Lay midwife, 78
Law of similars, 96–97
Licensed Practical Nurses (L.P.N.'s), 69
Licensed Vocational Nurses (L.V.N.'s), 69
Life expectancy, 4
Lister, Joseph, 158

Mastectomy, radical, 297
McMaster University, 13
Medicaid, 264–268, 277, 286, 328, 338
problems, 266–267
Medical care, cost of, 6
Medical education
continuing, 33, 35
Federal aid to, 13
Medical nurse specialists, 77
Medical Services representative, 216–217

Medicare, 249–264, 267–268, 277, 286, 328, 338
doctors' services, 256, 257
exclusions, 259
history, 249–251
home health benefits, 254–255
hospital coverage, 252, 253
hospital insurance, 251–255
limited coverage, 259–260
medical insurance, 256–258
nursing home (extended care) coverage, 252–254
out-patient hospital services, 256–258
out-patient physical therapy and speech pathology, 258
problems, 260–261
supplemental private insurance, 261–264
Mendelson, Mary, 286
Midwife
lay, 78
nurse, 78

Nader, Ralph, 337
National Academy of Sciences, 199
National Board for Certification in Dental Laboratory Technology, 51
National College of Naturopathic Medicine, 99
National Consumers League, 276–277
National Health Planning and Resources Development Act of 1974, 163–164
National Health Service Corps (NHSC), 32
National League for Nursing Education, 68
National Manpower Advisory Council, 31
National Organization for Women, 72
National Research Council, 199
Naturopathy, 98–100
New Drug Application (NDA), 197
Nightingale, Florence, 67
Nolen, Dr. William A., 178
Nurse midwife, 78

Nurse practitioners, 129–131
Nurses
    characteristics of, 71
    changing role of, 74–80
    family health practitioner, 77
    family practice, 77
    strike, 74
Nursing
    history of, 67–68
    personnel, 68–70
Nursing aides, 68–69
Nursing Homes, 271–288
    alternatives to, 272–275
    choosing, 277–284
    licensure and certification, 276–277
    problems, 284–287
    types, 275–276

Orderlies, 69
Osteopathy, 83–87
Osteoporosis, 55
Overcharged (dental care), 59

Palmer, Daniel D., 87
Pasteur, Louis, 158
Patient non-compliance, 341–342
Patient's Bill of Rights, 180, 333, 343, 367–369
Pediatric nurse practitioner, 76
Pharmacies, 219–220
    physician-owned, 223–224
Phocomelia, 198
Physical examination, 349
Physician assistants, 79, 129–131
Physicians
    education of, 11–14
    maldistribution of, 31–34
    unlimited free choice, 135–136
Plaque, 55
Podiatry, 90–92
Potter, William H., 21
Prescription Drugs, 195–228
    adverse reactions, 203–206
    advertising, 214–217
    generic, 338
    names, 207–210
    patient rights, 200–201
    prices, 210–214
    quality of, 201–203

safety of, 203
surveys, 338–339
Principles of Ethics of the American Dental Association, 54, 58
Prospective medicine, 342
Psychiatric aides, 69
Public Health Departments, 311–330
    child health conferences, 317–318
    education, 328–329
    environmental sanitation, 322–324
    family planning, 316–317
    health care project, 319
    health problems of senior citizens, 327–328
    laboratory, 324–325
    local, 313–329
    nursing, 325–326
    nutrition, 319–320
    records and statistics, 320
    services, 316–329
    state, 311–313
    structure, 314–315
Public health facilities, 334
Public Interest Research Group, 337–338

"Red tide", 323
Registered nurses, 70
Residency program, 12
Rutstein, Dr. David, 4, 300

Science and Health with Key to the Scriptures, 93
Semmelweiss, Ignaz, 158
Shopper's Guide to Surgery, 337
Social Security Act, 250
    Title 18. See Medicare
    Title 19. See Medicaid
Specialists
    kinds of, 17–19
    percent of, 15
Specialization, 14–24
    becoming a specialist, 16–17
    of dentists, 46–48
Staff privileges, 27–28
State Board of Dental Examiners, 60–61

State Consumer Agency, 61
Steinfeld, Jesse, 4, 6
Still, Andrew Taylor, 83
Subluxations, 88
Surgery, 23–24
Surgical privileges, 28–29

Taped telephone messages, 335–336
Tender Loving Greed, 286
Thalidomide, 198
Title 18, Social Security Act. *See* Medicare
Title 19, Social Security Act. *See* Medicaid

Trade names (drugs), 208
Trauma centers, 241

University of Miami School of Medicine, 13

Visiting Nurse Association, 274
Voluntary health agencies, 291–308, 336
    funds, 307–308
Voluntary health insurance, 5

Wilson, Gale, E., 94
Wisdom teeth, 57

X-rays, dental, 56